RACIAL JUSTICE AND THE LIMITS OF LAW

Bharat Malkani

With a Foreword by
Leslie Thomas KC

First published in Great Britain in 2024 by

Bristol University Press
University of Bristol
1–9 Old Park Hill
Bristol
BS2 8BB
UK
t: +44 (0)117 374 6645
e: bup-info@bristol.ac.uk

Details of international sales and distribution partners are available at bristoluniversitypress.co.uk

© Bristol University Press 2024

British Library Cataloguing in Publication Data
A catalogue record for this book is available from the British Library

ISBN 978-1-5292-3073-4 hardcover
ISBN 978-1-5292-3074-1 paperback
ISBN 978-1-5292-3075-8 ePub
ISBN 978-1-5292-3076-5 ePdf

The right of Bharat Malkani to be identified as author of this work has been asserted by him in accordance with the Copyright, Designs and Patents Act 1988.

All rights reserved: no part of this publication may be reproduced, stored in a retrieval system, or transmitted in any form or by any means, electronic, mechanical, photocopying, recording, or otherwise without the prior permission of Bristol University Press.

Every reasonable effort has been made to obtain permission to reproduce copyrighted material. If, however, anyone knows of an oversight, please contact the publisher.

The statements and opinions contained within this publication are solely those of the author and not of the University of Bristol or Bristol University Press. The University of Bristol and Bristol University Press disclaim responsibility for any injury to persons or property resulting from any material published in this publication.

Bristol University Press works to counter discrimination on grounds of gender, race, disability, age and sexuality.

Cover design: Nicky Borowiec
Front cover image: Adobe/4kate

This book contains graphic descriptions of racial injustices
and mistreatment of enslaved people. Racialized terms are discussed
in historic context, which necessitates their inclusion in this book.

Contents

Table of Cases		vi
Acknowledgements		viii
Foreword by Leslie Thomas KC		ix
Introduction		1
1	Racial Justice and Law: A Paradoxical Relationship	9
2	Racial Justice and Law: The Colonial Era	27
3	Racial Justice and Law: The 1900s and 2000s	54
4	The Use of Law to Tackle Racial Injustices: Contemporary Struggles	84
5	Antiracist Lawyering	121
Conclusion		136
References		146
Index		164

Table of Cases

England and Wales
Bahl v The Law Society [2004] EWCA Civ 1070
Begum v Secretary of State for Home Department [2023] H.R.L.R. 6 (Sp Imm App Comm)
Butts v Penny 2 Lev 201, 83 Eng Rep 518 (KB 1677)
Chamberlain v Harvey, 1 Ld Raym 146, 91 Eng Rep 994 (KB 1697)
Chief Constable of West Yorkshire Police v Khan [2001] UKHL 48
Constantine v Imperial Hotels Ltd [1944] KB 693
Diedrick v Chief Constable of Hampshire Constabulary and others [2012] EWHC 2144 (Admin)
G v Head Teacher and Governors of St Gregory's Catholic Science College [2011] EWHC 1452 (Admin)
Gregson v Gilbert (1783) 99 ER 629
Hillingdon London Borough Council v Commission for Racial Equality [1982] AC 779
Mandla v Dowell Lee [1983] 2 AC 548, 562
Pearne v Lisle (1749) 75 Amb ER 27
Pham v Secretary of State for the Home Department [2018] EWCA Civ 2064
R (Bapio Action Ltd) v Royal College of General Practitioners [2014] EWHC 1416 (Admin)
R (Begum) v Special Immigration Appeals Commission & Anor [2021] UKSC 7
R (Bridges) v South Wales Police [2020] EWCA Civ 1058 [199]
R (Daniels) v Prime Minister & Anor [2018] EWHC (Admin)
R (E) v JFS Governing Body [2009] UKSC 15
R (European Roma Rights Centre) v Immigration Officer at Prague Airport [2004] UKHL 55
R (Joint Council for the Welfare of Immigrants) v Secretary of State for the Home Department [2020] EWCA Civ 542
R (Limbu) v Secretary of State for the Home Department [2008] EWHC 2261 (Admin)
R (Roberts) v Commissioner of Police of the Metropolis and another [2014] EWCA Civ 69

R (Roberts) v Commissioner of Police of the Metropolis and another [2015] UKSC 79
R v Commission for Racial Equality, ex parte Prestige Group Ltd [1984] ICR 473
R v Secretary of State for Foreign Affairs ex parte Greenberg [1947] 2 All ER 550
Shanley v Harvey Eden 125, 28 Eng Rep 844 (Ch 1762).
Smith v Brown and Cooper 2 Salk 666, 91 Eng Rep 566 (KB 1701)
Smith v Gould 2 Ld Raym 1274, 92 Eng Rep 338 (KB 1706)
Social Science Research Council v Nassé [1979] 1 QB 144, CA, 172
Somerset v Stewart (1772) 98 ER 499
Taiwo v Olaigbe [2016] UKSC 31

Other jurisdictions

Brown v Board of Education of Topeka 347 US 483 (1954) (United States Supreme Court)
Commissioner for Local Government Lands and Settlement v Abdulhusein Kaderbhai [1931] AC 652 (Privy Council)
Loving v Virginia 388 US 1 (1967) (United States Supreme Court)
Nervais and Severin v The Queen [2018] CCJ 19 (AJ) (Caribbean Court of Justice)
Trop v Dulles 356 US 86 (1958) (United States Supreme Court)

Acknowledgements

In 2021, I was commissioned by the Baring Foundation to write a report on how civil society organizations have used legal action to tackle racial injustices. That report has led directly to this book, so in the first instance I would like to thank Jannat Hossain, Harriet Lowe, and David Sampson at the Foundation and Jacqueline Kinghan for connecting me with them. The Baring Foundation has also kindly granted permission to reproduce parts of that report in this book.

The report was premised on interviews with several people who work at the intersection of law and racial justice, and those interviews have shaped my thinking about the themes in this book. Thanks, therefore, to Jamila Duncan-Bosu, Sarah Mann, Alex Raikes, Shauneen Lambe, Aika Stephenson, Audrey Ludwig, Louise Whitfield, Sy Joshua, Alexandra Cox, and Angela Jackman.

When I started work on this monograph, I had conversations with more people whose knowledge and expertise have further sharpened my understanding of the relationship between law and racial justice. Thanks to Nisha Waller, Kenya Lamb, Naima Sakande, Abenaa Owusu-Bempah, Louise Taft, Connie N. Maina Sozi, and Miranda Grell for taking the time to speak with me. Several colleagues have also been generous with their time and have provided valuable and helpful comments on various chapters, so thanks to Jennifer Morgan, Daniel Newman, Ambreena Manji, Tom Hayes, Lizzy Wilmington, Barbara Hughes-Moore, Emily Kakoullis, Elen Stokes, Rachel-Cahill-O'Callaghan, Stewart Field, Ahmed Memon, and Steven Cammiss.

Helen Davis, Becky Taylor, and Grace Carroll at Bristol University Press have been patient, helpful, insightful, and supportive throughout. I'm sure there are others at BUP, such as the designer of the front cover, who have also put in a lot of effort to turn my work into a book, and so I'm thankful to them too. The two anonymous reviewers provided exceptionally helpful, detailed, and constructive feedback on an earlier draft, and much thanks goes to them for helping get that draft into a better shape. I am also immensely grateful to Leslie Thomas KC for taking the time to write such a thoughtful foreword.

Outside the world of law and race, Joyce provided space and time to write. But most of all, Zoe, Lucas, and Lily have put up with absences and absent-mindedness, and in their different ways have done the most to help me complete this book.

Foreword

Leslie Thomas KC

At the time of writing, I am chairing a joint advisory group for JUSTICE and INQUEST with the aim of developing a guide to raising issues of race at inquests for all relevant stakeholders. The aim of our guide is to: (1) provide information to practitioners on what the disparities are in relation to people from racialized backgrounds who die in or following state custody; (2) empower practitioners to identify when issues of race could be raised at an inquest into a death in state custody; (3) provide practitioners with guidance on the kinds of arguments that could be made in relation to the role of racism in state-related deaths and how to make these arguments effectively; and (4) develop guidance for all stakeholders, and in particular coroners, on how to identify issues of race and racism in cases where it may have played a role in a person's death. Accordingly, this work is relevant, timely, and a game changer.

Racial Justice and the Limits of Law is not just an academic exploration; it is a timely clarion call to justice. Having been immersed in the fields of civil liberties, human rights, and public law for over 30 years, I can attest to the resonance of the book's narrative with my own professional journey. In law school, we are gaslit into thinking that our justice system is one that stands for all, with Lady Justice being blindfolded as a symbol of impartiality. Yet, as the years have shown, she sometimes seems to possess an uncanny ability to discern skin colour and racial identity, leading many, including myself, to grapple with the systemic biases that disproportionately and adversely affect people of colour. As Martin Luther King Jr stated, "[i]t is not possible to be in favour of justice for some people and not be in favour of justice for all people".

In the ensuing chapters, Bharat takes us on a journey through history and the intricacies of the law and impressively captures the intricate relationship between the law and racial justice. Drawing from the introduction and the expansive scope of the work, I am deeply struck by the nuanced analysis that spans centuries, examining how legal and cultural influences converge to shape contemporary attitudes towards race.

In his writing, Bharat deftly encapsulates the historical imprints of law – wherein it acted as an instrument of racial oppression during the colonial era – and juxtaposes this legacy with the modern legal system that still grapples with both overt and covert racial prejudices. By understanding Britain's colonial past and the structural racism embedded in it, this book challenges its readers to confront and understand the law's historical role in perpetuating racial injustices.

The holistic approach that Bharat adopts is both commendable and audacious. Where other narratives might dissect isolated aspects of the law and racial justice, such as discrimination or law's association with slavery, this book provides a panoramic view. From the education system to employment, housing, and healthcare, we see that these problems, rooted deeply in the colonial era, manifest broadly across various sectors of modern society.

Bharat's insights, anchored in Critical Race Theory, are revelatory. He delves into concepts like 'structural racism', emphasizing that racism is not an aberration but is interwoven into the fabric of everyday societal practices. The exploration of race as a social construct, not as a biological given, further showcases how the law has both propagated racial categorizations and often failed to discern the changing implications of racism in society. By shedding light on 'intersectionality', Bharat illuminates the compounded challenges faced by individuals at the intersections of race, gender, age, and class – a nuance often overlooked by legal proceedings.

Particularly poignant is his emphasis on contemporary challenges and the new legal horizons appearing in racial justice's pursuit. Notably, the comprehensive coverage of topics highlights the multifaceted nature of racial injustice within legal spheres. But Bharat goes beyond merely critiquing; he elucidates pathways heralding change.

The theory of 'interest-convergence', suggesting that racial justice is sometimes only advanced when aligned with the interests of the dominant racial group, is deeply compelling. This perspective beckons readers to critically evaluate instances where the law might appear to be advancing racial justice, prompting them to question underlying motivations and potential implications.

The importance Bharat places on 'lived theory' resonates with the current global movement for racial justice. By emphasizing the paramountcy of the voices of those who've lived through racial injustices, he makes a call to action for legal practitioners to truly listen and respond. The story of the Colston Four serves as a pertinent example of how White allies, driven by a sense of responsibility, can play pivotal roles in this transformative journey.

This narrative acknowledges the law's dual nature – as a tool of systemic biases and a mechanism for emancipation – and it drives home a key message: while our legal system might reflect societal prejudices, it also houses an innate capability for metamorphosis and growth if used in the right way. Bharat shows us that way.

Yet, with all the transformative potential of the law, Bharat does not shy away from exposing its inherent limitations. He underscores that while legal interventions can address certain manifestations of racial prejudice, they cannot single-handedly erase deep-seated biases or heal the scars of historical injustices.

Bharat masterfully charts a roadmap – a vision to transcend the historical and deep-seated impediments that have long stifled the pursuit of racial justice. This work is a beacon of hope and a strategy for change, advocating for a justice system that recognizes and rectifies its own fallibilities. In a profession where many have grown weary and frustrated with the law's seeming inability to provide equitable justice, this book is a lifeline.

Every stakeholder in the justice system – from politicians, judges, and lawyers to policy makers – must delve into these pages. Bharat's work isn't just another book; it's a pioneering manual that provides us with the tools and knowledge to navigate this intricate landscape, all the time challenging and enlightening its readers to demand and effectuate change. Chapter 5, in particular, is a treasure trove of insights and revelations, a testament to the depth and breadth of Bharat's meticulous research and profound understanding. The challenges of the past and present are laid bare, but so too are the possibilities for a brighter, more just future.

It is incumbent upon us, law's guardians and practitioners, to heed this call and take tangible steps towards true racial justice. *Racial Justice and the Limits of Law* is more than a guide – it's an imperative.

Echoing Dr Martin Luther King Jr, "The arc of the moral universe is long, but it bends toward justice", this book stands as a testament to that sentiment. It serves as a reminder of the shared global endeavour of racial justice, urging every generation to rally collectively.

With profound respect for Bharat Malkani's seminal contribution, and with hope for a future that embraces racial equity.

Introduction

The 17th-century trade in enslaved people meets the 21st-century legal system

On 7 June 2020, during a protest in the city of Bristol in England against racial injustices, a statue of Edward Colston was hauled to the ground, rolled towards the docks, and pushed into the harbour. The statue had been erected in 1895, nearly two centuries after Colston had died, to commemorate his philanthropy in Bristol and his service as a local Member of Parliament. Although some Bristolians venerated Colston both during his lifetime and after his death, many others have been critical of him. He had been a member of the Royal African Company from 1680 until 1692, during which time the Company transported over 84,000 enslaved people from Africa to British colonies in the Caribbean and North America. On slave ships and on plantations in the colonies, Black Africans suffered all manner of horrific treatments and living conditions on the basis of their skin colour. Because of Colston's role in facilitating the enslavement of Black Africans, many people in Bristol had called for the statue to be taken down, or to have a plaque attached to it documenting his role in the trade of enslaved people. Bristol City Council, though, had resisted these calls.[1] When the protestors took matters into their own hands, they contributed to an ongoing conversation, both in Britain and abroad, about the appropriateness of maintaining statues of people who were involved in some of the worst racial injustices imaginable. Many celebrated the removal of what they considered to be a moral stain on the community, but others expressed anger at what they perceived to be an act of vandalism and an attack on British history.[2]

---

[1] On Edward Colston's role in the trade of enslaved people, see Mark Steeds and Roger Ball, *From Wulfstan to Colston: Severing the Sinews of Slavery in Bristol* (Bristol Radical History Group 2020). On Bristolians' relationship with Colston's legacy and their attempts to remove the statue through official channels, see Tristan Cork, 'How Bristol Challenged Colston for 100 Years' *Bristol Post* (7 June 2021).

[2] See Johannes Schulz, 'Must Rhodes Fall? The Significance of Commemoration in the Struggle for Relations of Respect' (2019) 27 *The Journal of Political Philosophy* 166 for a discussion of similar debates that have taken place in other countries. In the aftermath of

A few months after the protest, four people were charged under the Criminal Damage Act 1971 for their roles in the events that day, and a trial took place in Bristol Crown Court in December 2021. The 'Colston Four', as they came to be known, admitted to damaging the statue but argued that they had a 'lawful excuse' for their actions. The 1971 Act permits damage to property in certain circumstances, such as when acting to prevent a more serious crime from occurring. For example, we would excuse a person for damaging a door to a house if they did so to prevent a burglary. The Colston Four argued that the presence of the statue contravened the law against 'displaying indecent matter publicly', and that its presence was abusive and likely to unlawfully cause distress.[3] They removed the statue, they said, to prevent those crimes from continuing to occur. In their words, it was "wrong to celebrate an individual who had [committed] such crimes against humanity in such a multicultural city".[4] The defence went to great lengths to convince the jury that this was a case about racial justice and a lack of political will to tackle racial injustice, rather than a case about vandalism and criminal damage. The renowned historian David Olusoga provided expert testimony on Colston's role in the trade of enslaved persons, and Gloria Daniel, a descendant of an enslaved person, told the court that the presence of the statue caused distress to people like her whose ancestors had suffered under the system of slavery that Colston had supported.[5] They were, in effect, putting the 17th-century trade in enslaved persons on trial in 21st-century legal proceedings.

On 5 January 2022, a jury acquitted the Colston Four. Although we will never know the reasons for their decision, some have speculated that they did so because they sympathized with the defendants' struggle for racial justice.[6] Regardless of the jury's reasons, the trial laid bare the long-standing tension between the legal system and the struggle for racial justice, and it is

---

the protests in Bristol, the Mayor of Bristol established a commission to collect a range of views about the events that day. See We Are Bristol History Commission, 'The Colston Statue: What Next?' (2021), pp 43–55.

[3] Legal directions, Judge's Handout, in *R v Milo Ponsford, Sage Willoughby, Rhian Graham, and Jake Skuse* (on file with the author).

[4] Quoted in Graeme Hayes et al, 'We Attended the Trial of the Colston Four: Here's Why Their Acquittal Should Be Celebrated' *The Conversation* (7 January 2022).

[5] Sean Morrison, 'Colston 4 Found Not Guilty of Criminal Damage to Slave Trader's Statue' *The Bristol Cable* (5 January 2022). Also see Tom Lamont, 'How the Trial of the Colston Four Was Won: The Inside Story' *New Statesman* (2 April 2022).

[6] Hayes et al (n 4) (speculating that 'the jury's decision re-asserts what EP Thompson called the "moral economy" of the community – an act of absolution recognising the collective action of the defendants as being at the service of all of the community. The defence provided a frame for the actions that placed them within an ongoing community dialogue about the slave trade, Bristol's role within it and the veneration of a mass murderer').

this tension that is the subject of this book. On the one hand, the law in the Colston Four case was being used to *condemn* those who were protesting in favour of racial justice. This was not unusual: we will see over the following chapters that there is a long history of the law being used to stifle progress towards racial justice. On the other hand, the Colston Four were able to use the law to *advance* the cause of racial justice by arguing that the pursuit of racial justice trumps concerns about damage to property. This was also not unusual: we will also see throughout this book that racial justice campaigners have often been able to use the law to their advantage. Over the following pages, we will explore this paradoxical relationship between law and the struggle for racial justice with a view to understanding why and how the legal system in England and Wales has been both a help and a hindrance to racial justice campaigners.[7]

Law and the struggle for racial justice

There are three principal reasons why we might expect the legal system of England and Wales to assist the struggle for racial justice. First, we are routinely told that the legal system is underpinned by the principles of equality, fairness, and neutrality,[8] which appear to be allied to the idea of racial justice. Second, there are many substantive laws which seem to give effect to these principles, such as the Human Rights Act 1998, the Equality Act 2010, and the myriad laws that criminalize acts of racial hatred. Third, those involved in the administration of the legal system – the people whose duty it is to uphold these principles and apply these laws – can be trained to ensure that they do not act on any racial biases or prejudices. There have been several attempts to diversify the racial make-up of the legal profession, to ensure that legal officials reflect the views and experiences of racialized people.[9] Given these features of the legal system, it is not surprising to find examples of the law contributing to, or at least appearing to contribute to, the pursuit of racial justice. The decision in *Somerset v Stewart* in 1772 is credited with inspiring the anti-slavery movement and accelerating the abolition of slavery in the British Empire,[10] legislation such as the Equality Act 2010 has helped victims of discrimination, and many people have been

---

[7] Although this study is focused on England and Wales, much of the analysis applies to Scotland and Northern Ireland too.
[8] See, for example, Thomas Bingham, *The Rule of Law* (Penguin Books 2011).
[9] In 2020, the Courts and Tribunals Judiciary launched the 'Judicial Diversity and Inclusion Strategy 2020–2025', which aims to diversify the make-up of the judiciary. For a critique of the Strategy, see Keir Monteith KC et al, 'Racial Bias and the Bench: A Response to the Judicial Diversity and Inclusion Strategy (2020–2025)' (University of Manchester 2022).
[10] Peter Fryer, *Staying Power: The History of Black People in Britain* (Pluto Press 2018), p 134.

convicted for crimes that have been motivated by racial hatred, sending a signal that racism will not be tolerated.

Although we will examine how the law has advanced the struggle for racial justice in these ways and others, we will also explore the *limits* of law. For example, law has not stopped, and has instead facilitated, the racially discriminatory use of stop and search powers by the police. Law did not prevent, and instead helped create, the injustices faced by the Windrush Generation. And law has rarely helped, and has instead been used to criminalize, people of Gypsy, Roma, and Traveller (GRT) heritage. Over the following pages, we will see that these examples, and others, are not aberrations from an otherwise antiracist legal system.

This book takes a holistic approach to explaining the deeply rooted historical, cultural, and systemic reasons for the limits of law in the struggle for racial justice. It is holistic in two senses. First, it covers several centuries of legal developments, from the 1500s to the present day. Second, it addresses the use of law to tackle racism in several spheres of social life, including the education, criminal justice, employment, housing, and healthcare systems. In terms of the historical reasons for law's limits, we will see that the legal system was used to create and perpetuate racial injustices in the era of the British Empire, and that this legacy rears its head in the contemporary era in England and Wales.[11] In terms of cultural reasons, we will see that legal officials today tend not to understand what racial justice requires, and that these misunderstandings afflict the legal system's operation, even if on paper the law looks pro-racial justice. And in terms of systemic reasons, we will see that even when legal officials have good intentions, legal processes themselves are sometimes unhelpful, if not outright antithetical, to the pursuit of racial justice.

Although I cannot provide a definitive historical account of law's relationship with racial justice, and I cannot discuss every relevant piece of legislation or case, the holistic approach adopted here enables us to identify wider trends in the relationship between law and racial justice, and to join the dots between the works of those who have focused on more specific and discrete aspects of this relationship, such as racism in the criminal justice

---

[11] By exploring the legacy of colonial laws on the contemporary legal system, this book also contributes to the literature on the legacy of the British Empire on British society today more broadly. See, for example, Charlotte Lydia Riley, *Imperial Island: A History of Empire in Modern Britain* (The Bodley Head 2023); Peter Mitchell, *Imperial Nostalgia: How the British Conquered Themselves* (Manchester University Press 2021); Sathnam Sanghera, *Empireland: How Imperialism Has Shaped Modern Britain* (Penguin Books 2021); Afua Hirsch, *Brit(ish): On Race, Identity and Belonging* (Vintage Publishing 2018); Akala, *Natives: Race and Class in the Ruins of Empire* (Two Roads 2018).

system,[12] the efficacy of anti-discrimination laws,[13] the history of law and slavery,[14] and the effect of colonialism on legal education.[15] I hope this holistic overview is helpful for prospective and established lawyers who want to use their legal training to contribute to the struggle for racial justice, and helpful for activists who want to understand the benefits and drawbacks of the legal system.

Chapter outline

Chapter 1 sets out the theoretical basis for the study that unfolds over the later chapters. A definition of the term 'racial justice' is provided, which is followed by an explanation of six concepts from the discipline of Critical Race Theory (CRT) that are used throughout the book to explain and understand law's fraught relationship with the struggle for racial justice. The first is the concept of 'structural racism', which reflects an understanding of racism as something that is embedded in social life and institutions, rather than something that is incidental and aberrational from the normal course of social life.[16] The law, we will see, has played a role in structuralizing racism within society, and limits have subsequently been placed on law's competency to address structural racism. The second concept from CRT is the idea of race as a social construct, rather than a biological fact.[17] That is, people are not born into particular racial groups, but rather they are assigned to particular racial groups for social and political reasons. We will see that the law has contributed to the social construction of 'race' and 'racism', but that legal authorities are unable or unwilling to grapple with evolving understandings of race and racism.

---

[12] David Lammy, 'The Lammy Review: An Independent Review into the Treatment of, and Outcomes for, Black, Asian and Minority Ethnic Individuals in the Criminal Justice System' (2017).

[13] Shreya Atrey, 'Structural Racism and Race Discrimination' (2021) 74 *Current Legal Problems* 1.

[14] William M. Wiecek, 'Somerset: Lord Mansfield and the Legitimacy of Slavery in the Anglo-American World' (1974) 42 *University of Chicago Law Review* 86.

[15] Folúké Adébísí, *Decolonisation and Legal Knowledge: Reflections on Power and Possibility* (Bristol University Press 2023); Oluwaseun Matiluko, 'Decolonising the Master's House: How Black Feminist Epistemologies Can Be and Are Used in Decolonial Strategy' (2020) 54 *The Law Teacher* 547.

[16] Discussed in Chapter 1, but see Eduardo Bonilla-Silva, 'What Makes Systemic Racism Systemic?' (2021) 91 *Sociological Inquiry* 513.

[17] Discussed in Chapter 1, but see Kenan Malik, *Strange Fruit: Why Both Sides Are Wrong in the Race Debate* (Oneworld 2008).

The third concept that underpins the analysis in this book is that of 'intersectionality'.[18] Scholars and activists have recognized that people cannot be defined solely by their race, and that people also face injustices on the basis of other characteristics such as gender and class. For example, Black women have historically and contemporaneously faced injustices stemming from misogyny as well as racism. The legal system, we will see, has been slow to grapple with the nature of intersectional harms. The fourth insight from CRT is that of 'interest-convergence'.[19] Legal officials, we will see, have tended to advance the interests of racialized people when doing so serves the interests of, or at least is not detrimental to, the interests of the dominant racial group in society. In these cases, we can see how the law might actually sustain racial injustices under the guise of advancing racial justice. The fifth aspect of CRT that is relevant to understanding law's relationship with racial justice is the idea of 'lived theory', which involves centring the voices of those with lived experiences of racial injustice in legal action and campaigning.[20] The sixth aspect of CRT scholarship that informs this book is a recognition of the inherent limitations of legal processes. Law is not the panacea to society's problems, racial injustices or otherwise. The adversarial nature of many legal processes, for example, encourages an 'us versus them' attitude towards addressing social problems, which runs counter to the imperatives of racial justice.

These six aspects of CRT are also useful for determining appropriate terminology. For the reasons explained in Chapter 1, there are some ubiquitous terms that, on closer analysis, are inappropriate or unhelpful. These include terms like 'Black and Minority Ethnic' (BME) or 'Black and Asian Minority Ethnic' (BAME), and I explain why I prefer to use the term 'racialized person' instead. The terms 'equality', 'diversity', and 'inclusion' are also problematic for reasons set out in Chapter 1. Language plays an important role in the creation and perpetuation of racial injustices, and it is important to recognize the inappropriateness of such terms.[21]

With these key concepts in mind, we move on to Chapters 2 and 3 to see how the legal system has historically contributed to the problem of racism. Chapter 2 focuses on the colonial era. We will see how law was used to justify acts of imperial conquest; to create the idea of 'race'; and

---

[18] Discussed in Chapter 1, but see Kimberlé Crenshaw, *On Intersectionality: Essential Writings* (New Press 2022).

[19] Discussed in Chapter 1, but see Derrick Bell, '*Brown v. Board of Education* and the Interest-Convergence Dilemma' (1980) 93 *Harvard Law Review* 518.

[20] Discussed in Chapter 1, but see Avery F. Gordon, 'On "Lived Theory": An Interview with A. Sivanandan' (2014) 55 *Race & Class* 1.

[21] Jean-Jacques Weber, *Language Racism* (Palgrave Macmillan 2015).

to provide a veneer of moral legitimacy to racially unjust practices such as enslavement, displacement, and various social control measures across the British Empire. It is in this sense that law structuralized racism into all aspects of social life. Colonial legal systems, we will see, contributed to the problem of intersectional oppressions and routinely marginalized the voices of racialized people.

Chapter 3 picks up the story from the beginning of the 1900s. As the British Empire disintegrated and immigration to the metropole increased, laws were enacted which replicated the racial injustices of the colonial era. Immigration laws in the 20th century, we will see, sustained the two-tier racialized legal system that had developed during the age of Empire: one for people racialized as 'White British', and a more disadvantageous system for those racialized as something other than 'White British'. This brings us to the present day, and Chapter 3 ends with an overview of contemporary racial injustices in five social settings: the education, criminal justice, employment, housing, and healthcare systems.

Chapter 4 turns to the use of law to tackle racial injustices in the contemporary era. For the reasons set out at the beginning of the chapter, the substantive law has developed since the mid-1990s so that the legal system today generally has the appearance of being pro-racial justice, and thus racial justice activists have made greater use of the law to advance their cause. However, the turn to law has not been without its problems. Lawyers and campaigners have been encouraged, if not compelled, to frame their grievances within the language and discourse set by the legal system, and this is not always congruent with the nature of racial injustices. Focusing on access to justice as well as anti-discrimination laws, hate crimes law, and laws that require the promotion of positive race relations, we will see that advocates have struggled to use the legal system to address the six concepts from CRT that are outlined in Chapter 1. In this sense, whereas the racism of the law was *explicit* in the colonial and post-war eras, the racism of the law today is more *veiled*, in the sense that the substantive law masks the racially unjust outcomes of legal processes.

In Chapter 5, I offer some suggestions for how lawyers and racial justice campaigners might make more effective use of the law by adopting principles of 'antiracist lawyering'. I use definitions of 'antiracism'[22] and 'social justice lawyering'[23] to set out four principles of antiracist lawyering that will help lawyers address the six concepts of CRT that are needed to advance the cause

---

[22] Ibram X. Kendi, *How to Be an Antiracist* (The Bodley Head 2019).
[23] Austin Sarat and Stuart A. Scheingold (eds), *Cause Lawyering: Political Commitments and Professional Responsibilities* (Oxford University Press 1998); Jacqueline Kinghan, *Lawyers, Networks and Progressive Social Change: Lawyers Changing Lives* (Hart Publishing 2021).

of racial justice. These four principles are: reflection, creativity, collaboration, and accountability.

This is not to say that, at some point in the future, the legal system will unequivocally advance the pursuit of racial justice. Despite the potential for antiracist lawyering, it is clear that the legal system will at best provide racial justice campaigners with a form of 'cruel optimism'. This is the term used by Lauren Berlant to describe the contemporary social phenomenon of people constantly striving for the 'good life' – financial security, stable relationships, political and social equality – despite knowing that social systems in capitalist liberal democracies render achievement of these aims impossible.[24] Nasar Meer adopts this idea of 'cruel optimism' to explore how and why the struggle for racial justice is a perpetual one, with cyclical successes and failures rather than linear progress. In his view, 'there is no likely end to the struggle for racial justice, only the promise this heralds and the desire to persevere, even despite knowledge of likely failure'.[25] As we will see over the course of this book, law's relationship with racial justice is far from linear, with the occasional successful use of legal action often being followed by an Act of Parliament or judicial pronouncement that sets back the cause. In this sense, law generates a 'cruel optimism' among racial justice campaigners as they continually turn to legal action despite the system being set up to perennially disappoint them. It is with this in mind that the book ends with an outline of a UK Supreme Court case from 2021 involving a British woman called Shamima Begum, a name that will likely be familiar to many readers. Her case, I show, is the inverse of the Colston Four case. The latter involved the 17th-century trade in enslaved persons meeting 21st-century legal processes, resulting in the furtherance of racial justice; Begum's case involves a 21st-century problem – racialized terrorism – meeting a 17th-century legal solution – denial of legal personhood to racialized people – thus impeding the pursuit of racial justice.

Although legal action will not by itself bring about an end to racial injustices, I conclude by urging lawyers and campaigners to continue challenging such injustices wherever possible, using theories and practices of antiracism that address the six concepts of CRT that undergird the analysis in this book. Despite the shortcomings of the legal system, I think lawyers and campaigners ought to heed the sentiment expressed by the writer and racial justice activist James Baldwin: 'Not everything that is faced can be changed. But nothing can be changed until it is faced.'[26]

---

[24] Lauren Gail Berlant, *Cruel Optimism* (Duke University Press 2011).
[25] Nasar Meer, *The Cruel Optimism of Racial Justice* (Policy Press 2022), p 1.
[26] James Baldwin, 'As Much Truth as One Can Bear' *The New York Times Book Review* (14 January 1962).

1

Racial Justice and Law: A Paradoxical Relationship

Introduction

To understand the nuances and complexities of law's relationship with racial justice, we must first grapple with some definitional and conceptual issues.[1] In particular, we need to define the term 'racial justice'. We can then draw on insights from the discipline of Critical Race Theory (CRT) to set out six reasons why the legal system is not always a help in the struggle for racial justice.

A definition of 'racial justice'

Definitions of 'racial justice' will vary according to one's political or philosophical outlook,[2] but the definition adopted in this book runs as follows: *The struggle for racial justice is the struggle to ensure that a person's experiences of opportunities, treatment, and outcomes in social interactions and social processes are not affected by their skin colour or perceived or actual cultural background.* This requires some unpacking. People who have been racialized as 'Brown', 'Black', and anything other than 'White British' have suffered because they have not been given the same opportunities as White British people to participate in social processes such as education, healthcare, housing, employment, and so on. Even when they have had the opportunity to

---

[1] Portions of the text in this chapter have been reused from Bharat Malkani, 'The Pursuit of Racial Justice through Legal Action: An Overview of How UK Civil Society Has Used the Law 1990–2020' (Baring Foundation 2021). I am grateful to the Baring Foundation for their permission to reproduce parts of that report.

[2] Les Back and John Solomos (eds), *Theories of Race and Racism: A Reader* (3rd edn, Routledge 2022); Charles W. Mills, 'I – Racial Justice' (2018) 92 *Aristotelian Society Supplementary Volume* 69.

participate in these processes, they have suffered because they have been treated differently in those social processes, and they have not enjoyed the same outcomes as White British people.[3] Thus, the 'struggle for racial justice' is the struggle to create a society in which a person's life experiences are not shaped by their actual or perceived racial background.

Racial justice activists have tried to advance their cause in various settings, including homes, educational establishments, political debates, and elsewhere.[4] We are concerned with the legal system of England and Wales as a site in the struggle for racial justice. Victims of racism and campaigners for racial justice have long turned to the legal system for help because, in the United Kingdom's system of parliamentary democracy, their voices are often marginalized in political processes. However, although the principles of equality, fairness, and neutrality which are said to underpin the legal system *should* help advocates for racial justice, these principles are rarely adhered to in practice. We can turn to the discipline of CRT to identify six reasons why the law is of limited use in the struggle for racial justice.

The limits of legal action: insights from CRT

The complex and seemingly paradoxical relationship between law and racial justice has attracted considerable attention over several decades, giving rise to the discipline of CRT.[5] This term was coined by the organizers of a conference on race and law in the United States in 1989 to signify that they were examining the intersection of Critical Legal Studies, which focuses on how law perpetuates social inequalities, and studies of racism.[6] These scholars had been motivated to study law's role in perpetuating racial injustices because of the disjoint between the law on paper and the law in practice in the US. Throughout the 1950s and 1960s, campaigners in America had successfully deployed the legal system, securing notable gains in legislatures and courtrooms. These included the Civil Rights Acts of 1957 and 1964, the Voting Rights Act 1965, and the decisions of the US Supreme Court in *Brown v Board of Education* (1954) and *Loving v Virginia*

---

[3] See Chapter 3 for an outline of the various ways in which racialized people are disadvantaged in society today.

[4] There are many historical and sociological accounts of the antiracist struggle in the United Kingdom. See, for example, Azfar Shafi and Ilyas Nagdee, *Race to the Bottom: Reclaiming Antiracism* (Pluto Press 2022); Ambalavaner Sivanandan, *Communities of Resistance: Writings on Black Struggles for Socialism* (first published 1990, Verso 2019).

[5] For a useful introduction to CRT, see Richard Delgado and Jean Stefancic, *Critical Race Theory: An Introduction* (3rd edn, New York University Press 2017).

[6] Kimberlé Crenshaw et al (eds), *Critical Race Theory: The Key Writings That Formed the Movement* (New Press 1995), p xxvii.

(1967), which outlawed racial segregation in schools and prohibitions on interracial marriages respectively.[7] By the 1970s, though, scholars in law departments in American universities were questioning why racial injustices still persisted across the United States, including within the legal system, when racism had been formally repudiated by legal officials. The works of these scholars coalesced into CRT, and over the course of several years, many tenets of CRT have emerged which explain law's fraught relationship with racial justice. The discipline has extended beyond legal academia and is now a social as well as an intellectual movement which addresses all manner of ways in which racial injustices are created and sustained across law, politics, and society notwithstanding legal rejections of racism.

There have been some attempts to transpose the central tenets of American CRT scholarship to other jurisdictions, such as England and Wales,[8] but there is no need to because British-based scholars have actually long addressed the same concerns as American-based CRT scholars, just not necessarily under that name. For example, writing in 1972, before the phrase 'Critical Race Theory' had even been coined, Anthony Lester and Geoffrey Bindman explained the tension that is the subject of CRT enquiry when they wrote about law's relationship with racial justice in England and Wales in the following terms: 'With one face, the law embodies and reinforces racial inequality; with the other, it expresses and urges racial equality.'[9] Fifteen years later, and again before CRT was in vogue, Peter Fitzpatrick argued that 'racism is compatible with and even integral to law' in England and Wales.[10] These observations and claims have been reiterated more recently, particularly in light of legal developments that give the appearance of a legal system that is pro-racial justice. Writing in 2004, Patricia Tuitt explained how 'the violence of racial domination' is 'committed or facilitated by law',[11] and in 2021 Shreya Atrey asserted that 'law [in England and Wales] is not a neutral entity. Like other tools at the behest of the State, law too is implicated in the possibility of producing and reproducing racism'.[12] Social justice organizations such as the UK chapter of Black Lives Matter have also

---

[7] *Brown v Board of Education of Topeka*, 347 US 483 (1954); *Loving v Virginia*, 388 US 1 (1967).

[8] Mathias Möschel, *Law, Lawyers and Race: Critical Race Theory from the United States to Europe* (Routledge 2016).

[9] Anthony Lester and Geoffrey Bindman, *Race and Law* (Penguin Books 1972), p 14.

[10] Peter Fitzpatrick, 'Racism and the Innocence of Law' (1987) 14 *Journal of Law and Society* 119, 119. For essays on law's relationship with racial justice in other countries, see Peter Fitzpatrick (ed), *Nationalism, Racism, and the Rule of Law* (Dartmouth Publishing 1995).

[11] Patricia Tuitt, *Race, Law, Resistance* (GlassHouse Press 2004).

[12] Shreya Atrey, 'Structural Racism and Race Discrimination' (2021) 74 *Current Legal Problems* 1, 6.

drawn attention to law's role in racial injustices.[13] In 2022, researchers at the University of Manchester highlighted what they termed 'institutional racism in the justice system',[14] illustrating how legal processes might create or at least contribute to racial injustices despite the apparent condemnation of racism by legal authorities. Other British-based scholars who are not usually associated with the study of law have addressed law's relationship with racial justice in England and Wales in terms similar to CRT scholarship. These include the sociologists Stuart Hall[15] and Ambalavaner Sivanandan.[16] Thus, although the work of American scholars must be cited when outlining the following six key concepts of CRT, it should be emphasized that British-based legal and sociological scholars have also informed the development of these concepts.

Structural racism

The first key concept of CRT scholarship is the contention that racism is structural in society. American-based CRT scholars such as Derrick Bell and Kimberlé Crenshaw surmised that the legislative initiatives in the Civil Rights era in the US were inadequate because these laws treated acts of racial injustices as aberrations from the normal course of society, when racism was instead inherent and normal in social life.[17] Bell and Crenshaw, among others, pointed out that racism is not something *external* to society which afflicts social relationships from time to time and which can be cured by legislation and judicial decisions; rather racism is *part* of the social order, which includes the legal order. Racism is not the soft furnishings in a home that can be cleaned or removed when they become unsightly; racism is instead the foundations and the bricks and mortar of that house. Racism is one of the phenomena, like law, that *structures* societal relations.

'Structural racism' can be understood as the totality of three other types of racism – 'interpersonal racism', 'systemic racism', and 'institutional racism'. 'Interpersonal racism' refers to racism between people, such as racially motivated physical assaults or the shouting of racial abuse at a

---

[13] For information about the Black Lives Matter UK movement, see their website: https://ukblm.org
[14] Keir Monteith KC et al, 'Racial Bias and the Bench: A Response to the Judicial Diversity and Inclusion Strategy (2020–2025)' (University of Manchester 2022), p 6.
[15] Stuart Hall (ed), *Policing the Crisis: Mugging, the State, and Law and Order* (Macmillan 1978).
[16] Ambalavaner Sivanandan, 'RAT and the Degradation of Black Struggle' (1985) 26 *Race & Class* 1.
[17] Crenshaw et al (n 6). See also Richard Delgado and Jean Stefancic (eds), *The Derrick Bell Reader* (New York University Press 2005).

person. It also includes instances of racism committed by a person who is not overtly racist but who nonetheless holds unconscious biases. An example would be the landlord who prefers to let her property to a person racialized as 'White' rather than a person racialized as 'Black'. Layers upon layers of interpersonal racism feed into 'systemic racism', which refers to how systems in society, such as the housing system, reproduce these types of interpersonal racisms but on larger scales. When several landlords act in such a way, for example, we end up with segregated communities, with groups of racialized people living in poor housing conditions and in economically deprived neighbourhoods, because only unscrupulous landlords will let to them, which in turn leads to adverse impacts on health.[18] These social inequalities have an impact on organizations and institutions within that society, with 'institutional racism' referring to the practices, policies, and cultures of an organization, such as the police force, which have an adverse effect on people racialized as something other than White British. Continuing with the example of housing, the police might treat victims of crime from that economically deprived neighbourhood very differently from how they treat victims of crime from more affluent and White neighbourhoods. Indeed, the phrase 'institutional racism' was used to explain why the police failed to help the family of Stephen Lawrence, who was a victim of interpersonal racism. Lawrence's murder in 1993 was not investigated properly by the Metropolitan Police, which led to the collapse of the prosecution against the people who killed him. Sir William Macpherson, who chaired the public inquiry into the police's failure to adequately investigate the killing, explained that institutional racism is

> the collective failure of an organisation to provide an appropriate and professional service to people because of their colour, culture, or ethnic origin. It can be seen or detected in processes, attitudes and behaviour which amount to discrimination through unwitting prejudice, ignorance, thoughtlessness and racist stereotyping which disadvantage minority ethnic people.[19]

Lee Bridges has improved this definition by making it clear that institutional racism also refers to the operational policies and strategic priorities that

---

[18] Kevin Gulliver, 'Racial Discrimination in UK Housing Has a Long History and Deep Roots' (LSE British Politics and Policy Blog, 12 October 2017), Available from: https://blogs.lse.ac.uk/politicsandpolicy/racial-discrimination-in-housing

[19] Sir William Macpherson, 'The Stephen Lawrence Inquiry' (Cmd 4262-I, 1999), para 6.34.

inform the workings of the organization, rather than just the 'processes, attitudes and behaviour' of a few people who work in the organization.[20]

A key point to note is that these types of racism are interconnected and cyclical. Interpersonal acts of racism combine to create systemic racism, which leads to institutional racism, which generates interpersonal acts of racism, and so on. Sivanandan, former director of the Institute of Race Relations, made a similar point when writing that '[i]nstitutional racism is that which, covertly or overtly, resides in the policies, procedures, operations and culture of public or private institutions – reinforcing individual prejudices and being reinforced by them in turn'.[21] In the context of the United States, Eduardo Bonilla-Silva makes the same point with the example of the seemingly ordinary act of a White parent sending their child to a school that happens to be predominantly White. The parent might be thinking of the academic standards of that school, but this seemingly innocuous and legal act reproduces the effects of explicit racial segregation in schools that the legal system prohibits.[22] It is these sorts of everyday, ordinary actions and collective practices that combine to structuralize racism within society. Another key point to note is that although people of all races can be victims of interpersonal racism, structural racism in the UK only negatively affects those classed as something other than White British. This is because, as set out in the next chapter, during the era of the British Empire, societal structures were imbued with the idea of the supremacy of White British people. Thus, social institutions, practices, and cultures are set up to prioritize their interests over others.

Over the course of this book, we will see that legal authorities have been reluctant to address the problem of structural racism, preferring instead to focus on interpersonal acts of racism. Judges have tended to state that other authorities are better placed to tackle structural racism, and Reni Eddo-Lodge's account of structural racism offers a reason why. She illustrates that instances of structural racism are harder to identify than instances of interpersonal racism: 'Structural racism is an impenetrably white workplace culture set by [people with biases], where anyone who falls outside of the culture must conform or face failure.'[23] In other words, '[i]t doesn't manifest itself in spitting at strangers in the street. ... It manifests itself in the flick

---

[20] Lee Bridges, 'The Lawrence Inquiry: Incompetence, Corruption, and Institutional Racism' (1999) 26 *Journal of Law and Society* 298.

[21] Ambalavaner Sivanandan, 'The Great Cop Out: Public Accountability, Not Public Relations' (1998–99) 47 *Campaign Against Racism and Fascism* 2, 3.

[22] Eduardo Bonilla-Silva, 'What Makes Systemic Racism *Systemic*?' (2021) 91 *Sociological Inquiry* 513, 515.

[23] Reni Eddo-Lodge, *Why I'm No Longer Talking to White People about Race* (expanded edn, Bloomsbury Publishing 2018), p 64.

of a wrist that tosses a CV in the bin because the applicant has a foreign-sounding name'.[24] As she writes, the 'covert nature of structural racism is difficult to hold to account', whereas more explicit acts of interpersonal racism are easier to hold to account.[25]

It is worth noting that not all scholars use the same terminology in these sorts of discussions. Bonilla-Silva, for example, uses the term 'systemic racism' to describe what I have termed 'structural racism'. Ibram X. Kendi has suggested that the terms 'institutional racism', 'systemic racism', and 'structural racism' are 'redundant', and that we should just use the term 'racism' because '[r]acism itself is institutional, structural, and systemic'.[26] However, I think it is important to draw attention to the different ways in which racist incidents might occur, since we will see that the legal system differentiates between different types of racism.

Race and racism as social constructs

Another tenet of CRT that informs the analysis in this book is the contention that race is a social construct, rather than a biological or scientific fact. In the 18th century, scientific discourses emerged which asserted that people with different skin colour and facial features were biologically and qualitatively different from each other.[27] People with 'white' skin were considered to be intellectually, morally, and aesthetically superior to those with darker, 'black' skin. This, in turn, was used to justify the development of a two-tiered legal system, which allowed the mistreatment of those with darker skin.

This type of scientific racism came under sustained attack in the years following the Second World War. The Nazis had used scientific discourses to justify the Holocaust, and therefore governments and scientists after 1945 could no longer publicly state that there is a scientific basis to the belief in racial hierarchies.[28] Today, while some people still claim that there is a scientific basis to racial hierarchies, most governments and scientists tend to say that no significance or value should be attached to differences such

---

[24] Eddo-Lodge (n 23), p 65.
[25] Eddo-Lodge (n 23), p 64. Although it is *easier* to hold perpetrators of interpersonal racism to account, this should not be taken to mean that it is *easy* to hold them to account. As detailed in Chapter 3, there are notable cases of perpetrators of racist incidents evading justice. See, for example, Brian Cathcart, *The Case of Stephen Lawrence* (Penguin 2000).
[26] Ibram X. Kendi, *How to Be an Antiracist* (The Bodley Head 2019), p 18.
[27] Ali Rattansi, *Racism: A Very Short Introduction* (Oxford University Press 2007), p 31.
[28] Sebastián Gil-Riaño, 'Relocating Anti-racist Science: The 1950 UNESCO Statement on Race and Economic Development in the Global South' (2018) 51 *The British Journal for the History of Science* 281.

as skin pigmentation.[29] People are assigned to different racial categories and are treated differently, critical race scholars assert, for various political, cultural, social, and economic purposes, rather than because of any objective scientific findings. In other words, just as 'race' is not a static concept, neither is 'racism'. For example, the need for physical labour in the early days of the British Empire meant that Black people from Africa were classed as intellectually stilted in order to justify enslavement and forced labour in colonies in the West Indies and North America. More recently, the political need to be seen to be tackling the threat of terrorism has seen religion, or interpretations of religious texts, used as a marker for classing Muslim people in particular, and Brown-skinned people in general, as dangerous and antagonistic to so-called British values of tolerance and decency.[30] At other times and in other places, factors other than skin colour and religion have played a role in processes of racialization. For example, perceptions about culture and national origin have been used to inflict injustices on those considered to have 'white' skin, such as those of a Gypsy, Roma, or Traveller (GRT) heritage, and Jewish people. These people are not considered to be, for want of a better phrase, 'conventionally White'.

Even those classed as 'conventionally White' or 'White British' have been socially constructed for political and economic purposes. Racism, critical race theorists point out, was not only constructed with the aim of subjugating darker-skinned people but was also created to protect the interests of elite White people who hold positions of power in society. For them, racism provides cover for the subjugation of impoverished, working-class White people. The idea of racism works to convince impoverished White British people that racialized immigrants and 'money-grabbing' Jewish people for example are the cause of their problems. Racism thus disincentivizes impoverished Whites from joining forces with impoverished, working-class Black people, thus ensuring that working-class people are divided along racial lines and therefore do not present a unified threat to the middle and upper classes. But this is not to say that impoverished Whites faced the same injustices as those racialized as Black or Brown. Often, their skin colour or British-sounding name will provide some social advantages. W.E.B.

---

[29] For more detailed and nuanced accounts of the debates on whether 'race' is a biological or social construct, see: Angela Saini, *Superior: The Return of Race Science* (4th Estate 2019); Kenan Malik, *Strange Fruit: Why Both Sides Are Wrong in the Race Debate* (Oneworld 2008). Saini notes that scientific accounts of racial hierarchies exist today and were only hidden rather than debunked after the Second World War. Malik provides a nuanced account of how neither the 'scientific' account of race nor the 'social construct' account of race are, by themselves, accurate.

[30] Steve Garner and Saher Selod, 'The Racialization of Muslims: Empirical Studies of Islamophobia' (2015) 41 *Critical Sociology* 9.

Du Bois referred to this as the 'wages of whiteness',[31] which reflects the 'pay-offs' that people receive when racialized as White. This, however, can have a considerably detrimental effect on White-skinned people who have been racialized as something other than 'White British', such as those of a GRT heritage, and Jewish people. In later chapters, we will see how legal authorities have struggled to grasp the sorts of racial injustices these people have faced, as we tend to associate racism with skin colour.

Hall addressed the phenomenon of the ever-changing meaning of 'race' when he described 'race' as a 'floating signifier'.[32] When making the point that definitions of race and racial categories are not static, Hall wrote that race 'is constantly re-signified, made to mean something different in different cultures, in different historical formations, at different moments of time'.[33] Throughout this book, we will see that law has contributed to the social construction of 'race', has failed to recognize that racial inequalities are determined by the exercise of political and social power, and has failed to react to the changing nature of racial injustices.

Intersectionality and anti-essentialism

The previous section on race as a social construct alluded to the idea of social class, and a third concept that informs the analysis of law's relationship with the struggle for racial justice is the idea of 'intersectionality'. Angela Davis explained the idea of intersectionality from a feminist perspective in 1970 when she wrote that 'we cannot ... look at gender in isolation from race [and] from class'.[34] In her view, the subjugation of women in society was intricately tied to other forms of oppression such as racism and classism. In 1989, Crenshaw deployed the term 'intersectionality' to describe the problem of multiple sites of oppression that Davis was writing about.[35] She explained that race, gender, and class as grounds of oppression often intersected with one another, creating different types of oppression. Black men might suffer racism and classism, but they benefit from patriarchism.

---

[31] W.E.B. Du Bois, *Black Reconstruction in America: 1860–1880* (first published 1935, Free Press 1998).

[32] Stuart Hall, 'Race, the Floating Signifier: What More Is There to Say about "Race"?' in Stuart Hall, *Stuart Hall: Selected Writings on Race and Difference* (Paul Gilroy and Ruth Gilmore Wilson eds, Duke University Press 2021), p 359.

[33] Hall (n 32), p 362.

[34] Angela Y. Davis, *Freedom Is a Constant Struggle: Ferguson, Palestine, and the Foundations of a Movement* (Frank Barat ed, Haymarket Books 2016), p 41.

[35] Kimberlé Crenshaw, 'Demarginalizing the Intersection of Race and Sex: A Black Feminist Critique of Antidiscrimination Doctrine, Feminist Theory and Antiracist Politics' (1989) 1 *University of Chicago Legal Forum* 139.

White women might suffer sexism and classism, but they benefit from the 'wages of whiteness'. Black women, on the other hand, will often suffer racism, sexism, and classism simultaneously.

Audre Lorde expressed the importance of adopting an intersectional framework when highlighting in 1983 that the mainstream feminist movement of the time centred the voices of White middle-class women and relegated, if not totally ignored, the voices of Black, lesbian, and/or impoverished women.[36] In her view, the United States was a 'racist patriarchy', in the sense that the country privileged White men over and above all others.[37] By ignoring the lived experiences of Black, lesbian, and impoverished women, the American feminist movement that Lorde was critiquing was effectively strengthening the 'racist patriarchy' by reinforcing its norms. She therefore urged women who claimed to be feminists to not consciously or inadvertently subjugate other social groups. In other words, it is important that advocates for racial justice do not neglect other characteristics such as gender and class, as doing so will simply perpetuate social inequities and injustices.[38]

Although the concept of 'intersectionality' is usually associated with these American-based scholars, British Black feminists have long articulated similar ideas.[39] In the 1940s, for example, Claudia Jones drew links between colonialism and the 'triple oppression' that Black women face. She noted that imperialism was based on exploitation and created racism, thus generating class and racial injustices, but that Black women had suffered particular types of injustices under colonial rule because of their status as women.[40] The Organisation of Women of African and Asian Descent (OWAAD), established in 1978, agreed with Jones' claim that racialized women faced a 'triple oppression', noting that imperialists utilized 'racism to justify their rape of our countries and our people'.[41] OWAAD thus tied the fight for women's liberation to the struggle for racial justice and the imperative of anti-imperialism. In 1979, the organization Southall Black Sisters (SBS) was set up to campaign against the way immigration rules harmed Asian women.

---

[36] Audre Lorde, 'The Master's Tools Will Never Dismantle the Master's House' in *Sister Outsider: Essays and Speeches* (first published 1984, Crossing Press 2007), p 110.

[37] Lorde (n 36), p 110.

[38] For a detailed account of intersectionality as a framework for understanding interlocking oppressions, see Kimberlé Crenshaw, *On Intersectionality: Essential Writings* (New Press 2022).

[39] Oluwaseun Matiluko, 'Decolonising the Master's House: How Black Feminist Epistemologies Can Be and Are Used in Decolonial Strategy' (2020) 54 *The Law Teacher* 547.

[40] Matiluko (n 39), p 554.

[41] Cited in Matiluko (n 39), p 555.

Although SBS is primarily focused on campaigning for the rights of women, they have always recognized how women's rights are affected by racism and classism as well. As Oluwaseun Matiluko explains, then, 'the hallmarks of Black British Feminism are transnational solidarity, imperialism is the root of oppression, and that black women face oppression due to multiple factors, particularly, their race, their gender and their class'.[42]

It is not just feminists who have shed light on the importance of intersectionality. In 1974, Sivanandan assumed editorial duties of the journal *Race* and renamed it *Race & Class* in recognition that the two grounds of oppression were interlinked. The journal's Editorial Committee wrote: 'The concern of the journal continues to be with the oppression of black people in Britain, which necessarily involves the understanding of the place of black workers, and indeed of all migrant workers, within the entire working class ... hence the new title *Race & Class*.'[43] Similarly, we should not limit intersectional analyses to the categories of race, gender, and class. Discrimination on the basis of other characteristics such as disabilities and, as Lorde pointed out, sexual orientation can also compound racial injustices.

An important feature of theories of intersectionality is that these characteristics, and the harms inflicted on the basis of them, cannot be separated out. Lisa Bowleg explains this by comparing personal characteristics to the ingredients for baking a cake and notes that '[o]nce you've blended the cake, you can't take the parts back to the main ingredients'.[44] If a person has been treated unjustly because of a combination of their race, gender, and class, then we cannot separate those characteristics out and tackle each injustice separately. That is, we should not reduce the essence of a person to one characteristic, such as race. To engage in this sort of essentialism would be to replicate the essentialism of scientific accounts of racial differences, which sought to define a person according to their so-called biological race. Therefore, when addressing instances of racial injustices, we would hope for the legal system to be cognizant of how a person's other characteristics such as gender, class, disability, sexual orientation, and so on might compound the harms they have suffered. Throughout, though, we will see that legal processes do not generally accommodate the idea of intersectionality, which in turn means that these processes cannot adequately address the injustices suffered. Indeed, there is a real possibility that a judgment in favour of racial

---

[42] Matiluko (n 39), p 555.
[43] 'Editorial' (1975) 16 *Race & Class* 231, 231.
[44] Lisa Bowleg, '"Once You've Blended the Cake, You Can't Take the Parts Back to the Main Ingredients": Black Gay and Bisexual Men's Descriptions and Experiences of Intersectionality' (2013) 68 *Sex Roles* 754.

justice that does not address intersecting characteristics might, as Lorde warned, entrench other forms of oppression.

Interest-convergence

If the legal system is mired in racism, then the occasions on which the legal system appears to advance the cause of racial justice need explaining. Bell provocatively argued that US Supreme Court decisions which appeared to benefit Black Americans tended to also benefit White Americans and could therefore be explained on the basis that the interests of Black and White Americans converged. In his words: 'The interest of blacks in achieving racial equality will be accommodated only when it converges with the interests of whites.'[45] Bell used the decision in *Brown v Board of Education* in 1954 to explain this. In this case, the US Supreme Court ruled it unconstitutional to segregate schools along racial lines. When analysing the Supreme Court's judgment, Bell argued that the Court only ruled this way because the decision would also benefit White people. He identified three reasons why: elite Whites were concerned about the reaction of Black soldiers who were returning from the Second World War and the Korean War, segregated schools were tarnishing America's reputation worldwide at a crucial moment in the Cold War, and some Whites had come to believe that segregation was a barrier to industrialization and economic progress in the Southern states. Legal successes in England and Wales need similar interrogation, and we will see that the idea of 'interest-convergence' is often helpful when trying to make sense of apparent legal successes. For example, although David Scott does not use the term 'interest-convergence' when explaining the work of British anti-slavery campaigners in the 18th and 19th centuries, he is in effect referring to this concept when he explains that these campaigners only took action against slavery when it was jeopardizing the moral legitimacy of the British Empire.[46] In Chapter 2, we will see that the legal abolition of slavery in 1833 was hardly a victory for racial justice because, at the same time, British authorities were inflicting all manner of racial injustices across India and other colonies. If anti-slavery activists were really concerned with racial justice per se, they would have taken action against imperialism in all forms. This is a crucial point, since it means that even apparent legal successes are not really successes for racial justice if they serve the purpose of sustaining a society that prioritizes the interests of those classed as White British.

---

[45] Derrick Bell, '*Brown v. Board of Education* and the Interest-Convergence Dilemma' (1980) 93 *Harvard Law Review* 518, 523.

[46] David Scott, 'Abolitionism Must Come from Below: A Critique of British Anti-slavery Abolition' (2020) OpenLearn.

Lived theory

Critical race theorists have also emphasized the importance of centring the voices of those with lived experience of racial injustices. This is crucial for bridging the gap between theory and practice. All too often, theories of race and racism, and analyses of legislation and case law, can neglect the experiences of people and communities whose lives are profoundly affected by injustices. Sivanandan recognized the problems with this and thus ensured that his thinking was 'constantly being fed or being challenged by [my] immersion in "the facts on the ground"'.[47] He refused to use pre-ordained theoretical frameworks to address social problems but instead looked to how those 'on the ground' felt about the situation and resolved to tackle the problem from their point of view. Avery Gordon described this approach as a 'lived theory',[48] and this has been supported by the United Nations High Commissioner for Human Rights, who acknowledged in 2022 that 'lived experiences [are] key to achieve racial justice and equality'.[49]

Writing about the abolition of slavery in the British Empire, Peter Fryer notes that it was those with experience of racial injustice who freed themselves by resisting enslavement and escaping whenever possible.[50] Scott concurs, noting that it was 'slaves and former slaves [who were] genuinely radical and emancipatory social actors', rather than the White 'liberal anti-slavery abolitionists, such as Granville Sharp, Thomas Clarkson and William Wilberforce [who] all benefitted from either aristocratic patronage, wealth and/or had access to the political elite'. In his view, these activists were 'reformers who were looking to strengthen the moral legitimacy of the current social, political and economic order', which included other forms of labour exploitation within Britain and across Empire. In contrast, those with experience of slavery understood that the current social, political, and economic order was not compatible with their struggle for freedom.[51] As we will see throughout, when legal actors have ignored the voices of those with lived experience, they have either set back progress towards racial justice or have missed an opportunity to make progress. Today's lawyers and campaigners would therefore do well to learn from those with lived experience of racial injustices.

---

[47] Avery F. Gordon, 'On "Lived Theory": An Interview with A. Sivanandan' (2014) 55 *Race & Class* 1, 4.

[48] Gordon (n 47); Jasbinder S. Nijjar, 'Sociological Imagination, "Lived Theory" and Black Liberation: The Legacy of A. Sivanandan' (2018) *The Sociological Review Magazine*.

[49] Office of the High Commissioner for Human Rights, 'Lived Experiences Key to Achieve Racial Justice and Equality' (United Nations, 25 October 2022).

[50] Peter Fryer, *Staying Power: The History of Black People in Britain* (Pluto Press 2018), p 134.

[51] Scott (n 46).

The inherent limitations of legal processes

The preceding five tenets of CRT are largely focused on issues external to the legal system but which affect legal proceedings. The sixth tenet of CRT that informs the analysis of the limits of law is focused on the inherent shortcomings of the legal system and legal processes. The legal system of England and Wales comprises substantive laws (legislation and case law), and legal processes for ensuring that laws are adhered to and applied fairly. The term 'legal action' refers to the use of this system – these law and processes – to ensure that individuals, private organizations, and public authorities comply with their legal duties. The law can be used in many different ways. Drawing on Lisa Vanhala's work,[52] we might use legal norms to *empower* individuals and racial justice groups, so that people are aware of their legal rights and can stand up for themselves in the face of actual or potential racial injustices. For example, the organization StopWatch has created educational resources about individuals' rights when interacting with the police, with a particular emphasis on teaching racialized communities about their legal rights.[53] We might use the law to *inform* the wider public about racial injustices, or to persuade those in political power to change the law in light of such racial injustices. For example, the campaigning group Joint Enterprise Not Guilty by Association (JENGbA) have used the language of the law to raise public awareness of racial discrimination in certain aspects of the criminal law and have also engaged with lawmakers when lobbying for legislative changes.[54] But perhaps the action that most people think of when they hear 'legal action' is the use of litigation to *challenge* people or organizations who have allegedly not complied with their legal obligations. This might involve direct challenges to individuals or private companies, or applications to have the policies and practices of public authorities judicially reviewed for their compatibility with the law. In some instances, this is retrospective in that legal action is invoked after a breach of the law has allegedly occurred. In other instances, legal action can be prospective by ensuring that legal duties are complied with. And litigation might be focused on the particular facts of a specific case, or it might be strategic in that it seeks to secure changes that will benefit a broader range of people than just the parties to the case.[55]

---

[52] Lisa Vanhala, 'Framework for Better Use of the Law by the Voluntary Sector' (Baring Foundation 2016), pp 4–6.
[53] StopWatch, 'Rights and Wellbeing' project, Available from: https://www.stop-watch.org/what-we-do/projects/raw
[54] For more information about JENGbA's work, see https://jointenterprise.co
[55] Lisa Vanhala, 'Successful Use of Strategic Litigation by the Voluntary Sector on Issues Related to Discrimination and Disadvantage: Key Cases from the UK' (Baring Foundation 2017).

We are usually assured that however the law is made, and however it is enforced and applied, the legal system is neutral and impartial. Law's alleged neutrality is depicted by the symbol of the blindfolded – and thus unbiased – Lady Justice. However, the legal system is not some autonomous and monolithic entity with a mind and personality of its own. The legal system is a collection of principles, rules, procedures, and institutions that are created, implemented, administered, and staffed by people who have their own understandings of history, their own conscious and unconscious biases and prejudices, and their own political values and cultural identity.[56] The 'rule of law' might sound like a concept that tempers people's prejudices, ensuring that law prevails over personal whims, but the concept is a malleable one, defined by human beings with their personal biases. Indeed, we will see in Chapter 2 that the 'rule of law' was used to justify imperialism and the injustices of imperial rule during the era of the British Empire in ways that the idea would likely not be used now. Thus, the legal system's potential to promote racial justice is limited by legal officials' biases and understandings. We can see this in the context of both legislation and litigation.

There are many benefits to the creation of legislation to tackle racial injustices. Acts of Parliament have democratic legitimacy, are forward-looking, and can be preventative of harms. Legislation can be written to provide collective solutions to social problems such as racism,[57] with the Public Sector Equality Duty (PSED) that is contained in the Equality Act 2010 being one example of a prospective and collective measure to prevent racial injustices from occurring. The PSED, we will see in Chapter 4, requires public authorities to develop policies and measures that foster positive race relations. However, legislation is the product of political compromise and negotiation between people with very different conceptions of liberalism, different understandings of racial justice, and different electoral priorities.[58] This means that legislation rarely goes far enough to prevent racial injustices, with the parliamentary debates over the Race Relations Bill in the 1960s (discussed in Chapter 3) providing a stark illustration of the limits of legislation.

In terms of litigation, there are many examples of individuals securing some sort of redress in the courts for racial harms that they have suffered. While these are to be welcomed, we will see that litigation sometimes has the effect of reinforcing the erroneous belief that racial injustices are isolated

---

[56] See Peter Fitzpatrick and Alan Hunt, 'Critical Legal Studies: Introduction' (1987) 14 *Journal of Law and Society* 1.

[57] Thanks to Steven Cammiss for helping me formulate this point.

[58] For a thought-provoking account of how the idea of 'liberalism' actually fosters racial inequities, see Charles W. Mills, *Black Rights/White Wrongs: The Critique of Racial Liberalism* (Oxford University Press 2017).

events that can be attributed to individual aberrations from the legal rules and the normal course of society.[59] Litigation also rarely goes far enough, with victims of racism often explaining that racial injustices are 'lifelong' events that stay with them forever, and which legal action alone cannot fix.[60] Litigation also tends to be expensive and take a long time and can therefore be both financially and emotionally exhausting. And adversarial processes can be ill-suited to the pursuit of racial justice, exacerbating tensions between peoples and communities. Racial justice requires conversation and dialogue, teaching and learning, empathy and understanding. Adversarial legal processes, though, tend to involve argumentation and denial, a drive to win and a fear of losing.

A note on language

The critique of law's approach to racial injustice that takes place over the following chapters is premised on the six concepts of CRT that have been outlined in the current chapter. Before embarking on this study, though, a note on terminology is required. Despite the ubiquity of the terms in the literature, I have tried to avoid the phrases 'Black and Minority Ethnic' (BME) or 'Black and Asian Minority Ethnic' (BAME) because both these terms reinforce the discredited 'scientific' accounts of races, and they entrench the view that 'Whiteness' is the norm that all other races are to be compared to. With their focus on 'Black' and 'Asian', the terms also trivialize the racial harms suffered by those with white skin, but who are not considered to be 'conventionally White', such as Jewish people and those of GRT heritage.[61] And by suggesting that all those who are not conventionally White can be classed under one umbrella term, the terms BME and BAME fail to distinguish between the different types of racial injustices that different racial or ethnic groups suffer. For example, Black people of African descent experience different types of racial injustices than Black people of Caribbean descent, and GRT people suffer different types of racial injustices than both Black Africans and Black Caribbeans.[62] The terms also mask instances of racism *within* and *among* those not considered to be White British. There

---

[59] On the limits of rights-based approaches to law in addressing social problems that need collective solutions, see Mary Ann Glendon, *Rights Talk: The Impoverishment of Political Discourse* (Free Press 1995).

[60] Thanks to Sy Joshua for this observation.

[61] See, for example, Kalwant Bhopal, ' "What about Us?" Gypsies, Travellers and "White Racism" in Secondary Schools in England' (2011) 21 *International Studies in Sociology of Education* 315.

[62] See Chapter 3 for a discussion of how different racial groups face different types of racism in fields such as education, criminal justice, education, housing, and healthcare.

is considerable evidence, for example, of Indians holding prejudices against Black people.[63]

Another reason for rejecting the terms BME and BAME lies in the use of the word 'minority'. This implies that certain groups of people are mistreated because there are numerically fewer of them in society. However, numbers are not the issue. There are fewer children of billionaires, Folúkẹ́ Adébísí notes, than children of non-billionaires, yet they do not face the types of injustices that so-called 'BME' people face.[64] Adébísí suggests that power, rather than numbers, is the driving force of racial injustice, and law's inability to tackle the dimension of power is something that is addressed later in this book.

For these reasons, I have opted to use the phrase 'racialized people' or 'racialized person' instead, as I think this better captures the way in which people are assigned, however inappropriately, to racial categories for political, cultural, social, and economic purposes. Of course, as noted, people with 'white' skin are racialized as well, and perhaps a more accurate phrase to use would be 'people who have been racialized to their disadvantage'. This would be quite cumbersome to use throughout, though, and so I have generally shortened this to 'racialized people'.

Other terms that are ubiquitous in the literature, but which I try to avoid, are the terms 'equality', 'diversity', and 'inclusion', which are commonly abbreviated to 'EDI'. Almost all organizations now speak about their commitment to EDI, and the phrase seems positively antiracist because it appears to ensure that racialized people are treated equally to others and are heard and listened to as well. However, all three terms are problematic. The word 'equality' misses the point that people of different racial backgrounds do not enjoy the same starting point as each other by virtue of historical marginalization and oppression. The organization Black Equity Organisation explains why the term 'equity' is preferable to 'equality': 'Both concepts are essentially about fairness, but while equality sees everyone treated the same, equity achieves this by taking into account people's different starting points.'[65]

When companies speak about 'diversity', they are in effect speaking about 'diversity *from* Whiteness'. In other words, Whiteness is the norm which they will accept diversity from. When they speak of 'inclusivity', they are in effect speaking about including racialized people *within* 'White' spaces,

---

[63] See, for example, Anjalee Suthakaran, 'How Can We South Asians Dismantle Racism in our UK Communities?' (EachOther, 27 August 2020), Available from: https://eachot her.org.uk/how-can-we-south-asians-dismantle-racism-in-our-uk-communities

[64] Folúkẹ́ Adébísí, 'The Only Accurate Part of "BAME" Is the "And" ...' (African Skies blog, 8 July 2019), Available from: https://folukeafrica.com/the-only-accepta ble-part-of-bame-is-the-and

[65] 'Equity and Equality: What's the Difference?' (Black Equity Organisation nd), Available from: https://blackequityorg.com/#

which implies that White spaces are the norm which racialized people will be graciously welcomed into so long as they do not challenge the structures that may create and sustain racial injustices. A better phrase than EDI would be 'equity and intersectionality'. For example, rather than speak of a 'diverse' and 'inclusive' workforce, which assumes that Whiteness is the norm, we should instead speak of an 'equitable and intersectional' workforce, which does not indicate which 'race', if any, is the norm.

Conclusion

With these understandings of the six key concepts of CRT in mind, we can now explore how the relationship between law and the struggle for racial justice has evolved over the years. We will start with the use of law during the era of colonial rule, and readers are warned that in the next chapters it has unfortunately been difficult, if not impossible, to avoid repeating offensive terms, where quotes have been used to illustrate the depth of racism in law and society. Similarly, it has not been possible to avoid recounting harrowing incidents of racial injustices, including the horrendous mistreatment of enslaved people and the attempted degradation of people racialized as something other than White British. I am aware that these accounts will be upsetting for some readers, particularly those who have suffered racial traumas or whose ancestors are known to have suffered. I therefore apologise in advance to readers for some of the content that lies ahead.

2

Racial Justice and Law: The Colonial Era

Introduction

The legal system has long been used to create the idea of 'race' and racial differences and to structuralize racism within society. An early example is the Egyptians Act of 1530. A group of people, now thought to have originated in northern India, arrived in England around the turn of the 16th century, but because of their nomadic way of life they were viewed with some suspicion. As a result, a range of repressive laws were introduced, such as the 1530 Act which imposed a complete ban on the immigration of these people that came to be known as Gypsies (reflecting a contemporary belief that they had travelled from Egypt). Another Egyptians Act in 1554 subjected Gypsies who had been in England unlawfully for one month to the death penalty. These Acts reflected a belief that their way of life posed a threat to the social order, but the laws also shaped public attitudes towards Gypsies and other travellers such as Romani people for years to come.[1]

In this chapter, we will explore more broadly how law was historically used to structuralize racism within British society. The emergence of the British Empire, we will see, brought with it the development of a two-tiered legal system: one for those racialized as White British, and a more disadvantageous one for those who were colonized and racialized as something other than White British. We will first explore the use of law to justify imperialism, and we will then see how law was used to maintain imperial rule up to the turn of the 20th century.

---

[1] Derek Hawes and Barbara Perez, *The Gypsy and the State: The Ethnic Cleansing of British Society* (2nd edn, Policy Press 1996).

The use of law to justify imperialism

The British Empire was first and foremost a capitalistic endeavour. British imperialists were initially keen to accumulate wealth and power, but the ever-changing political, social, and economic context over several centuries meant that the Empire was ultimately a multifaceted and amorphous project. The seeds of imperialism were arguably sown when English rulers began assuming power in Ireland and Wales as early as the thirteenth century, but Empire-building took on new meanings when English settlers arrived in Jamestown, Virginia, in 1607. The establishment of settlements across North America and the West Indies, which has come to be known as the 'First Empire', mainly involved local rule, with only a degree of oversight from London. The American War of Independence and the loss of the North American colonies marked the shift towards the 'Second Empire', which ran from the 1780s and generally – but not always – involved territorial annexation across the globe, including large swathes of Africa and Asia, and direct political control from London.[2] By the mid- to late 1800s, Empire was an amalgam of different political entities including colonies, protectorates, dominions, consulates, and so on. It was an enormous empire too, with Queen Victoria at one point claiming over 450 million people as her subjects.[3]

Despite the variations in the type and level of control that the British exerted over different territories and peoples at different times, there was a common thread to Empire: in all cases, the acts of taking and exercising control were coercive acts which were motivated by a desire to accumulate wealth and power and which disregarded the views and welfare of local populations. The historian Caroline Elkins explains this: 'Coercion was central to initial acts of conquest and to the maintenance of rule over nonconsenting populations.'[4] To square coercive rule with the emerging conceptions of liberalism that were influencing policy makers and broader society in Britain, imperialists had to explain how the development of Empire was compatible with the 'rule of law' and its concomitant principles of 'liberty' and 'equality before the law'. This could have been an insurmountable paradox, since imperial rule clearly denied colonized people 'liberty' and 'equality' in both law and

---

[2] For more nuanced and detailed accounts of English rule in Ireland and the differences between the 'First' and 'Second' Empire, see D. Harkness, 'Ireland', P.J. Marshall, 'The First British Empire' and C.A. Bayly, 'The Second British Empire' in Robin Winks and Wm. Roger Louis (eds), *The Oxford History of the British Empire: Volume V; Historiography* (Oxford University Press 1999).

[3] Caroline Elkins, *Legacy of Violence: A History of the British Empire* (The Bodley Head 2022), pp 60–1.

[4] Elkins (n 3), p 35.

practice.⁵ As John McLaren explains, though, the 'rule of law' in the colonial era 'was a highly tensile notion. Its meaning varied depending on who was employing it and for what purpose'.⁶ Imperialists were able to construct a conception of the 'rule of law' that accommodated racism, and this had a long-lasting effect on law's relationship with the struggle for racial justice.

The logic of imperialists generally proceeded as follows. First, they described the indigenous people they encountered in their conquests as irrational, barbaric, and backwards. Second, they attributed these characteristics to skin colour, deploying pseudo-scientific accounts to support the claim that indigenous people were developmentally inferior to white-skinned people. Third, they argued that it was incumbent on the 'enlightened'⁷ British to introduce British values such as the rule of law to these populations, so that they could 'emerge into civilization'.⁸ The 'rule of law', therefore, not only justified imperial rule but demanded it too. Although Rudyard Kipling was writing in a slightly different context, he captured this sentiment when he described imperial rule for the alleged benefit of colonized people as the 'White Man's Burden'.⁹

In 1874, the Secretary of State for the Colonies, Lord Carnarvon, explained why, in his view, the implementation of British laws was central to the so-called 'civilizing' mission. He stated that the exportation of the British conception of the 'rule of law' to the colonies would bring an end to the alleged barbaric practices of native populations and would ensure that 'the humblest may enjoy freedom from oppression and wrong equally with the greatest'.¹⁰ Nearly a century later, Sir Kenneth Roberts-Wray, who was the legal advisor at the Colonial Office, claimed that 'British administration in overseas countries has conferred no greater benefit than English law and justice'.¹¹ The historian Shashi Tharoor notes that, for British imperialists, '[b]ringing British law to the natives was arguably one of the most important

---

[5] Martin J. Wiener, *An Empire on Trial: Race, Murder, and Justice under British Rule, 1870–1935* (Cambridge University Press 2009), p 2.

[6] John McLaren, 'The Uses of the Rule of Law in British Colonial Societies in the Nineteenth Century' in Shaunnagh Dorsett and Ian Hunter (eds), *Law and Politics in British Colonial Thought* (Palgrave Macmillan US 2010), p 71.

[7] For an introduction to the so-called 'age of enlightenment' in which these ideas came to the fore, see John Robertson, *The Enlightenment: A Very Short Introduction* (Oxford University Press 2015).

[8] These are the words of Lord Carnarvon, in 1874, quoted in Michael Lobban, *Imperial Incarceration: Detention without Trial in the Making of British Colonial Africa* (Cambridge University Press 2021), p 2.

[9] Patrick Brantlinger, 'Kipling's "The White Man's Burden" and Its Afterlives' (2007) 50 *English Literature in Transition 1880–1920*, 172.

[10] Lobban (n 8), p 2.

[11] Sir Kenneth Roberts-Wray, 'The Adaptation of Imported Law in Africa' (1960) 4 *Journal of African Law* 66, 66.

constituent elements of [their] mission'.[12] Just as the nature of Empire itself was protean, though, so too was the implementation of British laws. In some places, British laws replaced indigenous legal systems entirely; in other places, British laws were woven into existing legal systems and cultures.[13] In virtually all cases, though, perceptions of 'race' affected how different people experienced law. In India, for example, a penal code was drafted with the explicit purpose of 'legislating for a conquered race, to whom the blessings of our constitution cannot as yet be safely extended'.[14] Thus, as Tharoor explains, 'in its application during the colonial era, the rule of law was not exactly impartial. Justice, in British India, was far from blind: it was highly attentive to the skin colour of the defendant'.[15] Bal Gangadhar Tilak, who was a prominent campaigner for Indian independence, wryly noted in 1907 that the 'goddess of British Justice, though blind, is able to distinguish unmistakably black from white'.[16] In other words, two legal systems emerged: one for those deemed White and British and superior, and one for those racialized as something other than White British and deemed inferior. In some cases, the actual substantive law was different for these two classes of people; in other cases, the substantive law was the same but was applied very differently. We will see in Chapters 3 and 4 that the creation of a two-tiered legal system split across racial lines has had a long-lasting legacy, with Leslie Thomas KC noting in 2022 that even today 'it is a myth that Lady Justice is blind to colour'.[17]

The promise that British laws would be used to 'civilize' native populations was a false promise. It would not be in Britain's financial interests to ever grant indigenous populations equal legal rights to British colonizers. Indeed, once their 'backward traits' were attributed to skin colour, there was no way for these indigenous populations to 'emerge into civilization', since their skin colour was fixed. Thus, the emphasis of British rule turned to keeping colonized populations subjugated. As outlined later, their freedoms to move were restricted, they were made to work for low wages, and barbaric punishments were inflicted for even the most trivial transgressions of social and legal norms. Law was used to provide a veneer of legitimacy to the

---

[12] Shashi Tharoor, *Inglorious Empire: What the British Did to India* (Penguin Books 2017), p 89.
[13] Shaunnagh Dorsett and John McLaren, *Legal Histories of the British Empire: Laws, Engagements and Legacies* (Routledge 2014).
[14] Quoted in Tharoor (n 12), p 90.
[15] Tharoor (n 12), p 89.
[16] Cited in Elizabeth Kolsky, *Colonial Justice in British India* (Cambridge University Press 2010), p 4.
[17] Quoted in Haroon Siddique, 'Judiciary in England and Wales "Institutionally Racist", Says Report' *The Guardian* (18 October 2022).

mistreatment of racialized people. Put simply, then, racism was used to justify both the legal act of colonization ('they need our help') and the subsequent legal mistreatment of those populations ('they need to be controlled and disciplined').[18] It is to this legal mistreatment that we now turn, with a view to establishing how law embedded racism within social structures in both the colonies and, crucially, the metropole.

Law and slavery

Race-based slavery was a central feature of British rule in the American colonies and the West Indies, and the law that established and regulated slavery in the colonies had an impact on the substance and operation of the law in the metropole. This in turn embedded racial injustices into the fabric of society in the UK. In particular, enslaved Black Africans were denied legal personhood, sowing the seeds of a two-tiered legal system that was differentiated by race.

Law and slavery in the 1500s

The earliest known legal case to have involved the issue of slavery occurred in 1569, in the case of *Cartwright*. Cartwright had been accused of beating another man but had defended his actions on the basis that he had enslaved this man and could therefore do with him as he pleased. Although there is no official transcript of the case, a quote from the judgment was repeated in later cases: 'England was too pure an Air for Slaves to breathe in.'[19] Without the full transcript, there is no way of objectively contextualizing this statement, and historians are not certain what the phrase was intended to mean. Olusoga questions whether the statement reflected the specifics of Cartwright's case and merely prohibited the use of force against enslaved people, or whether the statement reflected a broader point about the illegality of slavery in England.[20] No statutes were ever passed to authorize slavery in England, and other cases in the 1500s suggest that legal authorities were keen to disavow slavery. For example, in 1587, a physician named Hector Nuñez lodged a petition with the Court of Requests in London when a Black man he claimed to have purchased and enslaved refused to carry out

---

[18] Tayyab Mahmud, 'Colonialism and Modern Constructions of Race: A Preliminary Inquiry' (1999) 53 *University of Miami Law Review* 1219, 1219 ('capacity and eligibility to freedom and progress were deemed biologically determined, and colonialism was legitimated as the natural subordination of lesser races to higher ones').
[19] See Peter Fryer, *Staying Power: The History of Black People in Britain* (Pluto Press 2018), p 116.
[20] David Olusoga, *Black and British: A Forgotten History* (revised edn, Picador 2021), p 118.

the duties that he assigned to him. When Nuñez sought to compel servitude through legal proceedings, he discovered that there had been no legal basis for the sale, and that English law did not recognize slavery within England. Since English common law provided no remedy, Nuñez petitioned the Queen directly, through the Court of Requests. There is no record of how the case was ultimately resolved, but the records that do exist nonetheless shed some light on how English law applied to Jewish people and those of African descent, and on how race has always been a social and legal construct. Openly practising Judaism was prohibited, but Jews like Nuñez were generally tolerated and enjoyed various legal rights and privileges, such as the ability to initiate legal action. Likewise, people from Africa were not presumed to be enslaved in ways that they would come to be in later years.[21]

Law and slavery in the 1600s

The development of the law on slavery was profoundly affected by the arrival of English settlers in what is now North America and Britain's involvement in the transatlantic trade in enslaved people. Sir John Hawkins and Sir Francis Drake were the first Englishmen to engage in this trade in 1564, but it was in 1672, when the Royal African Company was set up, that Britain's role in the trade increased substantially.[22]

An example of law's role in constructing the idea of race and racial differences can be found in 1655, when an enslaved woman of dual heritage named Elizabeth Key sued for her freedom and the freedom of her son in the British colony of Virginia. Key's mother was an enslaved Black woman, and her father was a free White Englishman. She argued that, in the absence of statutory law to the contrary, under English common law she should inherit the status of her father and therefore be free. Her suit reached the Virginia General Assembly, which decided 'that by the Common Law the Child of a Woman slave begot by a freeman ought to be free'.[23] There are three aspects of this case which are of interest here. First, the Assembly assumed the general legality of enslaving people who had been racialized as Black. Second, Key's success was met with a backlash, as lawmakers in Virginia responded by enacting a statute in 1662 that rendered the status of the child dependent on the mother instead. The law effectively created a production line of enslaved people from birth, and over time more laws were

---

[21] Carole Levin, 'Elizabeth's England and Others' in Carole Levin, *The Reign and Life of Queen Elizabeth I* (Springer International Publishing 2022), p 204.

[22] K.G. Davies, *The Royal African Company* (Octagon Books 1975).

[23] Taunya Lovell Banks, 'Elizabeth Key, Seventeenth-Century Virginia (US)' in Erica L. Ball et al (eds), *As If She Were Free: A Collective Biography of Women and Emancipation in the Americas* (Cambridge University Press 2020).

enacted in the colonies to legitimize, regulate, and perpetuate race-based slavery.[24] These laws categorized enslaved people as chattel, or property that slaveowners could dispose of as they wished. In this sense, they were denied legal personhood. Third, the case and the subsequent legislation entrenched the status of enslaved women as producers of enslaved people, presenting an early example of the problem of intersectional oppression described by Crenshaw and other critical race theorists. That is, enslaved Black women were to be oppressed in different ways from enslaved Black men on account of their gender as well as their race.

By the mid-1600s, then, we can see that the legal system in the metropole was officially silent on the issue of slavery, but that laws in the colonies were being developed which explicitly permitted slavery. For some time, these contradictory systems were able to operate side-by-side, but difficulties arose when slaveowners from the colonies travelled to the metropole and brought enslaved people with them. The absence of statutory law raised several questions that judges had to grapple with. Did the law relating to slavery in the colonies travel with the slaveowner and the enslaved, or were the judges to apply principles from municipal law? Could enslaved people be characterized as 'property' for the purposes of legal action? The Court of King's Bench addressed questions such as these in *Butts v Penny*, decided in 1677. The Court was presented with an action for trover, which was an action to recover the value of property that had allegedly been taken illegally. The property in this case was ten enslaved African people. The Court therefore had to determine whether enslaved African people could be categorized as property for the purposes of legal action. In an unambiguously pro-slavery opinion, the Court suggested that enslaved people from Africa could be classified as 'merchandise' for the purposes of legal transactions, because they were routinely bought and sold.[25] In other words, social customs determined the content of the law, and the Court made it clear that certain people could be classed as something other than human for certain legal purposes. The racial dimension of this cannot be understated. The Court justified enslavement on the grounds that 'negroes' were 'infidels' and therefore unable to be free.[26]

Although the opinion in *Butts v Penny* was pro-slavery and racially unjust, it had no precedential value. While the Court offered some suggestions for how the case could be decided, the judges did not issue a decisive ruling

---

[24] Known as 'slave codes', the first was established in 1661, which, among other things, controlled relationships between White people and enslaved Black people.
[25] *Butts v Penny* 2 Lev 201, 83 Eng Rep 518 (KB 1677). See William M. Wiecek, 'Somerset: Lord Mansfield and the Legitimacy of Slavery in the Anglo-American World' (1974) 42 *University of Chicago Law Review* 86, 89–90 for discussion.
[26] Wiecek (n 25), p 89.

because the Attorney General had asked to intervene in the proceedings. There is no record, though, of how the Attorney General intervened, or of the final judgment. Perhaps for this reason, Chief Justice Sir John Holt felt able to reject the *Butts* doctrine 20 years later. In *Chamberlain v Harvey*, decided in 1696, Holt stated that enslaved people could not be treated and disposed of as if they were 'chattel' or 'property', since that would imply they had no freedoms at all.[27] Instead, Holt ruled, enslaved people were akin to an apprenticed labourer, or 'a slavish servant'. This meant that although their freedom was restricted, their freedom was not removed entirely.[28] According to Holt, a slaveowner may have property rights in the enslaved person's *labour*, but they could not have property rights in the enslaved person's *body*. There are several aspects of this decision that are noteworthy. First, despite his rejection of *Butts*, Holt betrayed a view of racial capitalism – that the furtherance of White people's wealth depended on the subjugation of non-Whites. Second, the case marked an evolution in the relationship between law and slavery. In *Butts*, the Court had justified the enslavement of Black people on religious grounds – they were considered 'infidels'. In *Chamberlain*, though, the enslaved person in question had been baptized, and his lawyers argued that he should therefore now "acquire the privileges and immunities enjoyed by those of the same religion, and be intitled to the laws of England".[29] Because English statutory law was silent on slavery, they were able to argue that the common law should be developed in accordance with the presumption of liberty that was at the heart of 'the law of nature'. They also invoked Magna Carta and argued that in England, no person could hold property rights in another person. Although Holt's opinion did not go so far as to endorse these arguments, the proceedings laid the foundation for understanding the interplay between colonialism, racism, and law. The lawyers' arguments also highlighted the tension between the underlying principles of English law, which espoused the values of liberty and equality, and the substantive law of slavery, which was the antithesis of respect for liberty and equality. This tension between the promise of the law and the practice of the law in the context of racial justice is one that exists today, as we will see in later chapters.

Law and slavery in the 1700s

In *Smith v Brown and Cooper*, decided in 1701, Holt again appeared to strike a blow to the institution of slavery when he wrote: '[A]s soon as a negro comes into England, he becomes free; one may be a villein in England,

---

[27] *Chamberlain v Harvey*, 1 Ld Raym 146, 91 Eng Rep 994 (KB 1697).
[28] These cases are discussed at length by Wiecek (n 25).
[29] See Wiecek (n 25), p 92.

but not a slave.'[30] The case again involved the legal status of an enslaved person who had been brought to England, and the statement taken out of context could certainly appear to be anti-slavery. However, as historian William Wiecek points out, Holt also suggested a procedural mode by which the enslaved person's owner could recover the value of the person who had been sold.[31] In other words, Holt endorsed the sale of a human being, which can hardly be read as an attack on slavery. Five years later, in *Smith v Gould*, Holt and his colleagues on the King's Bench once again repudiated *Butts v Penny* and said that a human being could not be classed as 'property', while simultaneously finding a way for a slaveowner to assert title over an enslaved person.[32]

By the early 1700s, then, the law in the metropole was at best ambivalent about slavery. Judicial decisions were not favourable to the institution of slavery, but they were certainly not 'anti-slavery' or 'antiracist' as such. Merchants and slaveowners were nonetheless worried that the courts would soon unequivocally rule that once an enslaved person was brought from the colonies to England, they would automatically be free. Slaveowners in the colonies were fearful that this line of thinking would spread to the colonies, jeopardizing their livelihoods. Within the metropole, businesspeople with a commercial interest in slavery expressed concerns that such a ruling would stifle the ability of slaveowners to come to England for business. A group of influential traders, referred to as the West India Lobby (also known as the West India Interest), therefore asked the Attorney General and the Solicitor General for their views on the legal effect of bringing enslaved people from the colonies to the metropole, and the legal effect of baptizing enslaved people. In 1729, Sir Philip Yorke and Charles Talbot – the Attorney General and Solicitor General respectively – issued a short but clear opinion which suggested that the law was firmly on the side of slaveowners. It read, in its entirety:

> We are of Opinion, that a Slave, by coming from the West-Indies to Great Britain or Ireland, either with or without his Master, doth not become free, and that his Master's Property, or Right in him, is not thereby determined or varied. And that Baptism doth not bestow Freedom on him, nor make any alteration in his temporal Condition in these Kingdoms. We are also of Opinion, that his Master may legally compel him to return again to the Plantations.[33]

---

[30] *Smith v Brown and Cooper*, 2 Salk 666, 91 Eng Rep 566 (KB 1701).
[31] Wiecek (n 25), p 92.
[32] *Smith v Gould*, 2 Ld Raym 1274, 92 Eng Rep 338 (KB 1706).
[33] See Nicholas Leah, 'Confronting the Yorke–Talbot Slavery Opinion and Its Legacy within English Law' (Gatehouse Chambers, July 2021), Available from: https://gatehouselaw.co.uk/confronting-the-yorke-talbot-slavery-opinion-and-its-legacy-within-english-law

While this was not a definitive statement of the law, it was now clear what the two most senior legal officials in the country believed. First, they believed that enslaved people coming to Great Britain were not liberated upon arrival, and a slaveowner's property right in the enslaved person was not affected by travelling to the metropole. Second, they stated that baptism did not liberate an enslaved person or affect their status as an enslaved person. Third, they claimed that the law permitted slaveowners to forcibly remove enslaved people from the metropole and return them to the colonies against their wishes.

The Yorke–Talbot Opinion soon came to influence the development of English law. In 1733, Yorke was appointed Lord Chief Justice of the King's Bench, and between 1737 and 1756 he served as Lord Chancellor, taking the name of Lord Hardwicke. He took this opportunity to repudiate Holt's jurisprudence and to resurrect the reasoning set out in *Butts v Penny*. In *Pearne v Lisle*, he directly contradicted Holt by stating that enslaved people were essentially 'property' for the purposes of the law.[34] However, 13 years later, Hardwicke's successor – Lord Chancellor Henley – ruled that enslaved people *are* liberated upon arrival into Great Britain and *can* take legal action against their master.[35]

The ambiguous and often conflicting judicial decisions of the late 1600s and much of the 1700s were not reflective of statutory law, which was quite explicitly racist. Although there was no Act of Parliament that explicitly authorized slavery, there were many which assumed its legality and therefore legitimized the practice. For example, statutes were enacted in 1732 and 1752 that regulated the slave trade and confirmed slaveowners' property rights in enslaved persons respectively. The racial dimension of these laws was clear, with the charter of the Royal African Company in 1672 defining 'slaves' and 'negroes' as 'goods' and 'commodities'. In 1677, Solicitor General Sir Francis Winnington declared that 'negroes ought to be esteemed goods and commodities within the Acts of Trade and Navigation'.[36]

Somerset v Stewart (1772)

Against this legislative and judicial background, anti-slavery campaigners tried to take advantage of the absence of any statute that explicitly permitted slavery. In the mid-1700s, a young anti-slavery activist called Granville Sharp turned his attention to the Habeas Corpus Act, which had been passed in 1679. The Act stated that people deprived of their liberty must have an

---

[34] *Pearne v Lisle* (1749) 75 Amb ER 27.
[35] *Shanley v Harvey*, Eden 125, 28 Eng Rep 844 (Ch 1762).
[36] See Wiecek (n 25), n 39 and accompanying text.

opportunity to challenge their detention, and Sharp argued that this must be applicable to enslavement. In 1769, he set out this argument in a pamphlet which emphasized the humanitarian case against slavery.[37] According to Sharp, slavery was a 'gross infringement of the common and natural rights of mankind' and 'plainly coutrary [sic] to the laws and constitution of this kingdom'.[38] These might seem like obvious claims to make against slavery today, but they were quite radical claims in the mid-1700s for a White person to make.

By coincidence, in the same year that Sharp published his polemic against slavery, a slaveowner named Charles Stewart travelled from Virginia to London with an enslaved man called James Somerset, setting in motion a series of events that encouraged Sharp to put his thesis to the test and which had a profound impact on slavery in England and its colonies. Somerset escaped captivity in 1771, and when he was recaptured, Stewart had him shackled to a ship on the River Thames which was bound for Jamaica. Somerset's plight came to the attention of Sharp and other activists, who petitioned Lord Mansfield to issue a writ of habeas corpus, challenging the legality of his captivity. Mansfield was hesitant to rule one way or the other and instead urged the parties to settle the case outside the courts, but no agreement could be reached.[39]

When the dispute reached Lord Mansfield's court, Somerset's lawyers put forward a range of arguments. William Davy and John Glynn argued that if colonial laws were to apply in this case, then all colonial laws would have to apply in England, throwing the legal system into disarray. With that in mind, they focused on the jurisprudence of the English courts that had developed over the preceding decades, referring to the statement in the *Cartwright* case about the air of England being 'too pure for a slave to breathe'. Seemingly on behalf of all enslaved people, Davy argued: '[T]he moment they put their foot on English ground, that moment they become free. They are subject to the laws, and they are entitled to the protection of

---

[37] Granville Sharp, *A Representation of the Injustice and Dangerous Tendency of Tolerating Slavery; Or of Admitting the Least Claim of Private Property in the Persons of Men, in England* (Benjamin White 1769).

[38] Wiecek (n 25), pp 96–101.

[39] For an in-depth discussion and analysis of the legal arguments put forward in *Somerset v Stewart*, listen to the online webinar: Matthew Ryder KC and Alexandra Wilson, '"The Black Must Go Free": How a Legal Ruling on "Windrush Day" in 1772 Is as Relevant as Ever on Windrush Day 2021' (Matrix Chambers, 22 June 2021), Available from: https://www.matrixlaw.co.uk/resource/webinar-the-black-must-go-free-how-a-legal-ruling-on-windrush-day-in-1772-is-as-relevant-as-ever-on-windrush-day-2021. Listen in particular to the discussion by Matthew Ryder KC at 00:34–00:41. Also see Harry Potter, *Law, Liberty and the Constitution: A Brief History of the Common Law* (The Boydell Press 2015), chapter 18; Wiecek (n 25), pp 101–7.

the laws of this country.'[40] But Davy did not seem concerned with the racial dimension of slavery. He argued that it would be beneficial to declare slavery illegal in England because then no more enslaved people would be brought to England, and this would 'preserve the beauty and fair complexion of our people, which otherwise is in a probable way of becoming Morisco, like the Spaniards and Portuguese'.[41] This was an early example of what Bell would later term 'interest-convergence' – when a legal argument appears to advance the interests of racial justice but is only made because it also advances the interests of the dominant racialized group.[42] Francis Hargrave was also part of Somerset's team, and he put forward a more radical and antiracist argument by highlighting the "horrid train of evils" that accompanied racialized slavery. He urged Mansfield not to issue a ruling that would allow those 'train[s] of evil' to travel to England.[43]

Stewart's lawyers framed the case as one of commerce rather than morality. They argued that a ruling against Stewart would effectively liberate all enslaved Black people currently in England, at a cost of over £800,000. Mansfield, whose primary area of interest and expertise was commercial law, appeared sympathetic to this argument, noting that "setting 14,000 or 15,000 men at once loose by a solemn opinion, is very disagreeable in the effects it threatens".[44] He questioned the implications of abolition in the following terms: "[H]ow would the law stand with respect to their settlement? their wages? How many actions for any slight coercion by the master?"[45] As we will see, the desire to balance the interests of racialized people with other interests such as the economy has perennially hindered legal action against racial injustices.

Despite his concerns with commerce, Mansfield ultimately held in favour of Somerset. He reasoned that English law prevailed over colonial laws and noted that English law contained no provision that permitted Somerset's current detention or his forcible removal to Jamaica. One passage in particular of his judgment was seized upon by anti-slavery activists and has since become almost mythological. In his words:

> The state of slavery is of such a nature, that it is incapable of being introduced on any reasons, moral or political; but only positive law,

---

[40] Quoted in Olusoga (n 20), p 132.
[41] Quoted in Wiecek (n 25), p 103.
[42] Derrick A. Bell, 'Brown v. Board of Education and the Interest-Convergence Dilemma' (1980) 93 Harvard Law Review 518 (discussed in Chapter 1).
[43] Olusoga (n 20), p 132.
[44] Olusoga (n 20), p 130; James Oldham, 'New Light on Mansfield and Slavery' 27 Journal of British Studies 45, 47.
[45] Quoted in Wiecek (n 25), p 105.

which preserves its force long after the reasons, occasion, and time itself from whence it was created, is erased from memory: It's so odious, that nothing can be suffered to support it but positive law.[46]

This sweeping statement led anti-slavery activists and some courts to read Mansfield's opinion more broadly than he intended. Both the Court of Common Pleas and the King's Bench handed down judgments which stipulated that *Somerset* outlawed slavery in England. Justice Holroyd, for example, ruled in 1824 that when an enslaved person 'puts his foot on the shores of this country, his slavery is at an end'.[47] Mansfield's words galvanized the anti-slavery movement in both England and its colonies, with some historians going so far as to surmise that it hastened the abolition of the slave trade in 1807 and the abolition of slavery in 1833 in the British Empire, as well as the abolition of slavery in 1865 in what became the United States of America.[48] Crucially, though, the decision itself did not outlaw slavery in either England or its colonies.

In his far-reaching account of Black British history, Olusoga writes: 'Beyond 22 June 1772 ... James Somerset, the man whose personal freedom had become the subject of this epic trial, disappears from written words, his later life lost to us.'[49] This is an important point. There are biographies of Sharp and Lord Mansfield, but there is virtually no record of perhaps the most important person in this story. Had it not been for Somerset's bravery in escaping from enslavement, the case would never have been heard and the anti-slavery movement would not have been galvanized. Yet a common feature of legal cases and the reporting of such cases in this era is the silencing of the voices of the racialized. This is a problem that rears its head in legal cases today, as we will see in Chapter 4.

Despite the role of *Somerset* in accelerating the abolition of slavery, it was not an antiracist decision. Mansfield was at pains to clarify that his judgment did not abolish slavery in England or anywhere else but merely prohibited this particular escaped person from being forcibly returned to the colonies against his will. In other words, the judgment did not acknowledge the structural nature of racism in a polity that practised race-based slavery. The decision also did little to change attitudes towards racialized people in Britain,

---

[46] *Somerset v Stewart* (1772) 98 ER 499, 510.
[47] Quoted in Wiecek (n 25), p 110.
[48] On the effect of *Somerset* on British debates about slavery, see William R. Cotter, 'The *Somerset* Case and the Abolition of Slavery in England' (1994) 79 *History* 31. On the effect of *Somerset* on American debates about slavery, see Derek A. Webb, 'The *Somerset* Effect: Parsing Lord Mansfield's Words on Slavery in Nineteenth Century America' (2014) 32 *Law and History Review* 455.
[49] Olusoga (n 20), p 140.

highlighting the limits of legal action. Slaveowners soon worked out that if they changed the status of their enslaved person to an 'indentured servant', then they could be forcibly removed from England to the colonies, at which point they would be re-enslaved.[50] Developments outside the plantations of the American and West Indian colonies also suggest that *Somerset* should not be interpreted as a sign that the British legal system at large was concerned with racial justice. Just one year after the decision, the Government of India Act 1858 was passed which established parliamentary control over the East India Company, which effectively meant that Parliament was now complicit in the racial injustices being meted out by the Company in India. In that same year, Warren Hastings was appointed governor-general of Bengal, becoming one of the architects of British rule in India and its associated racial injustices.[51] And just two years after the decision in *Somerset*, Edward Long's influential *History of Jamaica* was published, in which the author regurgitated pseudo-scientific theories of racism when writing that Black people were developmentally inferior to Whites. Long had spent 12 years in Jamaica as a planter but also, crucially for our purposes, as a judge. His book, described by Fryer as 'highly respected both in his day and long after his death', therefore gave a veneer of legal legitimacy to racism and slavery.[52] Indeed, many slaveowners served as magistrates, and their racism often influenced their judicial decision-making. As Colin Bobb-Semple writes, magistrates 'were the people responsible for constant whipping and other forms of torture of enslaved Africans, in addition to performing their roles as justices. After emancipation, the planters continued to act as magistrates and dispensed justice, sometimes very harshly'.[53] Although the decision in *Somerset* in 1772 might have accelerated the abolition of the slave trade in 1807 and slavery in 1833, contemporaneous events in the 1770s meant that law's racism, and the racism of the British Empire, was still flourishing.

The Zong case (1783)

In 1783, Sharp and Lord Mansfield crossed paths once again in a case that arguably did the most of all legal cases to reveal the horrors of slavery and the trade in enslaved people and the ineptitude of the law in tackling these horrors. Two years earlier, on 18 August 1781, a British ship called *Zong* departed from the west coast of Africa carrying its crew and 442 enslaved

---

[50] Wiecek (n 25), p 108.
[51] Fryer (n 19), p 168.
[52] Fryer (n 19), p 168.
[53] Leslie Thomas KC, 'Foreword' in Keir Monteith KC et al, 'Racial Bias and the Bench: A Response to the Judicial Diversity and Inclusion Strategy (2020–2025)' (University of Manchester 2022), p 4.

Africans.[54] When the ship arrived in Jamaica on 22 December 1781, there were just 208 Africans on board. It was hardly unusual for slave ships to dock with fewer enslaved people on board than there were at the point of departure, because conditions aboard these ships were horrific and many people would die of sickness and disease. On many occasions, the enslaved would fight for their freedom and would subsequently be killed by the crew. However, the deaths on board *Zong* were different. At some point during the journey, after sickness had afflicted both the enslaved and crew members, the ship was mistakenly sailed past its intended destination. With sickness rampant and water supplies allegedly running low, the crew decided to kill some of the enslaved. It appears that somebody aboard the ship realized that if the enslaved people died from sickness, then the ship's owners would have to bear the cost of what was, in legal terms, unusable property. If, on the other hand, the enslaved people were thrown overboard with the aim of saving the ship, then the ship's owners could claim the loss on their insurance because the deaths – or 'loss of property' – would have been 'necessary' to save the ship and cargo. On 29 November, the crew pushed 54 women and children overboard, to their deaths. On 1 December, 42 men were thrown overboard. Some time later, 36 more people were pushed into the waters, where they drowned. Rather than be thrown overboard, a further ten Africans decided to jump. Although the ship's logbook was never retrieved and there was some dispute over the exact numbers, the courts in England accepted this version of events. In total, 142 people lost their lives.

The owners of *Zong* – a syndicate of businessmen led by William Gregson – initiated an insurance claim, stating that the enslaved were 'property' and that their deaths constituted a 'loss of cargo'. The question for the underwriters was whether the 'loss of cargo' was covered by the terms of the insurance. The Gregson syndicate stated the crew's version of events: throwing the enslaved overboard was 'necessary' to save the ship and the remaining cargo because of depleted water supplies and severe sickness. The insurers refused to pay, though, because in their view it was mismanagement that had led to the problems aboard the ship which in turn led to the enslaved people being thrown overboard. According to the underwriters, navigational errors and the failure to properly ration drinking water were attributable to the crew, and thus not covered by insurance. The Gregson syndicate challenged this in court, and on 6 March 1783 the case was heard before a jury, presided by Lord Chief Justice Mansfield. The jury decided in favour of the Gregson syndicate, effectively stating that the crew were legally entitled to jettison what they considered to be 'cargo' in order to ensure that *Zong* could make

---

[54] For a comprehensive study of the *Zong* affair, see James Walvin, *The Zong: A Massacre, the Law and the End of Slavery* (Yale University Press 2019).

it to Jamaica safely. Put another way: *Zong*'s crew had killed 132 enslaved Black people (with ten more jumping overboard in a vain attempt to save themselves), and the legal system awarded their employers money for this.

News of the jury's decision quickly spread. Olaudah Equiano, a formerly enslaved man who had come to play a prominent role in the anti-slavery movement, alerted Sharp to the trial and the events on board *Zong*, and they set about publicizing the mass murder. Sharp even explored the possibility of bringing murder charges against the crew, but these charges never materialized. While activists like Equiano and Sharp raised public awareness of the atrocities aboard *Zong*, the insurers appealed the jury's decision. The appeal was heard before Lord Mansfield and two other judges in the Court of King's Bench on 21–2 May 1783, and like all the slavery cases before it, this contributed to the law's construction of racial justice.

The shipowners' lawyers tried to frame the case around the concept of 'necessity', repeating the arguments at trial that it was necessary to throw the people overboard in order to save the ship, the crew, and the rest of the cargo. To make this argument, they referred to the legal judgments that characterized Black people as property rather than humans. One of their lawyers was the Solicitor General, John Lee, who stated that English law made 'our fellow Creatures of the Negro Cast ... the Subject of Property'. He argued that the insurance papers specified that the Africans were goods and property, and 'whether Right or Wrong we have Nothing to do with it'.[55] There are three salient points about this. First, we can see once again an attempt to classify human beings of a certain 'race' as something other than human, and therefore outside the boundary of law's protection of human beings. In other words, they are denied legal personhood. Second, the invocation of the idea of 'necessity' was a precursor to the use of 'emergency measures' to quell colonial unrest during the 19th and 20th centuries. This is explored later in this chapter, detailing how the idea of 'emergency measures' was used to justify official acts that were plainly contrary to orthodox understandings of the rule of law. Third, Lee's attempt to disentangle legal rules from moral imperatives – 'whether Right or Wrong we have Nothing to do with it' – is a theme that rears its head today, as legal officials focus on legal definitions of 'race' and 'racial justice' rather than moral definitions. We see this today, for example, in the refusal to consider the role of structural racism in the inquiry into the fire at Grenfell Tower in 2017.[56]

The insurers' lawyers tried to frame the case as one about 'humanity' rather than 'necessity'. They were supported and advised by Sharp, and his influence on their legal arguments was clear. For example, when discussing the ship's supply of water, one of the lawyers went so far as to claim that

---

[55] Walvin (n 54), p 145.
[56] See discussion in Chapter 4.

the enslaved Africans had an equal right to water as the crew. In Mr Pigot's words: "[A]s long as any water remained to be divided, these men were as much entitled to their share as the captain, or any other man whatever."[57] This was an extraordinary claim to make in 1783. If it was accepted that enslaved people on board a ship had equal rights to the captain and crew, then the whole enterprise of trading in enslaved people would be in jeopardy. Once again, we see the tension between the ideals of liberalism with its promise of equality on the one hand and the practical treatment of racialized people on the other. Another lawyer on the insurer's team added to this line of argument. Mr Heywood argued that his team appeared 'as Council for Millions of Mankind and the Cause of Humanity in general. ... To say that wantonly or by Ignorance a Capn may throw 132 lives overboard is a Proposition that shocks Humanity'.[58] Today, we would say that Heywood was raising the spectre of 'structural racism'. He was effectively saying that the case involved more than just the people directly involved by the facts of the case. He recognized that the facts of the case had implications for the whole of society, because racism afflicted 'Millions of Mankind'. His claim also had the hallmarks of what we today call 'strategic litigation'. He recognized that the decision in the case would go beyond the parties to the case and have much broader social effects.

As he did in *Somerset*, Mansfield found a way to decide the case without either condemning or condoning slavery and without tackling the structural nature of racism. During the hearing in May, he came across a fact that had not been disclosed at the March trial. According to the one witness who testified, it rained the day before the last group of enslaved people were thrown overboard. This cast doubt on the crew's claim about dwindling water supplies. Mansfield therefore ordered a re-trial to consider this new piece of evidence.[59] There is no record of a re-trial, and we can only presume that the matter was decided out of court. The hearings before Mansfield though revealed the extent to which the outright racist laws of the colonies had affected the law of the metropole. The commitment to liberty and equality which was presumed to underpin the legal system was shown to be a rhetorical commitment at best, as concerns with commerce and the economy entrenched the belief that racialized enslaved people could and should be treated as property rather than human beings. Nonetheless, the case helped the anti-slavery lobby. The public had more information now about what happened aboard slave ships, and public pressure led to the passage of the Dolben's Act in 1788, which regulated the trade in enslaved

---

[57] Walvin (n 54), pp 146–7.
[58] Walvin (n 54), p 147.
[59] *Gregson v Gilbert* (1783) 99 ER 629.

people. It was a modest piece of legislation, but it was becoming clear that the pro-slavery lobby was now on the defensive.[60]

Law and slavery in the 1800s

The fortunes of the anti-slavery lobby ebbed and flowed into the 19th century. In 1827, a full 55 years after *Somerset* had been decided, the High Court of Admiralty ruled that an enslaved person remained enslaved even after being brought to England. Grace James had travelled from Antigua to England with her mistress and had then returned to Antigua a year later. A customs officer, perhaps inspired by the rhetoric of anti-slavery arguments, argued that James had been freed once she landed in England and could therefore not be re-enslaved in Antigua. Lord Stowell, though, disagreed. He expressed concern with 'the public inconvenience that might follow from an established opinion that negroes became totally free in consequence of a voyage to England'. In his view, while the law might discourage slavery within the British Isles, 'the law uses a very different language and exerts a very different force when it looks to her colonies; for to this trade in those colonies it gives an almost unbounded protection'.[61] In their analysis of the case, Lester and Bindman surmise that 'Stowell, though an abolitionist, was troubled by the inherent disadvantages of taking judicial rather than legislative action against slavery in the colonies'.[62] Judicial action lacks the democratic legitimacy that legislative action enjoys, and Stowell understood that the political majority would disavow a decision that favoured the enslaved.

Slavery was eventually abolished in most of the British Empire by legislative action. On 28 August 1833, the Slavery Abolition Act received Royal Assent, and although Fryer has suggested that the 'gradual self-emancipation' of Black people 'is a matter of social rather than legal history',[63] he acknowledges that the decision in *Somerset v Stewart* had encouraged and enabled Black people to escape from captivity and had encouraged anti-slavery activists to pursue their cause with greater vigour and determination, which in turn made passage of the Act possible. This is not to say that abolition was now seen as a moral imperative, but rather that the actions of anti-slavery activists had affected the commercial viability of slavery to the point that opposition to abolition was weaker than it had been in previous years.[64] However, despite the benefits

---

[60] Fryer (n 19), p 133.
[61] Fryer (n 19), p 134.
[62] Anthony Lester and Geoffrey Bindman, *Race and Law* (Penguin Books 1972), p 34.
[63] Fryer (n 19), p 135.
[64] For a detailed account of the role of economic considerations in the abolition of the slave trade and slavery, see Eric Williams, *Capitalism and Slavery* (first published 1964, Penguin Books 2022).

of legislative action over judicial action, legislation is not a panacea for the problem of racial injustice. As the next section outlines, other events in the same decade as the abolition of slavery reveal how deeply rooted racism was in the legal order, including in the statute books.

Law and the social control of racialized populations

The abolition of slavery did not mark an end of racial injustices in the British Empire, either at home or in the colonies. Racialized populations across the Empire were denied freedom of movement, routinely monitored and were victims of brutal and disproportionate force whenever they resisted colonial rule.

Structuralizing racism through discrimination

In the same year that the Slavery Abolition Act was passed, the Government of India Act was also passed, and this provides a starting point for exploring how law was used to control and monitor racialized populations in myriad ways. The Act was primarily a means for renewing the Royal Charter that authorized the British-based East India Company to operate in India, where it had set up trading posts as far back as 1639. They were not the only foreign company to set up factories and trading relationships in India. Dutch, Portuguese, and French companies competed for business too. These companies developed relations with local princes and rulers and sought political influence in order to maximize profits. Tensions between these various rulers and companies led to the Battle of Plassey in 1757, which British forces won. The victory enabled the East India Company to assume a considerable degree of political control in India, and it soon became the largest employer in India.[65] However, Indians were only appointed to relatively lowly positions within the Company, and they came to resent the appointment of less able Europeans to more prestigious and well-paid positions. For this reason, the 1833 Act included a provision stating that no native of India 'shall, by reason only of his religion, place of birth, descent, colour, or any of them, be disabled from holding any place, office or employment' in the East India Company.[66] Lester and Bindman have described the 1833 Act as Britain's 'first anti-discrimination law'.[67] When

---

[65] For a detailed discussion of the East India Company, listen to William Dalrymple and Anita Anand, 'The East India Company' (16 August 2022), Available from: https://www.globalplayer.com/podcasts/42KuVh
[66] Lester and Bindman (n 62), p 383.
[67] Lester and Bindman (n 62), p 383.

considered alongside the Slavery Abolition Act of the same year, we might conclude that 1833 was something of a watershed moment, as law came to be used to advance racial justice. However, although the Government of India Act seems progressive on paper, it had little effect in practice. The directors of the East India Company issued a dispatch in 1834 that made it clear that although people would now be appointed to office based on merit alone, there was very little chance that natives of India would in practice meet the criteria for appointment to positions of power. In Lester and Bindman's words: '[A]lthough the new law required equal opportunities for Indians and Europeans alike to enter all branches of the administration, in practice Englishmen would continue to monopolize the covenanted service, which wielded the real power in India.'[68]

Even if the Act had been effective at outlawing discriminatory hiring practices, the law posed a problem for advocates of racial justice. If a decision-maker was admonished for acting discriminatorily, the legal system would in effect be saying that that decision-maker had deviated from the normal and acceptable state of affairs. But this could hardly be further from the truth and belied the structural nature of racism under British rule in India. In this sense, the Act provided a preview of what was to come in the metropole in 1965, when the first efforts to outlaw race discrimination in England suffered a similar fate: an anti-discrimination statute that masked the structural nature of racism.

The shortcomings of legal efforts to tackle discrimination were also apparent in Kenya. The 1931 case of *Kaderbhai* has been described as '[t]he worst instance in which racial discrimination was upheld by the Privy Council',[69] and to understand the case we need to go back to the early 1900s, when the British government encouraged Indians to move to the East Africa Protectorate to work primarily as labourers, farmers, and troops. From the outset, British officials were keen to ensure that Indians were restricted to the lowlands, so that the more pleasant highlands could be enjoyed by British imperialists and other Europeans. The government was not initially keen to impose legal restrictions on the movement of Indians, but it did not proactively enable Indians to move freely. After various negotiations and draft Bills, an Ordinance was passed in 1915 that M.P.K. Sorrenson describes as 'an ingenious compromise between the demands of European settlers for total exclusion of Indians from holding land, particularly in the highlands, and the concern of the Colonial Office to prevent discrimination from being written into the law'.[70] The Ordinance effectively allowed landowners to discriminate

---

[68] Lester and Bindman (n 62), p 387.
[69] Lester and Bindman (n 62), p 42.
[70] M.P.K. Sorrenson, *Origins of European Settlement in Kenya* (OUP 1968), p 175, quoted in Lester and Bindman (n 62), p 44.

against non-Whites in practice while not enshrining discrimination in law. For example, the Ordinance enabled the Commissioner of Lands to determine whether 'special covenants' could be inserted into leases but was silent on whether 'special covenants' could restrict people of particular races from enjoying the land in question. When the Commissioner announced that some town plots would be auctioned in Mombasa, he stipulated that only Europeans would be permitted to bid. He also announced that Asiatic and African people would not be permitted to reside in any houses built on the land unless they were a domestic servant. A British Indian person named Kaderbhai wanted to bid and challenged the Commissioner's diktat on the basis that there was nothing in the Ordinance that gave him the power to enact racially restrictive measures. The Commissioner's argument was that there was nothing in the Ordinance that expressly prohibited him from doing so. The case reached the Privy Council, which decided in favour of the Commissioner. Writing for the Privy Council, Lord Atkins stated they could only be concerned with 'the bare question of law – namely, the powers of the Commissioner under the Ordinance', and that '[q]uestions of policy, or, in other words, *how* the legal powers *should* be exercised, are not matters for the legal tribunal, but have to be determined by the appropriate constitutional authority'.[71] On the face of it, Lord Atkins appears to have simply upheld the principle of judicial neutrality, stating that his job is merely to determine whether laws have been complied with. However, he betrayed his partiality when he expressly accepted the suggestion that restrictions based on race were legitimate and rational because property values might decline if certain plots were purchased by non-White buyers.[72]

In at least two ways, the decision in *Kaderbhai* echoed the slavery decisions of the 1600s and 1700s. First, the judiciary accepted the argument that economic interests trumped the interests of racialized human beings. Second, Lord Atkins' exhortation that legal officials could not and should not engage in the propriety of a particular policy echoed Lee's exhortation in the *Zong* case that the insurance papers in question specified that the Africans were goods and property and 'whether Right or Wrong we have Nothing to do with it'.[73] And in many ways, the decision foreshadowed contemporary legal processes relating to the Grenfell Tower fire and the COVID-19 pandemic, discussed in Chapter 4. In short, the public inquiries into these disasters excluded consideration of the role of structural racism in the cause of the fire, and the role of structural racism in the disproportionate rate of deaths of racialized people respectively.

---

[71] *Commissioner for Local Government Lands and Settlement v Abdulhusein Kaderbhai* [1931] AC 652 (italics added).
[72] Lester and Bindman (n 62), p 46.
[73] Quoted in Walvin (n 54), p 145.

The use of law to control racialized populations

It was not just through surreptitious approaches to allowing discrimination that the legal system was used to control and monitor racialized populations across the Empire. It was also through the use of legislation to designate certain racial groups as 'criminal' and through the use of 'emergency measures' to quell rebellions. British rule in India once again provides a useful example of this.

Indians' discontent with the East India Company came to a head in 1857, when Indian soldiers who worked for the Company violently rebelled.[74] The rebellion was sparked by the introduction of a new rifle that the Indian soldiers, known as sepoys, would have to use. A rumour spread among the sepoys that to load the rifle, they would have to bite off the ends of cartridges which had been lubricated with a mixture of pigs' and cows' fat. Muslim and Hindu soldiers were dismayed by this affront to their religious beliefs. Even though these were just rumours, when considered in light of the other racial injustices that had been inflicted during Company rule, it was hardly surprising that the soldiers staged an uprising. The Company succeeded in quelling the rebellion, but this came at considerable reputational cost. The following year, under the Government of India Act 1858, the British government took over the Company's administrative and political powers. The 1858 Act established direct British political rule over India, and the ensuing years saw colonial rule entrench racial injustices in British law. The events of 1857 shattered any trust that the British had in native Indians, and thus British administrators sought to impose order and control over a population that was now considered unpredictable and untrustworthy. As Gyan Prakash has written, '[t]he lesson that the British drew from the Mutiny was that, if anything, colonial despotism had to tighten, not loosen, its noose; Indians were not to be appeased but rather should be ruled with an iron hand'.[75] Turning to pseudo-scientific reports that certain groups of Indians were inherently prone to criminality, the colonial government introduced the Criminal Tribes Act 1871. This gave legal effect to the belief that some people were born criminals, or at the very least would inevitably become criminals because of the families they were born into. British officials classified certain nomadic people as 'criminal', and the Criminal Tribes Act made it mandatory for all people born into these tribes to register with colonial administrators so that their whereabouts and actions could be

---

[74] Priyamvada Gopal, *Insurgent Empire: Anticolonial Resistance and British Dissent* (Verso 2019), chapter 1.
[75] Gyan Prakash, *Another Reason: Science and the Imagination of Modern India* (Princeton University Press 1999), p 4, quoted in Mark Brown, 'Race, Science and the Construction of Native Criminality in Colonial India' (2001) 5 *Theoretical Criminology* 345, 348.

monitored. If accused and found guilty of a crime, they would face harsher penalties than people not registered as a member of a 'criminal tribe'. The police were given powers to enforce the Act, which meant that people designated a member of a 'criminal tribe' were subject to surveillance and invasions of privacy.

The criminalization of certain tribes was not dependent on skin colour alone. Members of these tribes were generally considered to be of a lower social class, and the Criminal Tribes Act 1871 therefore highlights the intersection of race and class, with the concept of 'caste' coming to complement British approaches to 'race'.[76] Just as the law on slavery generated the intersectional oppression of Black women, so the social control of lower castes generated intersectional oppression in India along class lines. As outlined in the following chapters, this approach to criminalizing certain groups of people on the basis of racial differences and social class, and this approach to the imposition of collective punishments on people, has found modern iterations in the classifications of Gypsies, Roma, and Traveller (GRT) people's way of life as 'criminal', in the Matrix Gangs database that the police use to monitor predominantly young Black men of lower social classes, and in the use of the doctrine of 'joint enterprise' to tackle so-called gang violence.[77] The Criminal Tribes Act is also an example of imperialists' desire to order groups along racial lines, and the project of 'racial ordering' has continued through contemporary approaches to immigration law, as detailed in Chapter 3.[78]

It was not just in India that the law was used to stifle protests for racial justice and characterize racialized people as 'criminal'. On 11 October 1865, a group of several hundred Black men and women marched towards the town courthouse in Morant Bay, Jamaica, for reasons similar to those that had caused the uprising in India – protesting against rampant poverty, unfair taxes, and general injustices that were meted out along racial lines. A skirmish between the protestors and the volunteer militia led to Governor Edward John Eyre declaring martial law and suppressing the protestors with an extraordinary show of brutality. Over the next few days, hundreds of Black Jamaicans, many of whom had no involvement with the initial protest at all, were summarily shot or executed after show trials. Houses were burned to the ground, and over 600 men and women were flogged. George William Gordon, a local politician of dual heritage, was executed

---

[76] Brown (n 75).
[77] Jasbinder Nijjar, 'Echoes of Empire: Excavating the Colonial Roots of Britain's "War on Gangs"' (2018) 45 *Social Justice* 147 (drawing connections between the Criminal Tribes Act and more contemporary efforts to tackle 'gang' violence).
[78] On racial ordering, see Nadine El-Enany, *(B)Ordering Britain: Law, Race and Empire* (Manchester University Press 2020), chapter 1.

after a trial that barely had any semblance of due process. Just as the Indian Mutiny had led colonial administrators to rethink their approach to Indians, so too the approach to racialized people in Jamaica changed. 'After the Morant Bay Rebellion', writes Marouf Hasian Jr, 'the belief in racial hierarchies also ossified, and Afro-Jamaicans were re-characterized as unruly and untrustworthy colonial subjects'.[79]

There are numerous other examples of the use of brutal force to quell resistance to colonial rule, with the response to the Mau Mau uprising in Kenya being a particularly notorious example.[80] In 1895, the British government proclaimed a protectorate over East Africa and from 1902 had started to settle in the highlands in what is now called Kenya under the encouragement of Sir Charles Eliot, the British Commissioner for the Protectorate. The cooler climate in the highlands, and the apparent absence of settled habitants, made it attractive for British and European settlers. But the highlands had been home to people of the Kikuyu tribe. Over the ensuing decades, colonial authorities expropriated their land, compelled them to work for British farmers for low wages, and forced them to carry identity cards. Attempts by the Kikuyu to advance their interests through political processes were quashed, and political groups sympathetic to the Kikuyu were suppressed. These groups morphed into secret societies, and in 1952 one such society – Mau Mau – rebelled with force. At first, they attacked Kikuyu who were loyal to British settlers, and most of the victims of their violence were indeed members of the Kikuyu tribe. Just 32 White settlers were killed by Mau Mau over the next seven years, but their rebellion against colonial rule was met with a tremendous show of force by the British. Thousands of actual or suspected Mau Mau were captured and detained in concentration camps, where they lost their lives to disease and starvation. The few who were tried in special courts did not receive a fair trial and were in effect summarily executed.[81]

Priyamvada Gopal has documented other examples of resistance to colonial rule and the subsequent use by colonial authorities of 'emergency measures' involving collective punishment, the lethal use of force (often against civilians not involved in the insurgency), and other repressive measures.[82] The use of the term 'emergency measures' or 'State of Emergency' implied that colonial rule was ordinarily benign and that these measures were extraordinary and episodic departures from the norm. It is worth recognizing though that these measures were very much inherent

---

[79] Quoted and discussed in Gopal (n 74), p 84.
[80] Gopal (n 74), chapter 10; David Anderson, *Histories of the Hanged: Britain's Dirty War in Kenya and the End of Empire* (Weidenfeld & Nicolson 2005).
[81] Anderson (n 80).
[82] Gopal (n 74).

to colonial rule, which was premised on coercion and repression. Nasser Hussain explains this when contesting the portrayal of 'emergency measures' as episodic instances of state force. He notes that emergency powers were based on a 'claim of necessity' and were used to justify both 'discretionary authority in the *normal* institutional structure of the state, [and] in a more explicit crisis that requires the use of the military and martial law'.[83] That is, the 'claim of necessity' was invoked to justify colonial rule in the first place and was used to justify the two-tiered legal systems that were in place on a day-to-day basis to maintain rule. Nandini Boodia-Canoo makes a similar point: '[T]he period of colonialism represents an epoch during which violence, oppression and injustice in fact derived their legitimacy from legal rules.'[84] We can recall the invocation of the concept of 'necessity' in the *Zong* case to highlight the continuities between law's use during slavery and law's use a century after the abolition of slavery: it initially appears that the concept of 'necessity' was invoked to justify a departure from normal rules and principles, but the departure was more apparent than real. It is more accurate to say that the concept of 'necessity' was invoked *not* to justify a departure from the norm but when the horrors of the mistreatment of enslaved or colonized people were vivid rather than masked. That is, the mistreatment of racialized people was not an aberration from a system governed by the 'rule of law', but rather the 'rule of law' accommodated and enabled the mistreatment of racialized people, thus embedding such mistreatment into the structures of social life.

Conclusion

By the late 1800s, tensions had grown between European countries involved in imperialism, particularly with respect to the annexation of land in Africa. To prevent conflict between European nations, a conference was called to organize how these countries would 'share' the African continent between themselves. The Berlin Conference, which was held from November 1884 until February 1885, sparked what came to be known as 'the Scramble for Africa'.[85] Britain fared well among its European rivals, and by 1900 one in three Africans was a British colonial subject.[86] Cecil Rhodes' words in 1877 were being put into action: 'It is our duty to seize every opportunity of acquiring more territory and we should keep this one idea steadily before our

---

[83] Nasser Hussain, *The Jurisprudence of Emergency: Colonialism and the Rule of Law* (University of Michigan Press 2003), pp 134–5 (emphasis added).

[84] Nandini S. Boodia-Canoo, 'Researching Colonialism and Colonial Legacies from a Legal Perspective' (2020) 54 *The Law Teacher* 517, 517.

[85] Muriel Evelyn Chamberlain, *The Scramble for Africa* (3rd edn, Routledge 2013).

[86] Olusoga (n 20), p 401.

eyes that more territory simply means more of the Anglo-Saxon race, more of the best, the most human, most honourable race the world possesses.'[87]

The Scramble for Africa was justified with reference to pseudo-scientific accounts of racial hierarchies, such as that in the tenth edition of *Systema naturae*, which was published in 1758 by the Swedish biologist Carl Linnaeus. Linnaeus divided humankind into four groups, with 'European white' at the apex of the hierarchy, described as '[v]igorous, muscular. ... Very smart, inventive. Ruled by law'. 'Red'-skinned people from the Americas were described as '[i]ll-tempered, impassive. ... Ruled by custom'; whereas 'yellow'-skinned people from Asia were 'stern ... haughty, greedy. ... Ruled by opinion'. At the bottom of the hierarchy were black-skinned people from Africa, described as '[s]luggish, lazy. Crafty, slow, careless. ... Ruled by caprice'.[88] Craniometry and Social Darwinism were also used to 'prove' that White races were superior to the African races being conquered.

Colonial rule in Africa had more of a cultural effect on Britain than an economic one.[89] The British public, Olusoga writes, became fascinated with the people and tribes that explorers encountered as they ventured deeper into the continent. It did not take long for stereotypes to emerge: 'The Ndebele people were said to be savage warriors; the Yoruba were greedy and money-minded; the Zulu had a history of superstitious madness and blood-stained grandeur.'[90] More exhibitions took place in which African people were brought to Britain to be paraded for the voyeurism of White British people,[91] and this shaped the development of the legal system. As more Black Africans arrived in mainland Britain, more White British people grew concerned with the effects of the intermingling of Black people and White British people. There were particular concerns about sexual relationships between African men and White women, but there were other reasons why the influx of African visitors to Britain affected the development of the law. When African kings and other royalty visited Britain, beliefs about racial hierarchies were called into question as they tended to display the attributes of so-called 'civilized' White people.[92] This was something of a precursor to the 'good immigrant' narrative that has come to dominate legal, political,

---

[87] Quoted in El-Enany (n 78), p 22.
[88] These translations are taken from Ibram X. Kendi, *How to Be an Antiracist* (The Bodley Head 2019), p 41. See also Isabelle Charmantier, 'Linnaeus and Race' (Linnean Society of London, 3 September 2020), Available from: https://www.linnean.org/learning/who-was-linnaeus/linnaeus-and-race. Charmantier notes that the Linnean Society accepts that his work has provided 'the basis for scientific racism'.
[89] Olusoga (n 20), p 402.
[90] Olusoga (n 20), p 404 (internal quotations omitted).
[91] Olusoga (n 20), p 406.
[92] David Olusoga, for example, recounts the example of a royal visit in 1895 which generated headlines supportive of the three African kings who visited Britain. See Olusoga (n 20), p 417.

and social discourses of the contemporary era. That is, racialized people are welcome to mainland Britain only when they are considered to meet the ideals of the (White British) public. In his edited collection about the lives of immigrants in the UK today, Nikesh Shukla writes: '[T]he biggest burden facing people of colour in this country ... is that society deems us bad immigrants – job-stealers, benefit-scroungers, girlfriend-thieves, refugees – until we cross over in their consciousness, through popular culture, winning races, baking good cakes, being conscientious doctors, to become good immigrants.'[93] In the late 19th century, this attitude did not just attach to visiting kings. Communities of Black Britons emerged, with many leading relatively comfortable lives if they met or superseded the expectations of those who considered themselves native to Britain. These attitudes – that people were welcome if they met certain expectations – informed the development of immigration laws in the early 20th century, which continued the work of colonial laws in ordering and subjugating racialized populations. It is to the development of immigration laws that this book now turns.

---

[93] Nikesh Shukla (ed), *The Good Immigrant* (Unbound 2016), editor's note (paraphrasing the writer Musa Okwonga, who made this point to him in conversation).

3

Racial Justice and Law: The 1900s and 2000s

Introduction

The 20th and 21st centuries have brought changes and continuities in law's relationship with racial justice.[1] On the one hand, there has been a proliferation of laws that appear to be positively pro-racial justice, beginning with the Race Relations Act 1965. On the other hand, these laws have often proved to be ineffectual, and other laws have been enacted and used to subjugate racialized populations. This is partly because even though the British Empire disintegrated over the course of the 1900s, the legacy of colonial law survived. Hannah Arendt notably explained the 'boomerang effect' of imperialism, describing how imperialist practices in the colonies would come to shape practices in the metropole,[2] and in England and Wales we see that the racialized two-tiered legal system of the colonies has been replicated and reproduced in the metropole, primarily by immigration laws. These laws permit, and sometimes mandate, the differential treatment of people along racial lines. An outline of immigration laws prior to the Second World War sets the scene for understanding the post-war immigration legal regime, which in turn provides the context for understanding how racial injustices occur in England and Wales today.

---

[1] Portions of the text in this chapter have been reused from Bharat Malkani, 'The Pursuit of Racial Justice through Legal Action: An Overview of How UK Civil Society Has Used the Law 1990–2020' (Baring Foundation 2021). I am grateful to the Baring Foundation for granting permission to reproduce parts of that report in this chapter.

[2] Hannah Arendt, *The Origins of Totalitarianism* (first published 1951, Penguin Classics 2017), p 10.

Immigration laws predating the Second World War

At its height, the British Empire encompassed large swathes of the globe, and millions of people were classed as 'British subjects'. On the face of it, these 'subjects' could travel freely within the Empire. However, in practice, British authorities wanted to keep racialized populations under control, and so they implemented laws that restricted movement across borders, the effect of which is felt to this day. In the colony of Natal, for example, the Immigration Restriction Act 1897 required entrants to be in possession of £25, and to have knowledge of any European language. Although this applied equally to White British travellers and racialized subjects, its effects were discriminatory. Racialized subjects were often unable to speak a European language and would almost certainly not have what amounts to at least £3,000 in today's money.[3] It is for this reason that Bridget Anderson writes: 'The laws governing the movement of subjects within the Empire were an important means of manufacturing the category' of race.[4] That is, if a person did not meet the criteria, they were in effect being constructed as untrustworthy and in need of containment.

The Natal law provided the basis for the Aliens Act 1905. This was a response to concerns about the arrival in the metropole of impoverished Jewish people, who were fleeing persecution in Russia and Eastern Europe around the turn of the 20th century. Concerns were raised about the impact they were having on working and living conditions in the UK. The Aliens Act was therefore introduced with the aim of stemming the influx of Jewish refugees. Nadine El-Enany writes that the Aliens Act was 'an early instance of the use of immigration law on the British mainland as a means of preserving domestic white British supremacy'.[5] It was a clear attempt to delineate the beneficiaries of Britain's wealth and resources, accumulated through centuries of colonialism, along racial lines.

In 1919, when the UK was recovering from the turmoil of the First World War, a series of race riots broke out in major cities such as Cardiff and Liverpool. The cause of the riots can be traced to the cultural effects of colonialism. Britons had been taught that racialized people were morally, intellectually, and aesthetically inferior, but the war had brought many Black soldiers to the metropole who were now fraternizing with White British women in particular and being given jobs at a time of precarious employment opportunities for returning White soldiers. The disturbances in the mainland

---

[3] Nadine El-Enany, *(B)Ordering Britain: Law, Race and Empire* (Manchester University Press 2020), p 44.
[4] Bridget Anderson, *Us and Them? The Dangerous Politics of Immigration Control* (Oxford University Press 2013), p 35, quoted in El-Enany (n 3), p 45.
[5] El-Enany (n 3), pp 46–7.

were mirrored by disturbances in the colonies. In Sierra Leone, for example, Black residents expressed their anger when they were denied opportunities to work in British companies. These were soldiers who had served in the war, fighting for the British, and were now being treated discriminatorily. Such treatment has been echoed in more recent years with respect to the Gurkhas and Afghan security personnel, who have helped British soldiers only to be shunned when they have in turn needed help from the British.[6]

The race riots of 1919 influenced the enactment of the Aliens Order of 1920 and the Special Restrictions (Coloured Alien Seamen) Order in 1925. These provisions required all Black seamen in mainland Britain to register with the police and to prove their nationality. Previously, their status as subjects of the British Empire had been assumed, but the burden was now shifted so that they had to prove their nationality. The parallels with the Criminal Tribes Act in India (discussed in the previous chapter) are clear: racialized people were subject to control measures that their White counterparts were not, and the 1925 Order has been described as 'the first instance of state-sanctioned race discrimination inside Britain to come to widespread notice'.[7] To make matters worse, Black seamen sometimes would not carry a passport and had no means of proving their identity. Unable to demonstrate that they were in fact British subjects, these men had to register as 'aliens', making it far easier to deport them. Put another way, these British subjects were now exposed to the threat of deportation under legislation that had been designed to control and limit the arrival of non-British subjects.[8] In many respects, the 1925 Order foreshadowed the Windrush scandal that came to light in the 2010s, and which is discussed later in this chapter.

Immigration laws following the Second World War

Shortly before the onset of the Second World War, concerns with antisemitism had found legislative expression in the Public Order Act 1936. The Act did not expressly address the issue of racial animosity, but it

---

[6] On the refusal to allow Gurkhas the right to reside in the UK even though they had fought alongside British soldiers, see 'Home Secretary Announces Gurkhas Can Stay in Britain' *The Daily Telegraph* (21 May 2009), and *R. (Limbu) v Secretary of State for the Home Department* [2008] EWHC 2261 (Admin). On the reluctance of the British government to allow Afghan men and women to relocate to the UK even though they had helped British soldiers in Afghanistan, see May Bulman and Nicola Kelly, 'Revealed: UK Has Failed to Resettle Afghans Facing Torture and Death Despite Promise' *The Observer* (4 December 2022).

[7] Laura Tabili, 'The Construction of Racial Difference in Twentieth-Century Britain: The Special Restrictions (Coloured Alien Seamen) Order, 1925' (1994) 33 *Journal of British Studies* 54, 56.

[8] David Olusoga, *Black and British: A Forgotten History* (revised edn, Picador 2021), p 466.

was enacted to control extremist movements such as the British Union of Fascists. In this sense, we can see the use of law to tackle racial injustices in the 1930s, but the aftermath of the Second World War brought more changes to law's relationship with racial justice. Indeed, just two years after the war, the House of Lords issued a judgment that, while not antisemitic as such, showed indifference to the racism faced by Jewish people. Jewish refugees from the Holocaust were attempting to enter Palestine, but their ships were stopped by British authorities. A writ of habeas corpus was issued, claiming that the refugees were being unlawfully detained at sea. The writ was denied, and remarkably the Court made no reference to the Holocaust or to the fact that those on board were Jewish. The Court instead referred to them as 'immigrants'. While the decision was not discriminatory as such, the Court studiously framed the legal issues so narrowly as to render the racial injustices faced by those on board irrelevant to the question. Yet outside the Court, the racism faced by the Jewish people on board was central to their situation.[9]

Within the British mainland itself, the task of rebuilding the United Kingdom after the war was hampered by a severe shortage of workers, and British officials soon looked abroad for labour. At first, immigrants were largely welcomed. Several thousand Europeans were given permission, as well as financial and practical help, to move to the UK. This included people from Poland, Ukraine, Latvia, and Italy.[10] The arrival of these immigrants caused little consternation among governmental officials and the broader public, but there was considerable unease when it transpired that people from the West Indies were coming to help.[11] There was something quite incongruous about the difference in responses: West Indians were British subjects, whereas the Europeans who were welcomed were not. The Home Secretary at the time, James Chuter Ede, acknowledged that the difference in reaction could only be explained with reference to skin colour: "Some people feel that it would be a bad thing to give the coloured races of the Empire the idea that, in some way or other, they are equals of the people in this country."[12]

Despite some attempts to dissuade West Indians from travelling to the UK, there were no legal means to prevent their arrival, and on 22 June 1948 the steamship *Empire Windrush* docked in Tilbury, Essex, bringing a few hundred

---

[9] *R v Secretary of State for Foreign Affairs ex parte Greenberg* [1947] 2 All ER 550. For a useful analysis of this case and of how the English legal system has treated Jewish people, see Didi Herman, *An Unfortunate Coincidence: Jews, Jewishness and English Law* (Oxford University Press 2011).

[10] Amelia Gentleman, *The Windrush Betrayal: Exposing the Hostile Environment* (Guardian Faber 2020), p 99.

[11] Gentleman (n 10), pp 98–9.

[12] Quoted in Gentleman (n 10), p 103.

Black West Indians to live and work in the UK. By coincidence, this was the same day that Lord Mansfield had delivered his judgment in *Somerset v Stewart* 176 years earlier, and it was an event that would have a similarly profound effect on the relationship between law and racial justice in the UK. The arrival of *Empire Windrush* signalled the beginning of the large-scale immigration of Black Caribbeans to the UK,[13] and at first the legal system appeared to be used to facilitate racial equality. The Labour government introduced the British Nationality Act (BNA) in 1948 just one month after the arrival of the *Empire Windrush*, which created two categories of British citizenship: (1) Citizenship of the United Kingdom and Colonies (for British subjects in the UK and in its 48 colonies, including many in Africa, the West Indies, and South East Asia); and (2) Citizenship of the Independent Commonwealth Countries (referring to states that had gained independence, which at the time included Canada, Ceylon, Australia, New Zealand, India, Pakistan, South Africa, Southern Rhodesia, and Newfoundland).[14]

During Parliamentary debates on the passing of the Act, the Home Secretary rejected the concerns of those who thought "it would be a bad thing to give the coloured races of the Empire" equality, announcing instead that "we recognise the right of the colonial peoples to be treated as men and brothers with the people of this country".[15] It is in this sense that the BNA appeared to be giving effect to the principle of equality, as all British subjects enjoyed full legal rights to live and work in the UK, regardless of skin colour or cultural background.[16] However, it is arguable that the government of the day was only promoting the opportunities to work and live in the UK because Britain needed people to help regenerate the country. The BNA could also be read as a cynical attempt to hold the Empire together and thus preserve the project of White supremacy. This is because in the aftermath of the Second World War, colonized people were stepping up their claims to independence from British rule. In many cases, they used the language of liberalism and the rule of law – the same concepts that had been used to justify imperialism – to make the case for freedom.[17] Their calls were particularly hard to ignore in the aftermath of Nazi Germany's plans for racial

---

[13] Gentleman (n 10), p 9.
[14] See Randall Hansen, 'The Politics of Citizenship in 1940s Britain: The British Nationality Act' (1999) 10 *Twentieth Century British History* 67.
[15] Quoted in Gentleman (n 10), p 103.
[16] Gentleman (n 10), p 103; Randall Hansen, 'The Kenyan Asians, British Politics, and the Commonwealth Immigrants Act, 1968' (1999) 42 *The Historical Journal* 809, 815–16.
[17] Martin J. Wiener, *An Empire on Trial: Race, Murder, and Justice under British Rule, 1870–1935* (Cambridge University Press 2009), pp 1–19 ('Law in the Empire ... was both a tool to further British rule and a resource with which the colonized could tellingly criticize that rule').

conquest. Britain also did not have the finances, resources, or personnel to maintain a worldwide empire through coercive rule. The BNA, therefore, can be viewed as an attempt to persuade colonies to remain part of the British Empire, by presenting the view of Empire as compatible with the idea of equal rights, even though in practice it was not. In this sense, the law was being developed to mask the notions of White supremacy that underpinned colonial rule.[18] This is another example of 'interest-convergence', when the development of the law appears to be in the interests of racialized people but on closer inspection serves the interests of protecting White supremacy.[19] Indeed, developments in the colonies at around the same time suggest that British authorities were far from concerned with equality and racial justice. For example, we have already considered the brutal response to the Mau Mau rebellion in Kenya, which started just four years *after* the BNA was passed.

While British authorities were crushing the Mau Mau in Kenya, other Black people were following the path set by those on *Empire Windrush*, travelling to the UK to work in industries that were crucial to the regeneration of Britain such as the newly formed National Health Service, the railways, and the construction industry. These people collectively came to be known as 'the Windrush Generation' regardless of the name of the ship they arrived on. Despite their intentions to work and help rebuild British society, they suffered a range of race-based hostilities and mistreatment at the hands of private individuals and public officials. Amelia Gentleman's exposé contains first-hand accounts of the Windrush Generation being refused service in pubs and impoverished racial minorities being exploited by landlords and employers, for example.[20] The cruel irony of this should not be forgotten: it was the British who had enslaved and transported Black people from Africa to the Caribbean, and it was the British who now needed help from descendants of the enslaved to rebuild British society.[21] But centuries of pseudo-science being used to justify colonialism, enslavement, detention without trial, and other wrongs had left their mark on the psyche of the British population, leading to the racial injustices that were meted out when racialized people arrived to help rebuild Britain.

The extent of racism in the metropole during the 1950s led the Labour MP Archibald Fenner Brockway to propose a Racial Discrimination Bill in 1956 which would have outlawed acts of racial discrimination in various public places. However, this Bill, and eight similar Bills proposed by Brockway over the next

---

[18] El-Enany (n 3), p 14.
[19] Derrick Bell, '*Brown v. Board of Education* and the Interest-Convergence Dilemma' (1980) 93 *Harvard Law Review* 518 (see discussion in Chapter 1 of this book).
[20] See, generally, Gentleman (n 10); Reni Eddo-Lodge, *Why I'm No Longer Talking to White People about Race* (expanded edn, Bloomsbury Publishing 2018), p 23.
[21] Gentleman (n 10), p 114.

eight years, were never passed.[22] Public opposition to racial equality was simply too strong for any political party to advance the cause of racial justice.

The 1960s captured the paradoxical relationship between law and racial justice perhaps more vividly than any other decade. In 1960, the Conservative government enacted the Caravan Sites and Control of Development Act, which gave local authorities the power to close spaces that had been traditionally used by Gypsies and other travelling communities. Yet in 1965, the Labour government introduced the most progressive piece of racial justice legislation to date, with the Race Relations Act revolutionizing the opportunities for racialized people to make use of the law in their struggle for justice. This is not to say that the Act was without its problems, and its limitations are considered in more detail in the next chapter, but for now it is important to recognize that the 1965 Act was itself book-ended by two racist immigration laws: the Conservative government's Commonwealth Immigrants Act 1962, and the Labour government's Commonwealth Immigrants Act 1968. These both drastically curtailed the rights of racialized people to live and work in the metropole despite their historic ties to Britain. The Acts are worth considering in detail, as they laid the foundations for many of today's racial injustices.

Commonwealth Immigrants Acts of 1962 and 1968

Until 1962, the British Empire effectively constituted a single territory, and all British subjects were, on paper at least, free to enter the UK. The Commonwealth Immigrants Act 1962 put an end to this. The Act restricted the opportunities for so-called 'unskilled' immigrants from Asia and the West Indies to reside and live in the United Kingdom, but it permitted the arrival of similarly situated 'Commonwealth citizens' from places such as Canada, Australia, and New Zealand. The leader of the Labour Party at the time, Hugh Gaitskell, described the Act as "cruel and brutal anti-colour legislation", and Robert Winder has asserted that it 'was obvious that this was not an attempt to stop immigration per se, but to halt black immigration'.[23] This sent a clear message that law and policy were on the side of those who expressed racial animosity, rather than on the side of those who were experiencing racial injustices.

Just as Parliament was tightening control over immigration, so Britain was losing its grip over its colonies. In 1962 and 1963, for example, Uganda and Kenya respectively secured independence from British rule. The newly formed governments in these East African countries soon adopted policies

---

[22] Anthony Lester and Geoffrey Bindman, *Race and Law* (Penguin Books 1972), pp 108–9.
[23] Quoted in Gentleman (n 10), p 111.

of Africanization, and it was not long before people of Indian origin began to feel the effect of these policies. During British colonial rule, Indians had been considered to be higher in the racial hierarchy than Black Africans (but lower than Whites), and thus enjoyed relatively privileged opportunities, treatment, and outcomes in society. It was perhaps inevitable that upon independence, Black Africans would view the Indian population with suspicion and discontent. After all, Indians had benefitted from, and appeared to have been complicit in, the British authorities' subjugation of people of African origin. At first, Kenyan Asians used their British passports to travel to Britain to escape their declining living and working conditions, since they were unaffected by the 1962 Act's limitations on immigration.[24]

The British public's reaction to the arrival of East African Asians both shaped, and was shaped by, media and political depictions of 'coloured immigrants' taking over 'White British' people, with Enoch Powell playing a particularly prominent role in stoking public opposition to immigration.[25] In 1968, the Home Secretary, James Callaghan, rushed through another Commonwealth Immigrants Act, which imposed a further requirement that those wishing to move to the UK had to fulfil. In addition to holding a British passport that was issued in either London or Dublin – as opposed to being issued by colonial offices overseas – East African Asians now had to also show a 'qualifying connection' to the United Kingdom. In short, only those with a parent or grandparent who had been born, naturalized, or adopted in the UK could enter the country. The vast majority of East African Asians had no such connection, and thus their right to enter the UK was effectively curtailed.

Callaghan was in little mood to listen to concerns that the Act was racially discriminatory and went so far as to claim that the Act was needed in order to make the proposed Race Relations (Amendment) Bill that was to be introduced that same year more palatable to the public. In a memorandum, Callaghan wrote: '[T]he reception of the Race Relations Bill will be prejudiced in many minds, and support for it weakened, if people think that the numbers entering are unlimited or unreasonably high.'[26] He also wrote that 'the imminent Race Relations Bill will be a timely factor in helping us to show that we are aiming at a fair balance all round', betraying the view

---

[24] The historian Randall Hansen has argued that the exemption of Kenyan Asians from the 1962 Act was unintentional but nonetheless acknowledged by policy makers at the time. The decision to impose limitations upon them in 1968 was therefore something of a betrayal. See Hansen (n 16).

[25] Enoch Powell, 'Rivers of Blood' speech (Conservative Association meeting, 20 April 1968). See also Kevin Hickson, 'Enoch Powell's "Rivers of Blood" Speech: Fifty Years On' (2018) 89 *The Political Quarterly* 352.

[26] Quoted in Hansen (n 16), p 819.

that government should strike a balance between respecting the concerns of those with racial prejudices and respecting the welfare of actual or potential victims of racism. We can see, then, why this attitude created a paradoxical relationship between law and racial justice: on the one hand, it is used to appease those with racist sentiments; on the other hand, it protects racialized people when racists act on their prejudices.

Immigration laws from the 1970s

The 1962 and 1968 Acts did not quell concerns with immigration, and lawmakers responded with more legislation. The Immigration Act 1971 stated that only 'patrials' had a right to enter and stay in Britain. A 'patrial' was defined as someone who had a grandparent who had been born in the UK, or a parent who had been born or naturalized in the UK. The racial dimension of this cannot be understated: in 1971, 98 per cent of people born in Britain were racialized as White.[27] Moreover, White citizens of former 'settler colonies' such as Canada and Australia were more likely to have ancestors born in the UK, thus creating a system which favoured White immigrants. There were some protections for Commonwealth citizens who had arrived and settled in the UK before the commencement of the Act on 1 January 1973, though. By and large, if such people had been resident in the UK for five years, then they could claim a right of abode and thus came under the ambit of the 1971 Act and benefit from restrictions on deportations. Schedule 1 of the Act created a means for Commonwealth citizens to register themselves as a 'citizen of the United Kingdom and Colonies'.[28]

Speaking in 1978 when campaigning to be Prime Minister, Margaret Thatcher expressed how she would respond to public concerns with immigration. Noting that "people are really rather afraid that this country might be rather swamped by people with a different culture", Thatcher expressed a desire to limit the number of people immigrating to the UK. Without a hint of irony, she claimed that such restrictions were in the interests of racialized people, since otherwise they would face hostility: "[I]f there is any fear that it might be swamped, people are going to react and be rather hostile to those coming in. So, if you want good race relations, you have got to allay peoples' fears on numbers."[29] Once in power, Thatcher's government duly introduced more restrictions on immigration. The British

---

[27] El-Enany (n 3), p 4.

[28] For a review of these laws, see Amnesty International, 'Submission to the Windrush Lessons Learned Review' (2018).

[29] Gordon Burns, Interview with Margaret Thatcher (*World in Action*, 27 January 1978).

Nationality Act 1981 replaced the category of 'Citizenship of the United Kingdom and Colonies' with three types of citizenship: (a) British citizens, which included citizens of the United Kingdom and colonies with the right of abode in Britain; (b) British Dependent Territories citizens, which included persons in territories that, at the time, were still British colonies[30] (these people could register as British citizens after five years' residence in Britain); and (c) British Overseas citizens, which included all citizens of the United Kingdom and colonies who did not fall into one of the first two categories. People in this final category had no legal right to live or work in Britain, and they were considered to be 'aliens' for the purpose of immigration control and naturalization.[31] This made the criteria for securing the status of 'British citizen' all the more important.

The Act stipulated that citizenship would only be conferred to a person whose mother or father was a British citizen or was settled in Britain at the commencement of the 1981 Act. In other words, it was irrelevant whether one was born in the UK or not: what mattered instead was whether one's parents had been born in the UK or were considered 'settled' under the pre-1981 legislative provisions by, for example, registering themselves under the 1971 Act. The shadow Home Secretary at the time, Roy Hattersley, explained why this approach had a racially discriminatory effect even though the language used in the Act was facially race-neutral: "What is racist is that the difference between the two categories always works out ... in a way which disadvantages the black community and gives corresponding advantage to the white. That is why I again describe the Bill, irrespective of the Home Secretary's good intentions, as racist in outcome."[32] El-Enany writes that the 1981 Act 'severed a notionally white, geographically distinct Britain from the remainder of its colonies and Commonwealth. ... A territorially distinct Britain and a concept of citizenship that made Britishness commensurate with whiteness made it clear that Britain, the landmass and everything within it, belongs to Britons, conceived intrinsically as white'.[33] That is, Britain was now closing its borders to racialized people, the same people who had not long ago been coerced to submit to British rule.

Section 7 of the 1981 Act did account for those who could have registered under the 1971 Act but had not. It allowed such people to register as a British citizen if they had been ordinarily resident in the UK for five years. However, as the Windrush scandal which unfolded decades later revealed, there had been woefully inadequate attempts to ensure that such people

---

[30] Hong Kong, Bermuda, the British Virgin Islands, Gibraltar, and the Falkland Islands.
[31] El-Enany (n 3), p 128.
[32] Quoted in El-Enany (n 3), pp 127–8.
[33] El-Enany (n 3), p 4.

properly registered themselves as British citizens, as most were unaware of the changes being wrought by these legislative developments. In another effort to appear tough on immigration, Thatcher's government introduced the Immigration Act in 1988, which repealed whatever legal protections Commonwealth citizens had. Once again, those affected by the changes were either not made aware at all or were given incorrect advice.[34]

Developments in immigration law continued along this trajectory over the course of the 1990s and early 2000s. For example, the Immigration and Asylum Act 1999 introduced the practice of administrative removal instead of deportation in cases not involving criminality, which made it more difficult for individuals to challenge decisions against them. Deportation gives rise to a right of appeal,[35] but the only means of challenging administrative removal is judicial review, which is much harder to initiate. The 1999 Act made the Windrush scandal almost inevitable, as people could now be apprehended, detained, issued with removal directions, and put on to planes without having the option of a formal appeal process.[36]

Immigration laws and the 'hostile environment'

In 2012, the Home Secretary Theresa May introduced the idea of a 'hostile environment' in an article in *The Daily Telegraph*, announcing that private landlords, NHS staff, and employers would now be required to conduct checks on the immigration status of tenants, patients, and employees.[37] The stated aim was to make Britain a less welcoming place to potential economic migrants. This approach was formalized in the Immigration Acts of 2014 and 2016, which have contributed to the structuralized nature of racism in Britain today. Cautioning against the adoption of the measures, the Joint Council for the Welfare of Immigrants (JCWI) anticipated that the 2014 Act, which required private individuals to police other private individuals' immigration status, would 'divide society, creating a two-tier Britain, a return to the days of "no dogs, no blacks, no Irish" and of ill people with no access to healthcare walking the streets of Britain'.[38]

The JCWI was vindicated in 2017, when the *Guardian* newspaper began printing stories about Black British people who were being arrested, detained, denied legal rights, and ultimately removed from Britain and sent

---

[34] Wendy Williams, 'Windrush Lessons Learned Review' (19 March 2020), p 59.
[35] Although this has been restricted by the Immigration Act 2014.
[36] Thanks to Jen Morgan for helping me articulate this point.
[37] James Kirkup and Robert Winnett, 'Theresa May Interview: "We're Going to Give Illegal Migrants a Really Hostile Reception"' *The Daily Telegraph* (25 May 2012).
[38] Alan Travis, 'Immigration Bill: Theresa May Defends Plans to Create "Hostile Environment"' *The Guardian* (10 October 2013).

to Caribbean countries. This came to be known as the 'Windrush scandal', as it involved the deportation of people of the Windrush Generation who had lived and worked in the United Kingdom for, in some cases, several decades. To understand how the scandal unfolded, and the role of law in the creation of the scandal, we need to return to the Immigration Act 1971. This made it possible for people who arrived prior to 1 January 1973 – the date the Act came into force – to register their British citizenship, but many of the Windrush Generation were unaware of this. In any event, they were assured that registration was not compulsory, and that they retained their right to live and work in the UK. For some 40 years after 1973, this had generally not been a problem. However, the Immigration Act of 2014 now required everyone to prove their status whenever renting accommodation, applying for jobs, or accessing public services like the NHS. Many of the Windrush Generation though had not registered their citizenship and had no way of proving that they were in the UK lawfully. Many had travelled to the UK on their parents' passports, and for reasons unknown the Home Office had destroyed landing cards and other relevant documents that would have proved their legal status to live and work in the UK.[39] This left several thousand of the Windrush Generation in something of a legal black hole. Although lawyers soon learned of the problems and tried to help their clients, the scandal was brought to the public's attention by the journalist Amelia Gentleman, who explained the problem clearly: 'Britain's immigration legislation had profoundly changed since they arrived, without them noticing, pushing them across the invisible but crucial line that stands between legality and illegality.'[40] Unable to rent, work, or access healthcare, many fell into destitution, and many came to the attention of the Home Office, which ruthlessly detained and removed or deported them notwithstanding that they had lived and worked in the UK for several decades, and notwithstanding that they had a right of abode and so were exempt from immigration controls in the first place.

In her wide-ranging review of the Windrush scandal, set up by the government, Wendy Williams writes that the 'root cause' of the scandal 'can be traced back to the legislation of the 1960s, 70s and 80s, some of which, as accepted at the time, had racial motivations'.[41] As she writes, the Windrush scandal was the culmination of an 'immigration and nationality policy ... that saw non-white immigration as a problem to be solved'.[42] In May 2022, Gentleman revealed that an unpublished report by the Home

---

[39] Gentleman (n 10), p 149.
[40] Gentleman (n 10), p 191.
[41] Williams (n 34), p 12.
[42] Williams (n 34), p 52.

Office confirmed Williams' findings. The report apparently states that '[t]he British Empire depended on racist ideology in order to function, which in turn produced legislation aimed at keeping racial and ethnic groups apart. ... From the beginning, concern about Commonwealth immigration was about skin colour'. From the 1950s, according to the report, British officials shared a 'basic assumption that "coloured immigrants", as they were referred to, were not good for British society'.[43]

The effect of racism on the legal right to seek asylum

The legal restrictions placed on immigration from the 1960s did not, on the face of it, have any bearing on the right to seek asylum in the UK. Whereas 'immigrants' are those who voluntarily leave their home country, and are subject to a state's domestic immigration laws, asylum seekers are those who feel compelled to leave their country because they fear persecution at home and are subject to a process set by international law.[44] Even Thatcher suggested that those seeking asylum should be treated differently from those wanting to immigrate to the UK. Setting out her plans in 1978 to limit immigration, she said: "We do have to hold out the prospect of an end of immigration, except of course, for compassionate cases."[45] However, the racism that afflicted the development of immigration laws has had an impact on the process for seeking asylum in the UK. To explain why, we first need to recognize that the 'divide and rule' tactics of the British Empire meant that many places were inhospitable for people, with the partition of India and Pakistan a particularly notable example of the problems left by imperial rule. Britain's mismanagement of Indian independence led to violence along the border of India and Pakistan and the displacement of millions of people who sought refuge elsewhere. Teresa Hayter puts the problem in the following terms: '[S]ome [wars, conflicts, and repression] arise from centuries of imperialist control, and in particular the imperialists' divide and rule tactics and the boundaries they drew on maps. Imperialism in its modern guise has created new forms of impoverishment, which may exacerbate existing nationalist and ethnic tensions.'[46] If immigration routes are curtailed, though, then people who either want to or need to flee their home country will turn to the asylum system. As El-Enany writes: 'The removal of entry rights

---

[43] See Amelia Gentleman, 'Windrush Scandal Caused by "30 Years of Racist Immigration Laws" – Report' *The Guardian* (29 May 2022).

[44] Gina Clayton and Georgina Firth, *Immigration and Asylum Law* (9th edn, Oxford University Press 2021).

[45] Burns (n 29). Also see El-Enany (n 3), p 135.

[46] Quoted in El-Enany (n 3), p 136.

for racialised colony and Commonwealth citizens over the course of the 1960s, 1970s and 1980s produced the asylum route as one of the few means for historically dispossessed people to access Britain.'[47]

Throughout the 1980s, as claims for asylum in the UK increased, a narrative emerged that many, if not most, asylum seekers were in fact economic migrants who were trying to circumvent immigration laws. This narrative was coupled with the claim that resources in Britain are scarce, and British citizens would suffer if too many asylum seekers were granted refugee status. In 1993, John Major's Conservative government addressed these concerns in the Asylum and Immigration Appeals Act, which made it more difficult for people to seek asylum in Britain. The Home Secretary, Kenneth Clarke, echoed Thatcher in claiming that such measures were necessary to foster "good race relations" in the UK.[48]

Although the effects of these laws tended to be felt most keenly at border points where people tried to enter the UK, they would also have a profound effect throughout the UK. The Asylum and Immigration Act 1996, for example, made it a criminal offence to knowingly assist asylum seekers to gain entry to the UK through deception and gave extended powers to police and immigration officials to search and arrest asylum seekers. The 1996 Act also put employers at risk of criminal sanctions if they hired a person who was subject to immigration controls which placed limits on their right to work. In 1999, the Refugee Council claimed that these provisions had a detrimental impact on people with legitimate claims to asylum, as employers tended to avoid hiring them because of the burdensome documentation and the consequences of a criminal conviction in cases of error.[49]

The use of asylum law to structuralize racism was compounded by the international legal system relating to the protection of asylum seekers and refugees. The 1951 Refugee Convention applied only to displaced Europeans who were seeking refuge, with European states explicitly excluding non-European asylum seekers from the scope of the Convention.[50] This was despite the fact that the partition of India and Pakistan just three years earlier had displaced several million people from their homes. Although the 1967 Protocol to the Convention removed the geographical limitations to the 1951 Convention, this was introduced for reasons other than a belated concern with the welfare and rights of racialized asylum seekers.[51] As other scholars

---

[47] El-Enany (n 3), p 134.
[48] HC Deb 2 November 1992, vol 213, cc 21–120, 21, cited in El-Enany (n 3), p 144.
[49] El-Enany (n 3), p 147.
[50] Edwin O. Abuya et al, 'The Neglected Colonial Legacy of the 1951 Refugee Convention' (2021) 59 *International Migration* 265.
[51] See El-Enany (n 3), pp 139–40.

have explained, the international system of asylum law can actually serve to legitimize colonial wrongs by painting the former imperial state as a safe space that is ready to help those fleeing the harms being inflicted by the 'bad' former colony which has failed to govern itself properly, notwithstanding the argument that it was imperial rule that created the repressive conditions in the former colony.[52]

At the time of writing in late 2023, policies towards immigration and asylum continue to be imbued with racism. Despite the national and global condemnation of the Windrush scandal, the Conservative government has continued to legislate to make it harder for asylum seekers to claim refuge in the UK and has continued to dissuade racialized migrants from travelling to the UK. The Nationality and Borders Act 2022 (NBA), for example, was introduced in response to concerns with the numbers of people crossing the English Channel on small boats. Although there is some evidence to suggest that most people arriving on small boats have credible claims of asylum, the government has preferred to assert that the majority of such people do not need asylum and are instead trying to circumvent the laws that govern immigration.[53] The NBA is premised on the government's unfounded assertions and creates a two-tiered asylum system. Under the Act, those who arrive in the UK via an irregular route such as on a small boat might receive less protection and support than those arriving through an official route. The problem with this, though, is the paucity of safe, official routes for those fleeing persecution without relevant documentation such as passports and visas. The 2022 Act has also made it harder to establish refugee status and to appeal adverse decisions. Jennifer Morgan and Christel Querton have highlighted the deleterious effect the Act will have on women in particular, drawing attention to the problem of intersectional discrimination.[54]

The government has also introduced the Illegal Migration Act 2023, which precludes any asylum claims from even being heard if the person has

---

[52] El-Enany (n 3), p 139.
[53] Around 98 per cent of people arriving on small boats make a claim for asylum. The Home Office does not provide data on the outcomes of these asylum claims, but the Refugee Council has pointed out that most people arriving on small boats come from countries such as Iran, Iraq, Sudan, and Syria, and that the majority of people from these countries who apply for asylum are granted asylum. In the Refugee Council's view, this is a good indication that people crossing the Channel on small boats are likely to be recognized as being in need of protection. See Refugee Council, 'An Analysis of Channel Crossings & Asylum Outcomes: November 2021' (November 2021).
[54] Jennifer Morgan and Christel Querton, 'Access to Protection for Women Seeking Asylum in the UK' in Jane Freedman and Georgina Colby (eds), *Feminist Representations: Sexual Violence Against Women, Asylum, Voice and Testimony* (Proceedings of the British Academy series, Oxford University Press, forthcoming).

arrived via an irregular route having passed through a country where they did not face persecution. They would instead be automatically detained and either sent back to their home country or a country that is deemed 'safe'. It seems likely that at least some people arriving via irregular routes will be automatically sent to Rwanda as a 'third safe country', as part of an agreement between the UK and Rwanda.[55]

We can see, then, how '[i]mmigration law', in El-Enany's words, has become 'a crucial mechanism for ensuring that colonial wealth remains out of the hands of those from whom it was stolen'.[56] Immigration laws both create the idea of 'race' and delineate which 'races' have access to British laws, resources, and services. Lester and Bindman have explained why this structuralizes racism within British society: 'If our immigration laws are racially discriminatory in their aims and effect, it becomes difficult to persuade employers, workers, property developers and house-owners to treat people on their merits, regardless of race.'[57] As we will see in the next section, Lester and Bindman were arguably underplaying the effect of racist immigration laws when they wrote that such laws make it 'difficult to persuade' employers and so on to disregard race. Immigration laws, it can be argued, *compel* employers, property owners, and so on to treat people of different races differently.[58] It is in this sense that immigration laws structuralize racism today.

Racial injustices in the United Kingdom today

With the development of the legal framework in mind, we can turn to the numerous studies that illustrate how these laws contribute to the depth and breadth of racism in British society today. The following is a summary of the main research findings of racism in the fields of education, criminal justice, employment, housing, and healthcare, and readers are advised to consult the sources referred to if they want fuller accounts of racism in each field. The purpose of this broad overview is to set the scene for the next chapter, which looks at efforts to tackle racial injustices in these fields through the legal system.

---

[55] Office of the High Commissioner for Human Rights, 'UK Illegal Migration Bill: UN Refugee Agency and UN Human Rights Office Warn of Profound Impact on Human Rights and International Refugee Protection System' (United Nations, 18 July 2023); Enver Solomon, 'The Illegal Migration Bill Has Passed, and Here's What Will Happen: Children Lost, Abused and Exploited' *The Guardian* (18 July 2023).
[56] El-Enany (n 3), p 5.
[57] Lester and Bindman (n 22), p 14.
[58] The JCWI case is discussed in Chapter 4.

Education

We start with the education system, because this is a 'key site in the struggle for racial and ethnic equality in Britain'.[59] Educational institutions are where children will often mix with people of different races for the first time and over a sustained period. It is also where children spend much of their formative years acquiring knowledge and developing social and learning skills. Education also plays an important role in social mobility, helping shape a person's place in society. Schools as institutions, and schooling as a practice, then, are key drivers of race relations since it is in the education system where initial understandings of race and racism can be formed.[60] And experiences of education can have a knock-on effect on experiences of other social processes, such as criminal justice and employment. One's educational achievements, for example, can open or close the door to certain employment opportunities.

Current data suggest that a person's experiences of the education system will be affected by their race. Writing in 2020, Claire Alexander and William Shankley explained that '[e]ducation remains a primary arena for both the maintenance of entrenched racial stereotyping and discrimination. ... Concerns over structural racism, low educational attainment, poor teacher expectations and stereotyping, ethnocentric curricula and high levels of school exclusions for some groups remain entrenched features of our school system'.[61] To get a snapshot of the problems today, we can examine (a) rates of exclusions and suspensions from school, (b) the attainment gap, and (c) the school curriculum and the government's Prevent agenda.

Data from the Department for Education reveal that, year on year, Gypsy and Roma pupils, Irish Travellers, and Black Caribbean students tend to be excluded or suspended from school at higher rates than other racial groups.[62] Similar patterns can be found when looking at the academic achievements of different racial groups. Chinese and Indian students tend to achieve the highest grades at GCSE level, with White British, Pakistani, Black Caribbean, and Gypsy and Roma children achieving the lowest proportion of top grades.[63] Despite the tendency of White British pupils to achieve relatively low grades, they tend to receive higher awards at degree-level.[64]

---

[59] Claire Alexander and William Shankley, 'Ethnic Inequalities in the State Education System in England' in Bridget Byrne et al (eds), *Ethnicity, Race and Inequality in the UK: State of the Nation* (Policy Press 2020), p 94.
[60] Alexander and Shankley (n 59), p 94.
[61] Alexander and Shankley (n 59), p 94.
[62] Department for Education, 'Permanent Exclusions and Suspensions in England' (updated 8 August 2023).
[63] Department for Education, 'GCSE Results (Attainment 8)' (18 March 2022).
[64] Higher Education Statistics Authority, 'Undergraduate Degree Results' (22 November 2022).

Indeed, it is in this context that we can see clearly the unhelpfulness of the 'Black and Minority Ethnic' (BME) or 'Black and Asian Minority Ethnic' (BAME) labels, as there is considerable variation within racial groups. It is not particularly helpful to speak of 'Asians', for example, when Indians and Pakistanis face quite distinct outcomes.[65]

These disparities do not conclusively prove that racialized people are being discriminated against by educational providers, though. It might be that schoolchildren's home life or cultural background plays a more significant role in their success or otherwise at school. There are at least two rejoinders to such a view, though. First, even if this was the case, the imperative is on the education system to accommodate different people's home and cultural backgrounds. This is what is implied by the commitment to respecting diversity and fostering inclusivity – the idea that a system will cater to people of all backgrounds. What the data show instead, though, is that commitments to diversity and inclusivity are problematic for the reasons set out in Chapter 1: they presume the normativity of 'Whiteness', and education providers find it difficult to ensure equal opportunities, treatment, and outcomes within a framework that centres and prioritizes Whiteness.

A second rejoinder can be located in critiques of the 'Prevent' strategy. In 2014, the Department for Education announced that all schools will now be under a duty to 'actively promote the fundamental British values of democracy, the rule of law, individual liberty, and mutual respect and tolerance of those with different faiths and beliefs'.[66] This duty had first been set out in the Prevent Strategy in 2011, which is one of the United Kingdom's central policies to identify people at risk of being drawn into terrorism. While the Prevent Strategy is, on the face of it, race-neutral, there have been objections to the way in which the strategy has stigmatized Muslims.[67] Similarly, the focus in the guidance on the apparent 'Britishness' of values such as 'mutual respect and tolerance' is concerning because it reinforces assumptions about the superiority of 'British' norms over other cultures, implying that other cultures do *not* value 'mutual respect' or 'tolerance'. This quite explicitly mirrors the rationales for colonialism in the 17th and 18th centuries: that other societies are allegedly uncivilized. Likewise, the contention that 'mutual respect and tolerance' are 'fundamental British values' obscures the lack of respect and tolerance that characterized British

---

[65] On the unhelpfulness of the terms BME and BAME, see 'A note on language' in Chapter 1.
[66] Department for Education, 'Promoting Fundamental British Values as Part of SMSC in Schools' (November 2014).
[67] For a summary of the criticisms, see Lee Jerome et al, 'The Impact of the Prevent Duty on Schools: A Review of the Evidence' (2019) 45 *British Educational Research Journal* 821, 824–7.

rule in the colonial era. As Catherine Vincent argues, the requirement to promote British values 'proceeds through disavowal and amnesia about Britain's history of colonial violence and racialised structural inequalities in the contemporary state'.[68] She quotes Christine Winter and China Mills, who assert that '[t]he British values policy is more than a counter-terrorism strategy, it is a psychic defence mechanism that protects and privileges whiteness; denies the normalised state violence and radical exclusions on which liberal values have been built'.[69] In other words, the ways in which the Prevent Strategy structuralizes racism in the education sector is built upon the historical exclusions of certain racialized groups from British civic life.

The importance of securing racial justice within schools and throughout the education system can also be illustrated by what Jessica Perera has described as the 'pupil referral unit-to-prison pipeline', referring to the ways in which Black children in particular who have been excluded from school find themselves caught up in the criminal justice system.[70] Several civil society organizations have also explained why children who 'are outside of mainstream education are more vulnerable to becoming the victim of childhood criminal exploitation'.[71] The education system intersects with the criminal justice system in a number of ways, and racial injustices within the former can have a notable impact on racial disparities and injustices in the latter.

Criminal justice

It is perhaps in the criminal justice system that we see racism rear its head most vividly, and that we see the 'boomerang effect' of imperialism most strikingly.[72] The literature on racism within the criminal justice system is vast, encompassing numerous governmental reports and inquiries; academic research; and publications of civil society organizations that highlight the multiple and complex ways in which racialized people suffer injustices throughout the system.[73]

---

[68] Carol Vincent, 'Belonging in England Today: Schools, Race, Class and Policy' (2022) 58 *Journal of Sociology* 324, 332.

[69] Christine Winter and China Mills, 'The Psy-Security-Curriculum Ensemble: British Values Curriculum Policy in English Schools' (2020) 35 *Journal of Education Policy* 46, 60.

[70] Jessica Perera, 'How Black Working-Class Youth Are Criminalised and Excluded in the English School System' (Institute of Race Relations 2020).

[71] 4in10, Just for Kids Law, and Children's Rights Alliance for England, 'Race, Poverty and School Exclusions in London' (2020), p 5.

[72] J.M. Moore, 'The "New Punitiveness" in the Context of British Imperial History' (2015) 101 *Criminal Justice Matters* 10.

[73] For general overviews of racism and the criminal justice system, see: David Lammy, 'The Lammy Review: An Independent Review into the Treatment of, and Outcomes for,

There are some criminal laws that discriminate against racial groups, such as the Police, Crime, Sentencing and Courts Act 2022 which has put people of Gypsy, Roma, and Traveller (GRT) heritage at greater risk of arrest and criminal conviction if they reside in a roadside camp without authorization.[74] For the most part, though, it is criminal justice processes rather than the substantive criminal law that are racially unjust. Lord Scarman's inquiry in 1981, Sir William Macpherson's inquiry in 1999, and Baroness Casey's review in 2023 have all highlighted a problem of racism within the Metropolitan Police Force,[75] but the available data support the view that police forces across England and Wales discriminate along racial lines in the contexts of, for example, stop and search powers and arrest rates.[76] Notable incidents include a strip-search by police officers of a 15-year-old Black girl in her school in December 2020, with a Child Safeguarding Practice Review in 2022 finding that the police's actions were 'unlikely to have been disconnected from her ethnicity and her background as a child growing up on an estate in Hackney'.[77] The girl, referred to as 'Child Q', is in the process of bringing legal action against the police in relation to her treatment, and the case highlights the intersection of race, gender, class, and age.

Racialized people are not just more prone to be viewed as criminal by the police but are also less likely to be viewed as warranting protection. The most notorious example is the Stephen Lawrence case. The failure of the police and other agencies to provide appropriate services to people because of their colour, culture, or ethnic origin also reared its head in the Bijan Ebrahimi case. Ebrahimi was murdered in 2013 by one of his neighbours after being subjected to sustained racial harassment and violence. Ebrahimi had contacted Avon and Somerset Police on several occasions to report the harassment, but the police ignored his appeals for

---

Black, Asian and Minority Ethnic Individuals in the Criminal Justice System' (2017); Institute of Race Relations, 'Criminal Justice System Statistics' (14 September 2023); Ana Veiga et al, 'Racial and Ethnic Disparities in Sentencing: What Do We Know, and Where Should We Go?' (2023) 62 *The Howard Journal of Crime and Justice* 167.

[74] For an outline of how the Bill will affect people of GRT heritage, see Abbie Kirkby, 'Briefing on New Police Powers for Encampments in Policing, Crime, Sentencing and Courts Bill: Part 4' (24 March 2021).

[75] Lord Justice Scarman, 'The Brixton Disorders 10–12 April 1981' (Cmd 8427, 1981); Sir William Macpherson, 'The Stephen Lawrence Inquiry' (Cmd 4262-I, 1999); Baroness Louise Casey, 'An Independent Review into the Standards of Behaviour and Internal Culture of the Metropolitan Police Service' (March 2023). See also Tony Jefferson, 'Policing the Riots: From Bristol and Brixton to Tottenham, via Toxteth, Handsworth, etc' (2012) 87 *Criminal Justice Matters* 8.

[76] Lammy (n 73).

[77] Jim Gamble and Rory McCallum, 'Local Child Safeguarding Practice Review: Child Q' (City of London & Hackney Safeguarding Children Partnership, March 2022), para 5.73.

help. A Multi-Agency Review into his death concluded that institutional racism played a part in the police's failure to help: 'As an Iranian man living in this environment, Mr Ebrahimi was disadvantaged by the inappropriate responses by Avon and Somerset Constabulary and Bristol City Council to his racist victimisation. Representatives of those organisations displayed a distinct lack of understanding of his plight and, accordingly, unwitting prejudice against him.'[78]

Beyond racism in policing, research has highlighted that Black suspects are more likely to be charged by the Crown Prosecution Service (CPS)[79] and that racialized people are more likely to be found guilty and sentenced to harsher punishments than White defendants in similar circumstances. For example, the odds of receiving a prison sentence for drug offences are around 240 per cent higher for those classified as 'BAME' than for those who classify themselves as White.[80] Once in prison, racialized people have reported fewer positive relationships with prison staff than White British prisoners, and they are also more likely to report being victimized.[81] People of GRT heritage have reported particular difficulties with the prison system, with 27 per cent of GRT prisoners reporting feelings of depression, compared with an average of 15 per cent across all prisoners.[82]

The 'myth of Black criminality' has been well documented by sociologists such as Paul Gilroy and Stuart Hall,[83] and for present purposes it is important to emphasize how assumptions about Black criminality, and thus racial disparities and inequalities in the criminal justice system, are tied to the racial injustices of the colonial era. A stark illustration is the narrative of 'gang violence' and the measures adopted in response. The concept of a 'gang' is an amorphous one, but it loosely refers to instances where groups of people jointly engage in criminal behaviour. However, in criminal justice discourses, the term is almost exclusively reserved for instances of young Black people jointly engaging in criminal behaviour. That is, a group of White middle-aged men who conspire to commit white-collar crime will generally not be referred to as a 'gang' by the police or prosecution or media, whereas a group of Black youths engaged in drug-related criminal activities

---

[78] See David McCallum, 'Safer Bristol Partnership: Multi-agency Learning Review following the Murder of Bijan Ebrahimi' (Safer Bristol Executive Board, 17 January 2014, updated 25 October 2017), para 9.13.1.
[79] Aamna Mohdin and Carmen Aguilar García, 'Defendants of Colour More Likely to Be Charged than White People, Finds CPS Study' *The Guardian* (7 February 2023).
[80] Lammy (n 73), p 33.
[81] Lammy (n 73), p 50.
[82] Lammy (n 73), p 52.
[83] Stuart Hall (ed), *Policing the Crisis: Mugging, the State, and Law and Order* (Macmillan 1978); Paul Gilroy, 'The Myth of Black Criminality' (1982) 19 *The Socialist Register* 47.

will be.[84] The reservation of the term 'gang' for actual or suspected Black perpetrators of crime can be seen in the database the police use to keep track of actual or suspected gang members. In May 2018, it was revealed that the Metropolitan Police Force had 3,362 people registered on its Gangs Matrix database, of which 89 per cent were categorized as 'BAME'.[85] The racialized use of 'gang' narratives also finds expression in the doctrine of 'joint enterprise' in criminal law. This doctrine gives prosecutors the ability to prosecute multiple people for the same offence, without having to prove which person committed the actual criminal act in question. Although the doctrine of joint enterprise is facially race-neutral, in that it applies theoretically to all people of all races, research has consistently shown that Black youths are disproportionately charged and convicted under the law on joint enterprise.[86]

Patrick Williams has referred to the 'race–gang nexus' to highlight how Black people are now being construed as criminals in a collective sense,[87] and we can see the continuities with the Criminal Tribes Act 1871, which constructed certain Indian 'tribes' as inherently and collectively 'criminal'. Jasbinder Nijjar has explained how the contemporary 'war on gangs' finds it roots 'in a history of British colonial efforts to collectively control, punish, and exploit racial subjects constructed as criminal collectives'.[88] As Nijjar writes in relation to the Gangs Matrix database, the idea that certain racialized groups are 'networks of criminality' is just as prevalent today as it was in the colonial era. We can see, then, how the legacy of racist colonial-era laws structuralizes racism in British society today.

Employment

Criminal records can have an impact on someone's employment prospects after serving their sentence, and it follows that if there are racial disparities in convictions and sentencing, then there are going to be disparities in employment opportunities. But even those without a criminal record

---

[84] Becky Clarke and Patrick Williams, '(Re)Producing Guilt in Suspect Communities: The Centrality of Racialisation in Joint Enterprise Prosecutions' (2020) 9 *International Journal for Crime, Justice and Social Democracy* 116.

[85] Jasbinder Nijjar, 'Echoes of Empire: Excavating the Colonial Roots of Britain's "War on Gangs"' (2018) 45 *Social Justice* 147, 149.

[86] Clarke and Williams (n 84); Patrick Williams and Becky Clarke, 'Dangerous Associations: Joint Enterprise, Gangs and Racism' (Centre for Crime and Justice Studies 2016).

[87] Patrick Williams, 'Criminalising the Other: Challenging the Race–Gang Nexus' (2014) 56 *Race & Class* 18.

[88] Nijjar (n 85), p 149.

are subject to differential opportunities, treatment, and outcomes in the workplace on the basis of race. This is important because employment plays a vital role in a person's living standards and life chances. Work can be emotionally fulfilling, financially rewarding, or both. Study after study, though, has shown that race discrimination within the workplace has been a long-standing problem. We saw earlier in this chapter that immigrants to the UK in the post-colonial period struggled to access the labour market because of overt discrimination. Legislative initiatives to bar discriminatory practices have not eliminated the problem altogether, though. In 2017, an independent government review led by Baroness McGregor-Smith revealed striking 'underemployment and underpromotion of people from BME backgrounds'.[89] We can consider these two issues in turn.

McGregor-Smith found that while the employment rate for White workers was 75.6 per cent, it was just 62.8 per cent for racialized people. And while the unemployment rate for White workers was 11.5 per cent, it was 15.3 per cent for those from a BME background. A study by the Runnymede Trust in the same year also found that ethnic minority women had faced the biggest challenges to entering the workplace after the 2008 recession and the Coalition government's austerity measures. Funding cuts to training courses that were used by ethnic minority women effectively closed the door to employment for them.[90] However, we must be careful before concluding that these statistics demonstrate discriminatory attitudes among employers. There might be alternative explanations for the underemployment of racialized people. For example, racialized people might be searching for jobs ineffectively or might lack the social capital to find out about vacancies. To test this, researchers have periodically carried out experiments which have consistently shown that racialized people are underemployed because of discrimination, rather than differences in social capital or job search strategies. Anthony Heath and Valentina Di Stasio have summarized these experiments, which generally involve sending job applications and CVs that are substantially identical except for the made-up name of the applicant.[91] Taken together, the experiments, conducted between 1969 and 2017, reveal that 'white minority groups tend to face only modest risks of discrimination,

---

[89] Baroness McGregor-Smith, 'Race in the Workplace: The McGregor-Smith Review' (Department for Business, Energy and Industrial Strategy 2017), p 6, Available from: https://www.gov.uk/government/publications/race-in-the-workplace-the-mcgregor-smith-review

[90] Sarah-Marie Hall et al, 'Intersecting Inequalities: The Impact of Austerity on Black and Minority Ethnic Women in the UK' (Women's Budget Group and Runnymede Trust 2017).

[91] Anthony F. Heath and Valentina Di Stasio, 'Racial Discrimination in Britain, 1969–2017: A Meta-analysis of Field Experiments on Racial Discrimination in the British Labour Market' (2019) 70 *The British Journal of Sociology* 1774.

whereas applicants with black Caribbean, black African and Pakistani names all experience much greater, and more or less equally high, risks of discrimination'.[92] Black Caribbeans, for example, would have to 'make about 50 per cent more applications than their white British counterparts in order to receive a positive response'.[93]

Heath and Di Stasio attempted to make sense of this pattern, as we might expect legislative changes to at least reduce the risk of discrimination in hiring practices. They argue that '[t]he failure of legislation to reduce discrimination is not perhaps altogether surprising: there has been weak enforcement, little financial incentive for employers to change, and lack of monitoring'.[94] They then speculate that the continuing risks of discrimination might be attributable to 'subtle racism', which they surmise manifests itself in 'negative employer beliefs about the linguistic and work-related skills and motivations of minorities with a migration background from less-developed countries'.[95] They also draw the link between employment and education and criminal justice: 'Persisting negative stereotypes of non-white minorities in Britain may well be a result of the well known high rates of school exclusion for black youngsters, disproportionate rates of "stop and search", and over-representation of black and Muslim young men in prison.'[96]

Even when racialized people find themselves in employment, they suffer differential treatment in the context of promotions. In her review, McGregor-Smith writes that while '[a]ll BME groups are more likely to be overqualified than White ethnic groups ... White employees are more likely to be promoted than all other groups'.[97] She recommended that legislation be introduced to ensure that all companies and businesses which employ more than 50 people publish workforce data broken down by race and pay band.[98] Her review also shed light on what employees and employers think about the role of government in supporting progression of racialized employees in the workplace. Respondents to the Call for Evidence most commonly replied that 'the Government's role was to ensure enforcement of the legislation'.[99] However, in response, the government evaded responsibility: '[W]e believe that in the first instance, the best method is a business-led, voluntary approach and not legislation as a way of bringing about lasting change.'[100]

---

[92] Heath and Di Stasio (n 91), p 1789.
[93] Heath and Di Stasio (n 91), p 1787.
[94] Heath and Di Stasio (n 91), p 1794.
[95] Heath and Di Stasio (n 91), p 1794.
[96] Heath and Di Stasio (n 91), p 1794.
[97] McGregor-Smith (n 89), p 6.
[98] McGregor-Smith (n 89), p 16.
[99] McGregor-Smith (n 89), pp 78–9.
[100] Department for Business, Energy & Industrial Strategy, 'Government Response to Baroness McGregor-Smith' (nd), p 3.

Housing

Racism within the housing sector has received less scholarly attention than racism in education, criminal justice, and employment but is equally important because a person's living conditions will have an impact on other aspects of their life, such as access to schools, jobs, healthcare, and so on. Social scientists have documented patterns of migrants' housing in the UK, noting that as migrants arrived in the UK to undertake manual labour and public sector work in the mid-1900s, they generally settled in urban areas that were blighted by poverty. In some cases, specific employment opportunities shaped the settlement of migrants, with the textile industries in Lancashire and Yorkshire leading to dense populations of migrants in those areas, for example.[101] As Shankley and Nissa Finney note, '[d]iscrimination and racism have been found to shape the housing experiences of migrants and minorities historically', with private landlords sometimes refusing to let their properties to racialized people. In 2013, the Runnymede Trust found that 'over a quarter of Black Caribbean, Black African and Pakistani[s] ... have felt discriminated against when seeking a place to live'.[102] And when properties are let to racialized people, they experience worse living conditions. Social housing providers, for example, are known to allocate their least desirable properties to racialized people.[103] Awaab Ishak had just turned two years old when he died in 2020 because of, in the words of a senior coroner, 'a severe respiratory condition caused due to prolonged exposure to mould in his home environment'.[104] His parents had repeatedly raised concerns about the mould to their social housing provider, Rochdale Boroughwide Housing (RBH), but no attempts were made to improve ventilation or to fix the mould. After the coroner announced her verdict, RBH admitted that they had failed to act because they had made assumptions about Awaab and his family's lifestyle on the basis of their racial background. In particular, they had assumed that the mould was being caused by the family's bathing and cooking habits. In their words: 'We did make assumptions about lifestyle and we accept that we got that wrong. We will be implementing further

---

[101] William Shankley and Nissa Finney, 'Ethnic Minorities and Housing in Britain' in Byrne et al (n 59), p 151.

[102] Quoted in Sue Lukes et al, 'Slippery Discrimination: A Review of the Drivers of Migrant and Minority Housing Disadvantage' (2019) 45 *Journal of Ethnic and Migration Studies* 3188.

[103] Shankley and Finney (n 101), p 151.

[104] Joanne Kearsley 'Awaab Ishak: Report to prevent future deaths' (16 November 2022); Mark Brown and Robert Booth, 'Death of Two-Year-Old from Mould in Flat a "Defining Moment", Says Coroner' *The Guardian* (15 November 2022). See also Stephen Topping, 'The Nasty Stench of Racism Pervades the Tragedy of Little Awaab Ishak' *Manchester Evening News* (20 November 2022).

training across the whole organisation. We abhor racism in any shape or form and we know that we have a responsibility to all our communities.'[105] This was hardly the first time that housing authorities had failed to exercise care towards racialized persons. In the early hours of 14 June 2017, a fire broke out in Grenfell Tower, a 24-storey block of apartments in North Kensington, London. The tower had been clad in flammable material, which caused the initial fire to spread at incredible speed. Seventy-two people died, the vast majority of whom were from an ethnic minority background. Just as Ishak's parents had repeatedly raised concerns with their social housing provider, so too had the residents of Grenfell Tower. But once again, their worries were not taken seriously, with fatal consequences.[106]

Healthcare

Racial inequalities across these spheres of social life combine to have an effect on experiences and outcomes in healthcare settings. This was markedly pronounced during the COVID-19 pandemic in 2020, when it quickly became clear that racialized people were dying from COVID at a disproportionate rate. Baroness Doreen Lawrence chaired a review into the disproportionate rates of death and found that

> Black, Asian and minority ethnic people have been overexposed, under protected, stigmatised and overlooked during this pandemic – and this has been generations in the making. The impact of Covid is not random, but foreseeable and inevitable – the consequence of decades of structural injustice, inequality and discrimination that blights our society.

Lawrence's review draws together the effects of discrimination in employment and housing, for example, to show how these combined to create inequalities in healthcare during the pandemic. As she writes, 'Black, Asian and minority ethnic people are more likely to work in frontline or shutdown sectors which have been overexposed to Covid-19' and 'suffered disproportionately from the Government's failure to facilitate Covid-secure workplaces'. Similarly, '[t]he Government's decade-long failure to build social rented housing has pushed many families into the less regulated and less secure private rented market. Black,

---

[105] Robert Booth, 'Landlord Admits It Made Assumptions about Family in Mouldy Rochdale Flat' *The Guardian* (22 November 2022). Also see: Robert Booth, 'Social Landlord in England Said Mould Was "Acceptable" in Refugees' Homes' *The Guardian* (28 March 2023).
[106] See discussion in Chapter 4.

Asian and minority ethnic households are also disproportionately affected by the affordability crisis in housing', thus leading to poor-quality and overcrowded living conditions which exacerbated exposure to COVID-19.[107]

Whereas the pandemic drew attention to the intersecting features of class and race, the problem of racial injustices in maternity care illustrates the intersection of sexism and racism. In 2022, the charity Birthrights published the findings of a year-long inquiry into the disproportionate rates of harm that Black and Asian women suffered during pregnancy. The available data highlighted that racialized women were 'more likely to experience baby loss, become seriously ill and have worse experiences of care in pregnancy and childbirth, compared to white women'.[108] As noted by the Joint Committee on Human Rights: 'Seven in 100,000 white women die in childbirth, 13 in 100,000 Asian women, 23 in 100,000 mixed ethnicity women, and 38 in 100,000 Black women. The death rate for Black women in childbirth is therefore five times higher than for white women and it is increasing year on year.'[109]

The Birthrights inquiry found that 'systemic racism' (correlating to the idea of 'structural racism' that I have used in this book) is the root cause of the disparities in treatment and outcomes. Systemic racism includes 'individual interactions and workforce culture through to curriculums and policies'.[110] In other words, it includes interpersonal and institutional racism. The report includes instances of medical personnel failing to identify symptoms of sepsis and jaundice because of the patient's skin colour.[111] Examples of overt and covert racial prejudices by caregivers are ample, with treatment being based on assumptions and stereotypes about, for example, Black women's high pain threshold and Asian women's low pain threshold.[112]

Conclusion

We can see why, then, these five fields of social inquiry are helpful to a study of law's relationship with racial justice. The five fields are interconnected, illustrating how racial injustices cannot be siloed off into 'interpersonal' racist incidents or considered in separate social settings in isolation to one another. As Atrey writes, '[r]acism is thus more structurally rooted

---

[107] Baroness Doreen Lawrence, 'An Avoidable Crisis' (2021).
[108] Birthrights, 'Systemic Racism, Not Broken Bodies: An Inquiry into Racial Injustice and Human Rights in UK Maternity Care' (2022), p 9.
[109] Joint Committee on Human Rights, 'Black People, Racism and Human Rights' (2019–21, HL 165, HC 559), p 40.
[110] Birthrights (n 108), p 9.
[111] Birthrights (n 108), pp 47–8.
[112] Birthrights (n 108), p 53.

than ever before. Yet, it is more difficult to identify structural racism now given that it is "coded into" the "normal procedures" classified as neutral and as nothing to do with race'.[113] The difficulty in identifying structural racism, we will see in the next chapter, is a key reason why the legal system has not always been helpful to the struggle for racial justice despite the contemporary appearance of a pro-racial justice legal system. Another reason is the prevailing political mood. In the summer of 2020, following the Black Lives Matter protests that took place across the country and which provided the backdrop to the toppling of the statue of Colston in Bristol, Prime Minister Boris Johnson convened the Commission on Race and Ethnic Disparities (CRED) to provide a holistic review of racism in the UK. The Commission considered the concept of structural racism, offering a definition which closely aligns with the definition I offered in Chapter 1: 'Structural racism', the Commission wrote, is a phrase used 'to describe a legacy of historic racist or discriminatory processes, policies, attitudes or behaviours that continue to shape organisations and societies today'.[114] In its report, though, the Commission concluded that structural racism is *not* a problem in the United Kingdom today. Published in March 2021, the Sewell Report (named after the Chair of the Commission, Dr Tony Sewell) reads: 'The country has come a long way in 50 years and the success of much of the ethnic minority population ... should be regarded as a model for other White-majority countries.'[115] According to the Commissioners, there is no evidence of institutional or structural racism in the UK, and 'most of the disparities ... which some attribute to racial discrimination often do not have their origins in racism'. Instead of racial disparities having their origins in racism, the Commissioners wrote, the disparities are sometimes the fault of racialized people themselves. In their words, there are 'other reasons for minority success and failure, including those embedded in the cultures and attitudes of those minority communities themselves. There is much evidence to suggest, for example, that different experiences of family life and structure can explain many disparities in education outcomes and crime'.[116]

Given the innumerable studies of racial injustice across various fields of social life outlined earlier, it was little surprise that the Sewell Report was roundly criticized by politicians, racial justice organizations, scholars, and many others. Lord Woolley, who had previously led the government's Race

---

[113] Shreya Atrey, 'Structural Racism and Race Discrimination' (2021) 74 *Current Legal Problems* 1, 15.
[114] Commission on Race and Ethnic Disparities, 'The Report of the Commission on Race and Ethnic Disparities' (2021), p 36.
[115] Commission on Race and Ethnic Disparities (n 114), p 9.
[116] Commission on Race and Ethnic Disparities (n 114), p 11.

Disparity Unit, claimed the report showed "monumental disrespect and disregard of people's lived experiences, but above all a lost opportunity for systemic change".[117] The British Medical Association, the National Black Police Association, and many others issued similar statements decrying the tone and findings of the report, with several individuals and organizations who had given evidence to the Commission seeking to have their name removed from the final report.[118] Marsha de Cordova, a Member of Parliament for the Labour Party, described the report as a "divisive polemic" that downplayed institutional and structural racism, and the equalities spokesperson for the Liberal Democrats, Wera Hobhouse, expressed concern that the report would be used to excuse "shameful inaction" on issues of racial injustice.[119]

The report also attracted criticism from abroad, with the United Nations Working Group of Experts on People of African Descent stating that 'it is stunning to read a report on race and ethnicity that repackages racist tropes and stereotypes into fact, twisting data and misapplying statistics and studies into conclusory findings and ad hominem attacks on people of African descent'.[120] In 2023, the same UN Working Group conducted a ten-day fact-finding mission in the UK, and its report on racism in Britain today struck a very different tone from the CRED Report. According to the UN Working Group, discrimination against people of African descent in the UK is 'structural, institutional and systemic'. The Working Group raised particular concerns with 'impunity and the failure to address racial disparities in the criminal justice system, deaths in police custody, "joint enterprise" convictions and the dehumanising nature of the stop and (strip) search'.[121] Catherine Namakula, the Chair of the Working Group, said at an open meeting: "The law is in conflict with children of African descent, instead of the children being in conflict with it. They're not breaking the law, the law is breaking our children."[122] These findings echoed that of the United Nations Committee on the Elimination of Racial Discrimination, which observed in 2016 that, in the United Kingdom, 'persons of African

---

[117] Aamna Mohdin et al, 'No 10's Race Report Widely Condemned as "Divisive"' *The Guardian* (31 March 2021).

[118] Aamna Mohdin and Peter Walker, 'Bodies Credited in UK Race Review Distance Themselves from Findings' *The Guardian* (12 April 2021).

[119] 'Campaigners Criticise Government Race Report' (BBC News, 31 March 2021).

[120] Working Group of Experts on People of African Descent, 'UN Experts Condemn UK Commission on Race and Ethnic Disparities Report' (Office of the High Commissioner for Human Rights, 19 April 2021).

[121] Working Group of Experts on People of African Descent, 'UK: Discrimination against People of African Descent Is Structural, Institutional and Systemic, Say UN Experts' (Office of the High Commissioner for Human Rights, 27 January 2023).

[122] Aamna Mohdin, '"The Law Is Breaking Children": Black People in UK Tell UN of Daily Injustices' *The Guardian* (27 January 2023).

descent face institutional racism in their enjoyment of rights, including the specific areas of ... health, employment, education, stop and search practices and the criminal justice system'.[123]

In April 2023, following the largest survey on racial inequalities undertaken for over 25 years, researchers concluded that there remain 'substantial ethnic inequalities in outcomes across a range of domains of life', and that 'Britain is not close to being a racially just society'.[124] In their view, the CRED Report could only be explained as an attempt 'to even out inequalities across population groups and places (but not to reduce inequality) without paying attention to the fundamental causes of these inequalities'.[125] They offer a reason for why the Commission avoided addressing the causes of inequalities and focused instead on perceived cultural failings or defects of certain racialized groups. As they write, the Commission's approach was 'not surprising in relation to the recent and current political context in the UK, where we are faced with a series of ongoing and evolving policies related to culture, citizenship, community, segregation and migration that are populist and disregard the evidence base'.[126] This account also provides the context for understanding law's contemporary relationship with the struggle for racial justice. As explained in the next chapter, the Commissioners are not alone in holding these views, and racial justice campaigners and lawyers have struggled to convince legal officials of the structural nature of racism in the UK today.

---

[123] UN Committee on the Elimination of Racial Discrimination (CERD), 'Concluding Observations on the Combined Twenty-First to Twenty-Third Periodic Reports of the United Kingdom of Great Britain and Northern Ireland' (3 October 2016, CERD/C/GBR/CO/21-23), para 22.
[124] Nissa Finney et al (eds), *Racism and Ethnic Inequality in a Time of Crises: Findings from the Evidence for Equality National Survey* (Policy Press 2023), p 210.
[125] Finney et al (n 124), p 209.
[126] Finney et al (n 124), p 209.

4

The Use of Law to Tackle Racial Injustices: Contemporary Struggles

Introduction

The previous chapters have set out how law was used to embed racial prejudices and injustices into the structures of social life and the legal system. Although the use of law to structuralize racism has a long history stretching back several centuries, the use of law to *tackle* racial injustices, which is the subject of this chapter, has a much shorter lifespan to date. We have seen that Granville Sharp made use of the Habeas Corpus Act to challenge slavery in the 1770s, and Parliament passed a law outlawing race discrimination in the context of employment law in India in 1833,[1] but these were haphazard and disjointed attempts to use the legal system to challenge racial injustices. When the Black cricketer Learie Constantine was denied a room at the Imperial Hotel in London in 1943 on the basis of his skin colour, there was no law prohibiting discrimination on the grounds of race. Instead, he had to rely on provisions of tort and contract law to secure a remedy.[2]

In this chapter, we will see that contemporary attempts to use the law have been much more systematic, but that legal discourses, norms, and processes are not always conducive to racial justice. The chapter begins with an outline of some key legal milestones between 1965 and 1993, which are the years of the first Race Relations Act and the murder of the Black teenager Stephen Lawrence respectively. Lawrence's murder was something of an inflection point in law's relationship with racial justice, as policy makers and legislators responded to the public outcry by strengthening laws against racial discrimination and racial hatred. An outline of the post-1993 legal

---

[1] See the sections titled 'Somerset v Stewart (1772)' and 'Law and the social control of racialized populations' in Chapter 2 for further discussions of these two affairs.

[2] *Constantine v Imperial Hotels Ltd* [1944] KB 693.

framework is then provided, followed by an examination of how, despite the framework in place, lawyers and racial justice advocates have only been able to secure limited gains in the legal arena. The law, we will see, has failed to adequately promote racial justice for six reasons that map on to the tenets of Critical Race Theory (CRT) discussed in Chapter 1. First, legal authorities have set limits on law's competency to address structural racism. Second, legal officials have been slow to respond to evolving social constructions of race and racism. Third, legal officials have not grappled with the problem of intersectionality. Fourth, legislators and judges tend to only allow the law to promote racial justice when such a course of action is also in the interests of those considered to be White British. Fifth, legal officials often fail to take seriously the lived experiences of those who have suffered racial injustices. Sixth, various aspects of legal processes such as adversarialism and time limits mean that the system is either of limited use in advancing racial justice, or widens rather than narrows racial divisions.

The development of laws to tackle racial injustices: 1965–93

The enactment of the Race Relations Act in 1965 was a landmark moment in the struggle for racial justice in the UK, as it was the first time that domestic law expressly prohibited racial discrimination within mainland Britain.[3] The Act prohibited racial discrimination in public places such as restaurants and hotels and outlawed incitement to racial hatred. To enforce the anti-discrimination measures, a Race Relations Board was set up which acted as a conciliatory body between the person complaining of discrimination and the person or authority alleged to have committed unlawful discrimination. Although there were many positives in these developments, the Act had its shortcomings. It was limited in scope, which had the effect of legitimizing race discrimination in spheres of public and private life not covered by the Act. And the enforcement mechanisms were weak, since the Race Relations Board lacked investigative powers. Just three years later, the Act was amended to increase its scope and strengthen its effectiveness. The Race Relations (Amendment) Act 1968 broadened the prohibition on discrimination to housing, employment, and access to services such as the provision of mortgages. A Community Relations Commission (CRC) was introduced to work alongside the Board, to coordinate national initiatives which would foster harmonious community relations. Again, authorities and services that were omitted from the Act

---

[3] See, for example, Harry Goulbourne, *Race Relations in Britain since 1945* (St Martin's Press 1998), chapter 5.

were given implicit permission to discriminate on the grounds of race, and the CRC also lacked bite. Thus, although Lester and Bindman are correct to write that the 'adoption of a law actively to promote equality represented a radical departure from the traditional neutrality and passivity of our legal system',[4] they are also correct when highlighting the shortcomings of the Acts.[5] Mahesh Upadhyaya's experience of using the law is a case in point. In 1968, when looking for a home for his family, Upadhyaya was told by a housing company that they would not 'sell to coloured people because that will jeopardise the sales of our other properties'. Although the Race Relations Board initiated legal action on his behalf, and although the judge agreed that the company had unlawfully discriminated against Upadhyaya, the case failed on procedural grounds. Moreover, as Upadhyaya has explained, the process did little to improve 'race relations' because his employer and co-workers disapproved of his decision to pursue legal action. 'The atmosphere at work became charged and unpleasant', he recalls. 'Many people disagreed with my decision to pursue this case. ... As much as I wanted justice, I did not want to imperil my employment – it had taken years of back-breaking graft and hardship to reach this point and now I risked losing it all.'[6]

Ultimately, the efficacy of the Acts was tarnished by the context in which they were enacted. As outlined in the previous chapter, these Acts were introduced alongside immigration laws in 1962 and 1968 that were explicitly racist. During the passage of the Commonwealth Immigrants Act 1968, for example, the Home Secretary James Callaghan stated that the task of government was to create "a fair and balanced policy on this matter of race *relations*".[7] In other words, the government was not seeking to chastise those who expressed animosity against racialized people. With this in mind, it is little surprise to find that the Race Relations Act had minimal effect on social attitudes. As Ann Dummett explains, attitudes had been shaped and consolidated by concurrent immigration laws:

> [T]he failure of the Race Relations Act to educate the public in favour of racial equality was due, not to the fact that governments play no part in educating public opinion, but to the fact that governments had succeeded all too well in educating public opinion in *favour* of

---

[4] Anthony Lester and Geoffrey Bindman, *Race and Law* (Penguin Books 1972), p 15.
[5] Lester and Bindman (n 4), chapter 11.
[6] For an outline of the case and Upadhyaya's recollections of the time, see Rahul Verma, 'It Was Standard to See Signs Saying "No Blacks, No Dogs, No Irish"' (EachOther, 29 November 2018).
[7] Quoted in Wendy Williams, 'Windrush Lessons Learned Review' (19 March 2020), p 55 (emphasis added).

racial discrimination for a full seven years before the Race Relations Act of 1968.[8]

Lester and Bindman concur: '[I]t was widely supposed that Britain was confronted not with a race problem but with an immigration problem.'[9] In this sense, while the Race Relations Acts of the 1960s might at first appear to be a radical step towards the use of law to tackle racism, they are better understood as examples of 'interest-convergence' at play: the Acts were only introduced because, when read alongside the Commonwealth Immigrants Acts of 1962 and 1968, they did not disadvantage those classed as 'White British'.[10] Sivanandan explained that the law was designed not to punish racists but to encourage the integration of Black people into White British communities, institutions, and practices. This, when read alongside the immigration laws, would benefit the White population since they would be able to make use of Black labour while also keeping control over the population.[11] Sir Dingle Foot, the Solicitor General, offered another reason why the law would benefit the White population, telling Parliament that the legislation would ensure that Great Britain was in line with the United Nations' stance on racism, and would therefore "restore this country's image in the world".[12]

The 1970s saw further legal developments in the relationship between law and the struggle for racial justice. The North Kensington Law Centre was opened on 17 July 1970, and was modelled on Michael Zander's proposal to establish 'neighbourhood law firms' in areas blighted by poverty so that people who could not afford the services of a lawyer could benefit from free legal advice. Zander was inspired by developments in the United States, where civil rights campaigners had set up such firms to aid impoverished racialized people who needed legal assistance.[13] Over the ensuing decades, more law centres have been set up across the United Kingdom, and the Law Centres UK website highlights the links between law centres and the struggle against racism:

> Law Centres were inspired by the American Civil Rights movement in the 1960s and abide by its core values of equality, dignity, respect, and justice. Our first Law Centres grew up with the fights for racial

---

[8] Ann Dummett, *A Portrait of English Racism* (Penguin 1973), p 181.
[9] Lester and Bindman (n 4), p 16.
[10] See the section 'Interest-convergence' in Chapter 1.
[11] Ambalavaner Sivanandan, 'Race, Class, and the State: The Black Experience in Britain' (1976) 17 *Race & Class* 347.
[12] Hansard, HC Deb 3 May 1965, vol 711, col 1050.
[13] Michael Zander, 'How Law Centres Started Out' (Law Centres Network UK 2020).

justice at the Mangrove, in Notting Hill, in New Cross, in Tottenham, in Brixton, in Liverpool, in Bristol.[14]

The reference to 'the Mangrove' leads us to another event in 1970 that appeared to turn the legal system towards promoting racial justice. The Mangrove was a restaurant in Notting Hill that was owned and run by a prominent civil rights campaigner, Frank Crichlow. Over several months, the restaurant was repeatedly raided by the police because of Crichlow's political activism. Incensed by the police's harassment, the local community organized a peaceful protest. This was met with force by the police, and nine protestors were eventually arrested and charged with incitement to riot. Some of the Mangrove Nine, as they came to be known, represented themselves at trial the following year, and this gave them the opportunity to express their lived experience of racism to the jury. Others were represented by lawyers who eschewed traditional approaches to litigation, such as Ian MacDonald. These lawyers presented unique arguments relating to the unrepresentative racial composition of the jury, and police harassment of the Black community.[15] Their legal strategy worked, as the jury returned a verdict in the Mangrove Nine's favour. Remarkably, the trial judge – who had not shown much sympathy towards the defendants – stated that the trial had "regrettably shown evidence of racial hatred on both sides". This was the first time a legal official had explicitly and publicly accepted that there was a problem of racism within the police force.[16]

The success of the Mangrove Nine galvanized racial justice campaigners, as did the passage of the Race Relations (Amendment) Act in 1976. This introduced the concepts of 'direct' and 'indirect' discrimination, which are considered later, and established the Commission for Racial Equality (CRE), which was effectively a merger of the Race Relations Board and the CRC. At first, the CRE investigated organizations even in the absence of evidence that the organization was unlawfully discriminating against anybody. If there was general evidence of discrimination in the sector, or if the organization was a leading company in the sector, the CRE considered

---

[14] See 'Racial Justice and the Role of Law Centres in Dismantling Systemic Racism', Available from: https://conference.lawcentres.org.uk. Also see Law Centres Network UK, 'About Law Centres' (nd), Available from: https://www.lawcentres.org.uk/about-law-centres

[15] 'Obituary: Ian MacDonald' *Counsel Magazine* (20 November 2019).

[16] Robin Bunce and Paul Field, 'Mangrove Nine: The Court Challenge against Police Racism in Notting Hill' *The Guardian* (29 November 2010); Catherine Baksi, 'Landmarks in Law: When the Mangrove Nine Beat the British State' *The Guardian* (10 November 2020).

itself permitted, if not duty-bound, to investigate that company's policies and practices. However, although the CRE had more powers than its predecessors, it encountered considerable resistance from the courts, which condemned the CRE for the way in which it exercised its investigatory powers. In 1979, Lord Denning compared the CRE's investigations to that of the Inquisition,[17] and in a series of cases in the early 1980s the House of Lords created a 'reasonable suspicion' test, saying that the Commission could only investigate if it had acquired some evidence of unlawful discrimination and if a 'reasonable [person]' would suspect unlawful discrimination on the basis of that evidence.[18] As Bob Hepple writes: 'These decisions, coupled with a lack of adequate resources, placed serious restrictions on strategic enforcement, allowing discriminatory practices to continue unchecked.' After more adverse judicial decisions, the number of investigations conducted by the CRE declined sharply.[19]

This is not to say, though, that the courts were completely hostile to the use of law to tackle racial injustices. In *Mandla v Dowell Lee*, decided in 1983, the House of Lords adopted a wide definition of the terms 'race' and 'ethnicity' for the purposes of the 1976 Act. The Court could have excluded Sikhs, Jews, and such like on the basis that they are a religious group rather than a racial or ethnic group, but the Lords instead declared that the criteria for classification as a racial group included factors such as 'a long-shared history', 'a cultural tradition' such as religious observance, 'a common geographical origin, or descent from a small number of common ancestors', and a common language, literature, or religion.[20]

Law's relationship with the struggle for racial justice faced another inflection point in 1993, when Stephen Lawrence was killed on the evening of 22 April by a group of men who were explicitly motivated by racial animosity.[21] Despite multiple leads and compelling evidence against several suspects, the Metropolitan Police botched the investigation, and all charges against the suspects were dropped. The public outcry against the racist attack and the failings of the police compelled the government of the day, and subsequent governments, to introduce policy and legislative initiatives to show that they were taking the problem of racism in society seriously. When speaking of the *contemporary* legal framework as it pertains to racial justice, then, we can take 1993 as a starting point.

---

[17] *Social Science Research Council v Nassé* [1979] 1 QB 144, CA, 172.
[18] *R v Commission for Racial Equality, ex parte Prestige Group Ltd* [1984] ICR 473; *Hillingdon London Borough Council v Commission for Racial Equality* [1982] AC 779.
[19] Bob Hepple, *Equality: The Legal Framework* (2nd edn, Hart Publishing 2014), pp 183–4.
[20] *Mandla v Dowell Lee* [1983] 2 AC 548, 562.
[21] Brian Cathcart, *The Case of Stephen Lawrence* (Penguin 2000).

The contemporary legal framework

The post-1993 legislative landscape looks considerably more antiracist than the pre-1993 landscape. For example, the following Acts of Parliament passed after 1993 all tackle some form of racial injustice: the Crime and Disorder Act 1998 prohibits forms of racial hatred; the Human Rights Act 1998 and the Race Relations (Amendment) Act 2000 contributed to the anti-discrimination legal framework; the Criminal Justice Act 2003 and the Racial and Religious Hatred Act 2006 bolstered prohibitions against racial hatred; and the Equality Act 2010 (and its precursor, the Equality Act 2006) further strengthened laws against discrimination, harassment, and victimization. The Equality Act 2010 also introduced the Public Sector Equality Duty (PSED), which requires public authorities to not only eliminate discrimination, harassment, and victimization on the basis of race and other protected characteristics but to also 'advance equality of opportunity between persons who share a relevant protected characteristic and persons who do not share it' and 'foster good relations between persons who share a relevant protected characteristic and persons who do not share it'.[22] Put together, we can identify a three-pronged legislative attack on racial injustices: (a) laws that prohibit discrimination, harassment, and victimization in various contexts; (b) laws that prohibit the verbal or physical manifestation of racial prejudices or hatred; and (c) laws that require and facilitate proactive measures to ensure that discrimination and other racial injustices do not occur in the first place. There are other legal provisions that do not explicitly address racism yet which can nonetheless be used to tackle racism, but we will primarily focus on these three types of laws.

Before we can assess this framework, though, we ought to be clear that governments since 1993 have not uniformly legislated in favour of racial justice. For example, in the same year that Lawrence was murdered, Parliament excluded asylum seekers from social housing under the Asylum and Immigration Appeals Act 1993. The next year, the Criminal Justice and Public Order Act 1994 removed the duty on local authorities to provide sites for Gypsies and Travellers and enabled local authorities to remove property and vehicles from public sites.[23] Even several of those Acts which appear to be pro-racial justice are, on further inspection, problematic. For example, the Race Relations (Amendment) Act 2000 extended the scope of the 1976 Act by including public authorities such as the police within

---

[22] Equality Act 2010, s 149(1).
[23] For an account of how legislation has negatively affected people of a GRT heritage, see Derek Hawes and Barbara Perez, *The Gypsy and the State: The Ethnic Cleansing of British Society* (2nd edn, Policy Press 1996), p 130.

its ambit, as well as private organizations that performed public functions. The Act also placed a duty on public authorities to promote racial equality and empowered the Home Secretary to impose specific duties on those authorities. The CRE was also given more powers to enforce those duties. However, while these were all positive measures, the Act did not apply to certain areas of public policy, such as asylum and sentencing. Thus, like its predecessors, this gave the appearance that racism within those areas of public policy was acceptable. As Lee Bridges writes, 'by its exceptions and omissions, [the Race Relations (Amendment) Act 2000] may actually serve to legitimate racism in key areas of public policy, rather than outlaw it'.[24]

The Equality Acts of 2006 and 2010 have also been subject to principled and practical criticisms notwithstanding the appearance of commendable aims. Prior to 2006, race, sex, and disability discrimination were outlawed by different Acts of Parliament,[25] and each had its own commission: the CRE, the Equal Opportunities Commission, and the Disability Rights Commission respectively. The 2006 Act was an attempt to harmonize and simplify the discrimination law framework, bringing these three characteristics and six others – age, gender reassignment, marriage and civil partnerships, pregnancy and maternity, religion or belief, and sexual orientation – under one banner.[26] The Act also created the Equality and Human Rights Commission (EHRC), which subsumed the work of the commissions that had previously focused on race, sex, and disability. While on the one hand it is preferable not to silo off each ground of discrimination, there is a danger that the creation of one overarching commission means that the focus and expertise of the specialist commissions, including the CRE, has been lost.[27]

More recently, the Police, Crime, Sentencing and Courts Act 2022 has put more Gypsy, Roma, and Traveller (GRT) people at risk of criminal prosecution by restricting the lawfulness of residing in roadside camps.[28] And, as outlined in the previous chapter, immigration laws such as those passed in 2014, 2016, and 2022 continue to create divisions along racial lines. We can say, then, that in the contemporary era the substantive law has the appearance of being predominantly, but not absolutely, in favour of racial justice.

---

[24] Lee Bridges, 'Race, Law and the State' (2001) 43 *Race & Class* 61, 74.
[25] The various Race Relations Acts, Sex Discrimination Act 1975, Disability Discrimination Act 1995.
[26] Equality Act 2010, ss 4–12.
[27] For a summary of the concerns, see Hepple (n 19), p 179.
[28] Police, Crime, Sentencing and Courts Act 2022, part 4. See Samuel Burgum and Ryan Powell, 'The Policing Bill Will Criminalise Gypsy and Traveller Families – There Is a Better Approach' *The Conversation* (25 January 2022).

One reason for the persistence of racism within the legal system is that the system is as much a social system as education, criminal justice, and so on. It should therefore come as no surprise to find that the legacy of colonialism and racist immigration laws rears its head within the legal system at large. Indeed, this is just further evidence that racism is structural. There are various ways in which racism manifests itself in legal processes, illustrated well in recent memoirs by two barristers, Alexandra Wilson and Leslie Thomas KC.[29] Both recount the barriers they faced when studying for and working at the Bar on account of their race, with Thomas writing that 'the attitudes of the people who administer this system today can at times be as racist and colonialist as those who created it in the 1960s and 1970s'.[30] Their views are supported by a ground-breaking study of racial bias within the judiciary, published in 2022. The authors of 'Racial Bias and the Bench' argue that 'institutional racism in the justice system' is at least partly attributable to the system being 'presided over by judges' who display overt as well as covert racial prejudices.[31] Although the research is described as an exploratory study (based on the views of 373 legal professionals who responded to a survey on perceptions of racism within the judicial system), the evidence marshalled is striking. The report is replete with accounts of judges acting in racially biased ways towards defendants, and when delivering legal directions or rulings.[32] The information on the racial make-up of the judiciary is sobering. Just 1 per cent of the judiciary in England and Wales are Black, a figure that has not changed since 2014.[33] Attempts to diversify the judiciary have been ineffectual, with ethnic minority female solicitors being the least likely of all groups to be appointed as a judge.[34] And attempts to train lawyers and judges about racial bias and prejudices were also said to be lacking, with less than half of respondents reporting having received any training in the preceding three years.[35]

It is with this in mind that we can see why racism still permeates the legal system and legal processes of England and Wales, though perhaps not as viscerally as in the colonial era. And it is this background that helps

---

[29] Alexandra Wilson, *In Black and White: A Young Barrister's Story of Race and Class in a Broken Justice System* (Endeavour 2021); Leslie Thomas, *Do Right and Fear No One: A Life Dedicated to Fighting for Justice* (Simon & Schuster 2022).
[30] Thomas (n 29), p 422.
[31] Keir Monteith KC et al, 'Racial Bias and the Bench: A Response to the Judicial Diversity and Inclusion Strategy (2020–2025)' (University of Manchester 2022), p 6.
[32] Monteith et al (n 31), p 6.
[33] Monteith et al (n 31), p 31, citing Ministry of Justice in England and Wales, 'Diversity of the Judiciary: Legal Professions, New Appointments and Current Post-holders' (2022).
[34] Monteith et al (n 31), p 32.
[35] Monteith et al (n 31), p 22.

contextualize the cases in which the legal system has struggled to grapple with the six key concepts of CRT that are vital to advancing racial justice. It is of course not possible to consider every relevant case, but we will start with the problem of access to justice. We can then move on to a consideration of discrimination law, race hate crimes, and the legal duty to promote race equality.

Access to justice

It is all very well to have a raft of substantive laws that appear to protect racialized people and condemn racial injustices, but the law will mean little if people are not able to access it in the first place. There are several reasons why people might struggle to access the justice system, including financial constraints,[36] time limits, and the concept of justiciability. Although these barriers are faced by all users of the justice system, racialized people in particular have struggled to surmount these obstacles.

The Legal Aid and Advice Act of 1949 established the modern system of legal aid, which aims to ensure that those without the financial means to hire a lawyer are nonetheless able to access legal advice. This is to give effect to the principle that all are equal before the law, and that people's experiences of the legal system should not be affected by their wealth or otherwise. Since the 1980s, though, successive governments have imposed greater restrictions on access to legal aid. The Legal Aid, Sentencing, and Punishment of Offenders Act 2012 has been the source of the most severe cuts in modern times, with some areas of law being removed from the scope of legal aid, including most private family, employment, welfare benefits, housing, and non-asylum immigration law matters.[37] The Law Society has reported that these changes have resulted in vulnerable groups being unable to access free legal advice, noting that 'the level of need arises from the nature of the client, rather than the category of law involved'.[38] Since racialized people often lack political and social power and fall into lower socio-economic classes, it follows that racialized people have been disproportionately disadvantaged by cuts to legal aid. A 2015 report found that the removal of legal aid from certain employment matters has seen the number of race discrimination cases drop by 61 per cent, for example.[39] The

---

[36] See, for example, Jon Robins and Daniel Newman, *Justice in a Time of Austerity: Stories from a System in Crisis* (Bristol University Press 2021).

[37] Law Society, 'Access Denied? LASPO Four Years On; A Law Society Review' (June 2017), p 6.

[38] Law Society (n 37), p 6.

[39] Helen Anthony and Charlotte Crilly, 'Equality, Human Rights and Access to Civil Law Justice: A Literature Review' (Equality and Human Rights Commission 2015), p 92.

cuts to legal aid provide an example of how class intersects with race: those of a lower socio-economic background are going to struggle to access the law, whereas those from a more affluent background might be able to use the law to their advantage.

Cuts to legal aid have also affected the work that lawyers can do. Legal aid lawyers today have highlighted the increased bureaucratization of the process for securing legal aid, meaning that much of their time is spent filling out paperwork rather than investigating allegations of racial injustice. Even the EHRC has struggled to initiate legal action during the era of austerity. The EHRC has legal powers to undertake inquiries and investigations and to initiate judicial reviews and to intervene in individual cases. However, David Isaac, who chaired the Commission from 2016 until 2020, has drawn attention to the effect of budgetary cuts. When the Commission in its current guise was established in 2011, it had an annual budget of £70 million. Writing in 2020, Isaac notes that this has been cut by 70 per cent to just £17.1 million. In March 2023, the budget remained at £17.1 million. As Isaac writes: 'The fact that EHRC's current budget is less than the budget of one of its legacy commissions – the Commission for Race Equality (CRE) – in 2005–2006 speaks volumes about the lack of adequate funding for the promotion and sponsorship of equality and human rights in this country.'[40]

At the time of writing, a number of organizations have responded to the legal aid crisis by allocating money to help people initiate legal action to tackle racial injustices. In 2021, the EHRC announced a Race Legal Support Fund, to which lawyers can apply to help finance race discrimination claims.[41] Similarly, from 2021 the Baring Foundation has ringfenced £2 million over a period of five years to help fund legal challenges to racism, with a particular focus on racism in the criminal justice system.[42] And in 2022, the Law Centres Network UK ran a two-day conference to explore the role of Law Centres in tackling systemic racism.[43] It is hoped that these sorts of initiatives will help impoverished racialized people with access to legal assistance.

---

[40] David Isaac CBE, 'Reflections on the EHRC' (2020) 6 *European Human Rights Law Review Reflection* 578, 580.

[41] Equality and Human Rights Commission, 'New Legal Fund to Tackle Race Discrimination' (23 November 2021), Available from: https://www.equalityhumanrights.com/en/our-work/news/new-legal-fund-tackle-race-discrimination

[42] Lucy de Groot, 'New Baring Foundation Funding for Racial Justice' (Baring Foundation, 4 February 2021), Available from: https://baringfoundation.org.uk/blog-post/new-baring-foundation-funding-for-racial-justice (the Foundation announced £3 million in total for racial justice work, of which £2 million is earmarked for the use of law for social change).

[43] The conference was titled 'Racial Justice and the Role of Law Centres in Dismantling Systemic Racism'. For a review, see Law Centres Network, 'Law Centres Cap Off an

Even when a person is able to access legal assistance, they still must make sure that they are initiating legal action within certain time limits, and these limits can act as a barrier to justice. In certain employment law matters, for example, claims need to be made within three months. However, one of the key problems for racialized people is dealing with the emotional trauma of suffering race-based discrimination and injustices. It can take time for a person to gather their strength and feel confident enough to initiate legal proceedings. The tight time limits are therefore particularly problematic in racial discrimination cases.[44]

A further problem lies in the idea of justiciability. Courts will not listen to all grievances, only those that are considered appropriate for judicial inquiry. We saw in the case of *Kaderbhai* in 1931 that the Privy Council refused to consider whether the Commissioner could or could not exercise his powers in a racially discriminatory manner, ruling instead that the Commissioner had not gone beyond the powers vested in him under the Ordinance in question.[45] In Lord Atkins' words, the Privy Council was only concerned with 'the bare question of law – namely, the powers of the Commissioner under the Ordinance', and that '[q]uestions of policy, or, in other words, how the legal powers *should* be exercised, are not matters for the legal tribunal, but have to be determined by the appropriate constitutional authority'.[46] This view – that certain questions are not appropriate for judicial inquiry – was repeated in the public inquiry into the Grenfell Tower fire. The issue of race had been central to discussions about the fire because the vast majority of the residents who died were from an ethnic minority background. When an inquiry was launched into the circumstances of the disaster, a group supporting victims and their families urged the inquiry to consider how race and class contributed to the tragedy. The Grenfell Next of Kin group urged the chair to consider whether the cost-cutting measures that contributed to the spread of the fire would have been sanctioned 'if the tower block was in an affluent part of the city for an affluent white population'. They accused the authorities who were responsible for the maintenance of the tower of 'contemptuous disregard' for the residents. 'Systemic racism', the group argued, 'goes deep to the heart of the problem

---

Intensive Year with a Focus on Racial Justice' (22 December 2022), Available from: https://www.lawcentres.org.uk/policy/news/news/law-centres-cap-off-an-intensive-year-with-a-focus-on-racial-justice

[44] Bharat Malkani, 'The Pursuit of Racial Justice through Legal Action: An Overview of How UK Civil Society Has Used the Law 1990–2020' (Baring Foundation 2021), pp 25–6.

[45] See discussion in 'Law and the social control of racialized populations' in Chapter 2.

[46] *Commissioner for Local Government Lands and Settlement v Abdulhusein Kaderbhai* [1931] AC 652 (italics added).

that caused the catastrophe'.[47] This was not the first time such a request had been made. Two years earlier, a similar request had been denied. Sir Martin Moore-Bick refused to extend the terms of reference of the inquiry, and his decision withstood a judicial review challenge in the High Court, which echoed Lord Atkins in *Kaderbhai* when it ruled that

> [t]he inclusion of such broad questions within the scope of the Inquiry would raise questions of a social, economic and political nature which in my view are not suitable for a judge-led inquiry. They are questions which could more appropriately be examined by a different kind of process or body, one which could include persons who have experience of the provision and management of social housing, local government finances and disaster relief planning.[48]

The decision of the Chair of the inquiry and of the High Court meant that the inquiry was precluded from considering how, historically, the allocation of social housing has been shaped by 'racialized distinction[s] between deserving and undeserving'.[49] We saw in the previous chapter that racism in the housing sector is very much a structural issue, and the High Court was effectively stating that the Court could not consider the issue of structural racism.

In her commentary on the decision, Patricia Tuitt writes that 'justiciability is a distinctly legal concept that enables the law to identify with the racial capitalist logics at play in the allocation of social housing'.[50] In other words, the Court's use of the concept of justiciability had the effect of legitimizing the role of racism in the allocation and provision of social housing. Writing many years before the Grenfell disaster and the inquiry, Peter Fitzpatrick highlighted the issue at stake here: '[R]acism marks the constitutive boundaries of law, persistent limits on its competence and scope.'[51] That is, we see time and time again that when racial injustices are challenged, limits are placed on law's ability to tackle that injustice. Put another way, the law will not be extended to deal with issues of structural racism, even though law

---

[47] Mark Townsend, 'Grenfell Families Want Inquiry to Look at Role of "Race and Class" in Tragedy' *The Guardian* (26 July 2020), Available from: https://www.theguardian.com/uk-news/2020/jul/26/grenfell-families-want-inquiry-to-look-at-role-of-race-and-class-in-tragedy

[48] *R (Daniels) v Prime Minister & Anor* [2018] EWHC (Admin) [11].

[49] Robbie Shilliam, *Race and the Undeserving Poor: From Abolition to Brexit* (Agenda Publishing 2018), p 159.

[50] Patricia Tuitt, 'A Concise Note on Peter Fitzpatrick's "Racism and the Innocence of Law"' (2021) 17 *International Journal of the Law in Context* 36, 39.

[51] Peter Fitzpatrick, 'Racism and the Innocence of Law' (1987) 14 *Journal of Law and Society* 119, 122.

played a central role in the structuralizing of racism during the colonial era. The effects of this should not be understated. The law is not only defined by what it is; it is also defined by what it is not. By omitting the problem of structural racism from its ambit, the law is effectively legitimizing structural racism, or at the very least is giving the impression that structural racism is not an 'injustice' in legal terms.

Access to justice, then, is hampered by legal officials' unwillingness to grapple with structural racism or the intersection of class and racial injustices. But even when the justice system is accessible, racialized people have continued to struggle to make use of the law.

Discrimination, harassment, and victimization

Discrimination on the basis of race occurs when a person receives 'less favourable treatment' or a 'particular disadvantage' because of their perceived race.[52] The obvious examples are the person who is refused a job because of the colour of their skin or who is stopped and searched by a police officer who does not stop and search a person of a different race in similar circumstances. On the face of it, the legal system appears to take the problem of discrimination seriously.[53] Since 1833, eight different Acts of Parliament have been passed which seek to address race discrimination in some shape or form. We have already considered the legislation applicable in India during colonial rule[54] and the four Race Relations Acts in 1965, 1968, 1976, and 2000. These were augmented by the Human Rights Act 1998 which requires all provisions in the European Convention on Human Rights to be enjoyed by all people without discrimination. Contemporary anti-discrimination law is found in the Equality Act 2010 and its precursor 2006 Act. Many people have benefitted from the Equality Act and its prohibitions on discrimination, but the legal framework is not infallible. By examining some of the case law on 'direct' and 'indirect' discrimination, we will see how the law has struggled with the six concepts that were outlined in Chapter 1. The problem of intersectionality is particularly acute in discrimination law, and we will consider that as a separate matter.

---

[52] Equality Act ss 13 and 19.
[53] There is a considerable body of literature on discrimination law, and the outline provided here is by no means a comprehensive study of the legal framework. For a more thorough account, see Hepple (n 19); Sandra Fredman, *Discrimination Law* (3rd edn, Oxford University Press 2022). On race and discrimination law in particular, see Sandra Fredman (ed), *Discrimination and Human Rights: The Case of Racism* (Oxford University Press 2001).
[54] See 'Law and the social control of racialized populations' in Chapter 2.

Direct discrimination

Section 13 of the 2010 Act, which mirrors previous statutory law on discrimination, defines 'direct discrimination' as occurring when a person treats another 'less favourably' than others because of their race, or when people are segregated on the basis of race even if they are treated equally. Direct discrimination can be described as overt discrimination and is perhaps the most obvious type of discrimination. The prohibition on direct discrimination is strict, in that there are virtually no lawful exceptions to the rule. In some cases, legal action has proven to be effective. In 2004, for example, the House of Lords ruled that Roma people had been directly and unlawfully discriminated against by British immigration officers stationed at Prague Airport.[55] The officers had been stationed there in response to a rising number of asylum claims from Czech nationals of Roma origin, and it followed for Lady Hale that the scheme was 'inherently and systemically discriminatory and unlawful' since Romani people were effectively being specifically targeted by the scheme.[56] The Court accepted that people of Roma origin had been subjected to more rigorous questioning by the officers than others and emphasized that the 'whole point of the law is to require [authorities and suppliers of services] to treat each person as an individual, not as a member of a group. The individual should not be assumed to hold the characteristics which the [authority or service supplier] associates with the group'.[57]

A 2009 case, though, highlights some problems with the judiciary's approach to direct discrimination cases. The question was whether the Jewish Free School's admissions policy was directly discriminatory, since it gave preference to students who were recognized as Jewish under the criteria set by the Office of the Chief Rabbi. In particular, the school gave preference to (a) students whose mothers were Jewish by birth, (b) students whose mothers had converted to Judaism in line with principles of Orthodox Judaism, and (c) students who had themselves converted in line with Orthodox Judaism. The Supreme Court was divided, with a 5–4 majority reluctantly holding that this policy contravened the duty to not discriminate on grounds of ethnic origin.[58] Lord Phillips made it clear that the court 'has not welcomed being required to resolve this dispute' because he considered this to be a case where

---

[55] *R (European Roma Rights Centre) v Immigration Officer at Prague Airport* [2004] UKHL 55 ('*Roma Rights*').
[56] *Roma Rights* (n 55) [97].
[57] *Roma Rights* (n 55) [74].
[58] *R(E) v JFS Governing Body* [2009] UKSC 15 ('*JFS*'). Although the case was decided under s 1 of the Race Relations Act 1976, the provision is materially similar to s 13 of the Equality Act 2010.

'giving preference to a minority racial group' is justifiable. He was at pains to make it clear that although the Court was ruling that the school's policy was racially discriminatory, '[n]othing that I say in this judgment should be read as giving rise to criticism on moral grounds of the admissions policy ... let alone as suggesting that these policies are "racist" as that word is generally understood'.[59] In other words, the Court emphasized that legal definitions of 'racism' are different from social understandings of 'racism'. As critical race theorists have explained, though, 'race' itself is a social construct, and so if the law is going to be effective in tackling racial injustices, it must be flexible to accommodate socially evolving definitions of 'race' and 'racism'.

Didi Herman has argued that the decision is problematic because it highlights the extent to which Jewish people are not protected under English law.[60] She notes that up until this case, no claim for race discrimination against Jewish people had ever succeeded under the Race Relations Acts, and it is ironic that the first time a Jewish person has succeeded in their claim, the discriminator in question is an Orthodox Jewish school. The decision is also problematic because it seems to assume that race and religious belief are always two sides of the same coin. Although religious observance is a factor that can determine membership of a racial group, the two are not always synonymous, and on the facts, the school's admission policy was based on religious rather than racial grounds. To put this more prosaically: we can confidently say that the Nazi regime was racist against Jews because the regime would have killed anybody perceived as Jewish regardless of whether they practised Judaism or not. In other words, Nazis were not concerned with religious belief per se. The school, on the other hand, was primarily concerned with religious practice and observance but was not concerned with Jewish people as an ethnic group. Herman concludes that '[o]ne of the ironies of the *JFS* decision is that as the court calls the school a racial discriminator, the judges themselves indulge in some of the clumsiest racial discrimination we have seen'.[61]

Indirect discrimination

Section 19 of the Equality Act 2010 describes 'indirect discrimination' as occurring when there is a 'provision, criterion, or practice' that on paper applies to all persons equally, but which in effect disadvantages a person or group of people because of their race. This can be described as covert

---

[59] *JFS* (n 58) [8]–[9].
[60] Didi Herman, *An Unfortunate Coincidence: Jews, Jewishness and English Law* (Oxford University Press 2011), pp 126, 157.
[61] Herman (n 60), p 165.

discrimination. There are several cases that highlight the problems with the judiciary's indirect discrimination jurisprudence.

In *Taiwo v Olaigbe*, decided in 2012, the UK Supreme Court betrayed a lack of understanding of how race is socially constructed and law's role in constructing categories of race.[62] It also highlighted the enduring problem of intersectionality. The case was an employment dispute involving two women from Nigeria, from impoverished backgrounds, who had been brought to the UK as domestic workers. They worked for a wealthy couple; the husband was from Nigeria, and the wife from Uganda. The workers' mistreatment at the hands of their employers was severe: they were underfed and had their passports taken from them; they were physically and verbally abused; they were paid less than the minimum wage, with no terms and conditions of employment; and they were required to work virtually around the clock, with no holiday entitlement. As Lady Hale noted at the beginning of the Court's judgment, English law does not tolerate '[t]he mistreatment of migrant domestic workers by employers who exploit their employees' vulnerable situation'. Hale explained the legal framework:

> Depending on the form which the mistreatment takes, it may well amount to a breach of the worker's contract of employment or other employment rights. It may also amount to a tort. It may even amount to the offence of slavery or servitude or forced or compulsory labour under section 1 of the Modern Slavery Act 2015 or of human trafficking under section 2 of that Act.[63]

However, as she emphasized, 'the law of contract or tort do not provide compensation for the humiliation, fear and severe distress which such mistreatment can cause'.[64] Compensation, Hale explained, could only be made 'if the employer's conduct amounts to race discrimination under the Equality Act 2010 or its predecessor the Race Relations Act 1976'.[65] It followed that the Supreme Court needed to determine whether the mistreatment in the case amounted to discrimination on the basis of race. The employment tribunals had found that the mistreatment of the workers was contingent on the employees' 'precarious immigration status',[66] in that the employers would not have treated workers with British passports in a similar way. The Supreme Court accepted this finding and therefore enquired

---

[62] *Taiwo v Olaigbe* [2016] UKSC 31 ('*Taiwo*'). For a useful analysis of this case, see Shreya Atrey, 'Structural Racism and Race Discrimination' (2021) 74 *Current Legal Problems* 1.
[63] *Taiwo* (n 62), [1].
[64] *Taiwo* (n 62), [1].
[65] *Taiwo* (n 62), [2].
[66] *Taiwo* (n 62), [2].

whether 'immigration status' amounted to 'race' under the definitions of 'race' in the 1976 and 2010 Acts. According to section 9 of the 2010 Act, 'Race includes – (a) colour; (b) nationality; (c) ethnic or national origins'. The workers argued that since immigration is intrinsically linked to nationality, it must follow that discrimination on the basis of immigration status constitutes race discrimination. The Supreme Court disagreed:

> The reason why these employees were treated so badly was their particular vulnerability arising, at least in part, from their particular immigration status ... it had nothing to do with the fact that they were Nigerians. The employers too were non-nationals, but they were not vulnerable in the same way.[67]

The Court failed to acknowledge, though, that the concept of nationality itself is not limited to national origin (in this case, Nigeria). Nationality, for the purposes of immigration status, is constructed by factors such as race, class, and gender. Thus, the employers' immigration status was relatively secure not because they were from Nigeria and had valid visas but because of their class. The employees' vulnerable immigration status, on the other hand, was due to their class (domestic workers), gender (women), and race (Black). Understood this way, we can see that 'nationality' narrowly construed is just one factor that shapes a person's immigration status, but that race and other intersecting characteristics are other factors that play a crucial role in determining a person's immigration status. Thus, race was constitutive of, if not determinative of, the employees' vulnerable immigration status. In this sense, the discriminatory treatment was due in part to the employees' race, class, and gender.

A second case that illustrates the shortcomings of indirect discrimination law is a housing case from 2020.[68] The Immigration Act 2014, which formalized much of May's 'hostile environment' policy, required private landlords to carry out immigration checks on prospective tenants. The JCWI initiated judicial review proceedings, arguing that the 'Right to Rent' scheme, as it was dubbed, violated Articles 8 and 14 of the European Convention on Human Rights. The scheme was directed at 'irregular immigrants', which includes (a) people without leave to enter or remain in the UK, and (b) people with such leave but with conditions attached that prevent them from occupying private residences. The JCWI argued that, in practice, the scheme led to landlords discriminating against people who

---

[67] *Taiwo* (n 62), [26].
[68] *R (Joint Council for the Welfare of Immigrants) v Secretary of State for the Home Department* [2020] EWCA Civ 542 ('*JCWI case*').

did not have 'British passports and especially those without British passports and without ethnically British attributes such as name'.[69] In other words, it led to discrimination against racialized people who were not obviously 'ethnically British'. The Court held in favour of the Secretary of State, and the judgment sheds light on the inadequacy of a legal system that is more responsive to individual grievances than to structural racial injustices. Moreover, the judgment shows an unwillingness to acknowledge and address law's role in creating racial injustices.

After surveying the evidence, the Court agreed that the scheme affected a person's right under Article 8 of the Convention 'to respect for his private and family life, his home and his correspondence'. Writing for the Court, Lord Justice Hickinbottom found that the scheme had a discriminatory impact:

> [T]hose who had a right to rent, but did not have British passports (or, particularly, had neither such passports nor ethnically-British attributes), were the subject of discrimination on the basis of their actual or perceived nationality; and that that discrimination was caused by the Scheme in the sense that, but for the Scheme, that level of such discrimination would not have occurred.[70]

However, despite this finding, the Court ruled that there was an 'objective and reasonable justification' for the difference in treatment. First, there was a legitimate aim to the scheme, which was to create a coherent immigration system. Second, the scheme was rationally connected to that aim, in the sense that it would contribute to the achievement of that aim. Third, the Court ruled that there was no 'less intrusive measure' that could have been adopted which would have not been to the detriment of the pursuit of the aim in question.[71] Fourth, the Court ruled that, on balance, the impacts of the measure on an individual's human rights were proportionate to the benefits of the scheme.

With respect to this fourth consideration of proportionality, the Court referred to the nature of the parties to the case: the claim was not brought by an individual who was claiming they had been discriminated against, but it was instead a general challenge to the legality of the statutory provisions themselves.[72] A challenge to the validity of legislation on the basis of the proportionality test, the Court held, 'faces a high hurdle'.[73] The JCWI

---

[69] *JCWI case* (n 68), [4].
[70] *JCWI case* (n 68), [66].
[71] *JCWI case* (n 68), [113].
[72] *JCWI case* (n 68), [4].
[73] *JCWI case* (n 68), [117].

would have to show that the scheme was incapable of *ever* being operated in a proportionate way. Despite evidence that many landlords were in fact discriminating against 'regular migrants' because of their non-British sounding name or absence of a passport, the Court ruled that it was not the scheme itself that was causing the discrimination, but rather it was individual landlords who were at fault. Thus, it could not be said that the scheme inevitably caused migrants with a non-British sounding name to be discriminated against. Writing separately, Lord Justice Davis asserted: 'My conclusion thus is that, to the extent that there is discrimination, the Scheme (and thereby the State) is not responsible for it. As will be gathered, I take the view that it is landlords, by their own actions, who are.'[74] Even though the other two justices did not explicitly agree with Davis, they still did not get to grips with the racial injustice at hand. The JCWI had argued that the scheme made it 'rational' or 'logical' for landlords to discriminate, as it was in their material interests to do so. Hickinbottom rejected this claim, stating that while discrimination by landlords 'may have been foreseeable, or even inevitable', it was not necessarily 'rational' or 'logical' for landlords to do so.[75] Hickinbottom did not appreciate how law and policy shaped people's behaviour and values, and how immigration laws have historically and contemporaneously been imbued with racism and have shaped social systems such as the housing sector so that it is 'rational' and 'logical' for individuals to discriminate against racialized people. Moreover, by placing a higher burden on the applicants because the case was a general challenge to the legality of the statutory provisions, rather than an individual claim, the Court was effectively making it more difficult to challenge structural racism. Indeed, echoing the housing case of *Kaderbhai* from the colonial era, Hickinbottom explained that

> in the field of human rights, our courts have recognised that certain matters involving controversial issues of social and economic policy are by their nature more suitable for determination by the democratically-elected Parliament or the democratically-accountable executive than by the courts, such that, unless manifestly without reasonable foundation, their assessment should be respected.[76]

One of the most striking cases which underscores the inadequacy of discrimination law, and which highlights the legal system's tendency to marginalize the voices of those with lived experience of racism, is *R (Roberts)*

---

[74] *JCWI case* (n 68), [165].
[75] *JCWI case* (n 68), [69].
[76] *JCWI case* (n 68), [128].

v Commissioner of Police of the Metropolis and another, decided in 2015 in the UK Supreme Court.[77] The case involved a challenge to s 60 of the Criminal Justice and Public Order Act 1994, which can be invoked by the police when it is believed that there is risk that serious violence will occur in a locality, and which gives officers the power to stop and search individuals even by the police when the officer does not have reasonable grounds to suspect that the particular individual is engaged in any criminal activity. On the day in question, the use of s 60 powers had been authorized in the London Borough of Haringey and was used by an officer to stop and search Mrs Roberts, who is of African-Caribbean heritage, after she stepped off a bus. Mrs Roberts resisted, stating that she would rather have her bag searched in the privacy of a police station, but the officer persisted and eventually arrested Roberts on suspicion of handling stolen goods. No charges were made when it transpired that the goods on her person belonged to her. Roberts pursued legal action, alleging breaches of her rights to liberty (Article 5) and private life (Article 8) under the European Convention on Human Rights. She also invoked Article 14, claiming that she had been discriminated against on the basis of race.

The Divisional Court and the Court of Appeal rejected the arguments that there had been a breach of Article 5 and held that although there had been an interference with her right to private life under Article 8, such interference was lawful as it was 'in accordance with the law' and proportionate to the goal of preventing crime. On the Article 14 claim, Roberts' lawyer argued in the Court of Appeal that '[o]fficial statistics demonstrate that section 60 is used disproportionately to search black people in London. The official statistics are sufficient to mean that there is prima facie discrimination that the state must justify'.[78] Justice Kay, though, declined to engage with the statistical evidence on the basis that such statistics were 'controversial and give rise to difficult issues of interpretation'.[79] Kay then went on to acknowledge that s 60 had attracted criticism, 'particularly among some ethnic minority communities in London'. However, in his view, '[t]hat is a proper subject for debate elsewhere … it does not have the potential to render justiciable a specific allegation of discrimination in this particular case'.[80] Here, we see the limits of legal action when there is no explicit interpersonal racism, even if an individual's conduct has clearly been driven by structural racism.

Roberts appealed the Article 8 finding, but not the findings on Articles 5 and 14. This meant that the Supreme Court could have decided the appeal

---

[77] *R (Roberts) v Commissioner of Police of the Metropolis and another* [2015] UKSC 79.
[78] *R (Roberts) v Commissioner of Police of the Metropolis and another* [2014] EWCA Civ 69 [31].
[79] *Roberts (CA)* (n 78), [32].
[80] *Roberts (CA)* (n 78), [34].

without reference to race at all. However, the Justices addressed the racial element of the case. In rejecting the appeal, Lady Hale made a number of comments that betrayed a lack of understanding of the structural nature of racism, and she outright ignored the lived experiences of Black people who have been subjected to disproportionate use of stop and search powers. First, she acknowledged that '[a]ny random "suspicionless" power of stop and search carries with it the risk that it will be used in an arbitrary or discriminatory manner in individual cases'. However, she went on to say that the use of random and unpredictable searches was for the benefit of Black people because they are the ones most likely to be affected by, in her words, 'gang violence'. 'While there is a concern that members of these groups should not be disproportionately targeted', Hale wrote, 'it is members of these groups who will benefit most from the reduction in violence, serious injury and death that may result from the use of such powers. Put bluntly, it is mostly young black lives that will be saved if there is less gang violence'.[81] Her statements directly contradicted the statements that she had made in the *Roma Rights* case, in which she had emphasized that the 'whole point of the law is to require [authorities] to treat each person as an individual, not as a member of a group. The individual should not be assumed to hold the characteristics which the [authority] associates with the group'.[82] That is, in *Roma Rights* she was not willing to accept the claim that there was good reason to treat all those of Roma origin the same and insisted on treating individuals as individuals, whereas in *Roberts* she was willing to accept that it is justifiable to stop a Black individual because they are part of a group that (allegedly) benefits from s 60 powers. Moreover, though, Hale's assertions that s 60 powers benefit the Black community were made without reference to any evidence. Indeed, affected communities have consistently said that they would prefer a public-health approach to tackling knife crime and violence, and they have consistently argued that stop and searches increase distrust between communities and police officers, making a criminal justice approach to tackling knife crime and violence ineffective and counterproductive.[83]

A case that sheds light on the limits of adversarial legal processes can be found in a 2010 challenge to a school's uniform and appearance policy.[84] The school in question prohibited boys from wearing their hair in a 'cornrows' style, and an 11-year-old boy of African-Caribbean heritage was subsequently

---

[81] *Roberts (SC)* (n 77), [41]
[82] *Roma Rights* (n 55), [74].
[83] See, for example, Art Against Knives et al, 'Holding Our Own: A Guide to Non-policing Solutions to Serious Youth Violence' (2023), Available from: https://www.libertyhumanrights.org.uk/wp-content/uploads/2023/04/HoldingOurOwn_Digital-SinglePages.pdf
[84] *G v Head Teacher and Governors of St Gregory's Catholic Science College* [2011] EWHC 1452 (Admin) ('*G*').

prevented from attending the school while he kept his cornrow hairstyle. The boy and his mother challenged the policy on the grounds that it was indirectly discriminatory against African-Caribbean boys in particular. An expert educational psychologist commissioned on behalf of the pupil explained why cornrows had cultural significance for certain racialized groups such as Black Caribbeans, and the High Court ruled that although the policy applied to all students, it clearly had a disproportionate impact on certain racialized groups, without valid justification.[85] Crucially, though, the boy in question had been accepted at another school before the claim in this case was lodged, and it is at least questionable whether a claim would have been lodged had the boy faced returning to the school. The adversarial process pitted the schoolchild against the school and its governors and staff, and even if the boy had felt it necessary to pursue legal action, it is not a stretch to imagine how difficult his life would be in school if he had had to return to that same school.

Intersectionality and discrimination

It was noted earlier that, during the drafting of the Equality Act, concerns were raised about the prospect of each ground of discrimination being watered down if subsumed under one Act. However, it is also arguable that this approach draws attention to the problem of intersectional discrimination. By bringing the nine protected characteristics under one umbrella, the legislation draws attention to the interconnectedness of these grounds of discrimination rather than siloing them off in different Acts of Parliament. Indeed, the drafters of the legislation were cognizant of the need to tackle intersectional discrimination and included a provision which prohibits 'combined discrimination'. Section 14 of the Equality Act stipulates that a person unlawfully discriminates against another if, 'because of a combination of two relevant protected characteristics', they treat that other person 'less favourably than [someone] who does not share either of those characteristics'. However, this provision has not been enacted, and this has rendered it difficult for lawyers and judges to grapple with the spectre of intersectional discrimination in legal proceedings. Iyiola Solanke explained the problem well when she wrote in 2016 that '[t]he difficulty has been in finding a method to incorporate intersectionality into a legal framework'.[86] Atrey agrees that 'the framework of discrimination law has proven to be too resistant' to providing redress for intersectional discrimination.[87]

---

[85] G (n 84), [42]–[48].

[86] Iyiola Solanke, *Discrimination as Stigma: A Theory of Anti-discrimination Law* (Hart Publishing 2016), p 133.

[87] Shreya Atrey, *Intersectional Discrimination* (Oxford University Press 2019), p 2.

One of the key difficulties with addressing intersectionality in the current framework is that an appropriate comparator must be found. For example, if a Black person claims to have been discriminated against, the court can assess their claim by examining whether a non-Black person would have experienced the same treatment or outcomes because of the policy or practice in question. However, if a person claims they were discriminated against on the basis of being both Black and female, then it is not immediately clear what comparator a court would need. Would a Black male suffice, or a White female? Or would they need to consider how a non-Black male would have experienced the policy or practice in question? The case of *Bahl v The Law Society*, decided by the Court of Appeal in 2004, raised this exact issue. Dr Bahl, a Black Asian woman with British nationality, stood accused of bullying colleagues at work. She in turn complained that her employer's handling of the complaints had been marred by both race and sex discrimination. The Employment Tribunal stated: 'We do not distinguish between the race or sex of the Applicant in reaching this conclusion. Our reason for that is simple. The claim was advanced on the basis that Kamlesh Bahl was treated in the way she was because she is a black woman.'[88] Since no Black person or female had ever held the position that Bahl had occupied, the Employment Tribunal could not compare her treatment to that of a White female or Black male office holder. The Court of Appeal found that the Tribunal had made an error of law in failing to 'identify what evidence goes to support a finding of race discrimination and what evidence goes to support a finding of sex discrimination'.[89] Lord Justice Peter Gibson went on to write that '[i]t would be surprising if the evidence for each form of discrimination was the same'.[90] In other words, he expected the Tribunal to consider each ground of discrimination separately, rather than together. He could not conceive that a person might be treated in a particular way because they are a 'Black woman', and that their treatment as a Black person, or as a female, could not be separated from each other. Returning to the analogy of baking a cake that was made in the discussion of intersectionality in Chapter 1, Gibson was effectively trying to separate the ingredients of a cake after it had been baked.[91] For this reason, and others, Atrey suggests that instead of 'having intersectionality awkwardly fit the single-axis model,

---

[88] Quoted in the Court of Appeal judgment in *Bahl v The Law Society* [2004] EWCA Civ 1070 [135] ('*Bahl*').
[89] *Bahl* (n 88), [137].
[90] *Bahl* (n 88), [137].
[91] See Lisa Bowleg, '"Once You've Blended the Cake, You Can't Take the Parts Back to the Main Ingredients": Black Gay and Bisexual Men's Descriptions and Experiences of Intersectionality' (2013) 68 *Sex Roles* 754, and discussion in 'Intersectionality and anti-essentialism' in Chapter 1.

discrimination law could be re-centred around intersectionality'.[92] She creatively constructs a theory of discrimination law that is built around the idea of intersectionality, and although it is not the place here to engage in a discussion of what the law *could* be, Atrey's analysis is useful for highlighting the inadequacies of the current legal framework. If the legal system is going to adequately tackle racial injustices, then it must explicitly address the concept of intersectionality.

Harassment and victimization

Sections 26 and 27 of the Equality Act prohibit 'harassment' and 'victimization' on the basis of protected characteristics, including race. Harassment includes words and acts that are unwanted by the person they are directed at, and which are connected to one of the protected characteristics under the Act. Section 40 put employers at risk of liability if a third party harassed one of their employees, and the employer did not take sufficient steps to protect their employee. This provision was repealed in 2013 by the Enterprise and Regulatory Reform Act, and the case of Lloyd Odain illustrates both the strengths and weaknesses of the current law.

Mr Odain had been contracted by HM Prison and Probation Service (HMPPS) to work as a probation officer, but he was subjected to what the EHRC described as 'multiple incidents of racial discrimination and harassment' by another contractor. The unwanted acts included 'making monkey chants' to Mr Odain while he was talking with colleagues.[93] His complaint to his employers, though, went unheeded, leaving Odain with little choice but to leave his job. When he initiated legal proceedings, HMPPS agreed that monkey chants had been made but argued that it was not required to protect workers employed through third parties from harassment from other workers who were also employed through third parties. At a preliminary hearing, the judge ruled that HMPPS might still be vicariously liable for harassment if it could be shown that HMPPS had outsourced its statutory functions to the person accused of harassment.[94] Rather than proceed to a full hearing, HMPPS offered an out-of-court settlement which Mr Odain accepted. This might appear to be an instance of the successful use of law to tackle a racial injustice, but the settlement did not include an admission of liability, or an apology, or a commitment to review its policies and processes relating to the protection of staff from racial (and other types

---

[92] Atrey (n 87), p 2.
[93] Equality and Human Rights Commission, 'Contractor Who Suffered Monkey Chants and Racial Abuse at Probation Service Wins Payout' (24 August 2023).
[94] Thanks to Louise Taft for clarifying the grounds of legal action in this case to me.

of) harassment. Moreover, it took over three years just for Mr Odain to get to the preliminary hearing, with HMPPS fighting its corner tooth and nail. The financial and emotional toll of the proceedings virtually compel people in Mr Odain's position to accept less than satisfactory out-of-court settlements, which in turn stymies the extent to which law can be used to advance the goal of racial justice.

The prohibition on victimization addresses the concerns raised about the appropriateness of adversarial proceedings in the struggle for racial justice. We have seen that people may feel reluctant to initiate legal proceedings under the Equality Act because of a fear of repercussions, but section 27 makes it clear that a person who is involved in proceedings under the Act must not be victimized, or treated detrimentally, because of their involvement. This relates to people who do what is called a 'protected act', namely institute proceedings under the Act; give evidence or information in relation to proceedings under the Act; do 'any other thing for the purposes of or in connection with this Act'; or make an allegation that another person has contravened a provision of the Act. When determining whether or not a person has been victimized on the basis of doing a 'protected act', courts and tribunals must consider whether a person who had *not* done that protected act would have been treated the same way. As Lord Hoffmann has explained, though, the law does not change the social fact of tensions between the person doing a 'protected act' and the other party, and the other party may then reasonably treat that person differently:

> [O]nce proceedings [under the Equality Act] have been commenced, a new relationship is created between the parties. They are not only employer and employee but also adversaries in litigation. The existence of that adversarial relationship may reasonably cause the employer to behave in a way which treats the employee less favourably than someone who had not commenced such proceedings.[95]

Race hate crimes

'Hate crimes' are those crimes that are motivated by, or which include, hostility towards a person because of some immutable characteristic, such as race, religion, sexual orientation, disability, and transgender identity.[96] These crimes are particularly egregious because of the double impact they have on the victim. They suffer both the physical or verbal abuse and the

---

[95] *Chief Constable of West Yorkshire Police v Khan* [2001] UKHL 48 [59].
[96] Law Commission, 'Hate Crime Laws: Final Report' (Law Com No 402, 2021), para 1.1.

attempted degradation of who they are as a person. Hate crimes also cause wider secondary harms to other people in the community who share the same characteristics as the victim, as they are reminded that they too are vulnerable to being attacked because of a personal characteristic that goes to the heart of their identity.[97]

Crimes that are motivated by hostility to a person's actual or perceived racial background – as opposed to religion, sexual orientation, disability, or transgender identity – are the most common types of 'hate crime', or at least the most commonly reported types of hate crime.[98] The law has developed in a somewhat piecemeal fashion, and so it is worth setting out the legal framework before exploring the utility of the law in promoting racial justice.

The race hate crimes legal framework

Legislators were initially concerned with racist *words* rather than racist *actions*, with section 6 of the Race Relations Act 1965 outlawing 'incitement' to commit racial hatred. This was supplemented by prohibitions on hate speech in the Public Order Act 1986, parts 3 and 3A of which criminalize the 'stirring up' of hatred on the basis of race. Section 3 of the Football (Offences) Act 1991 prohibits racist chanting during football games, and section 127 of the Communications Act 2003 makes it an offence to use a public electronic communications network to disseminate materials or words that are likely to stir up racial animosity.

The development of legislation to tackle *acts* of racial hatred finds its roots in the aftermath of the murder of Stephen Lawrence in 1993, with the Law Commission stating that this case was 'one of the major spurs for the introduction of racial hate crime laws'.[99] Since the late 1990s, a dual system for tackling acts of racial hatred has emerged. First, there are substantive criminal offences that outlaw racially motivated acts. People convicted under these laws are convicted of committing a 'racist crime', such as 'racially aggravated assault'. Second, there are sentencing provisions that can be invoked to ensure that a person's sentence reflects the role of racial animosity in the crime committed. Persons sentenced under these provisions are convicted of a general crime, such as 'assault', but their sentence will reflect the role that racism played in the commission of the general offence. We can consider these two types of laws in turn.

---

[97] Paul Iganski, 'Hate Crimes Hurt More' (2001) 45 *American Behavioral Scientist* 626.
[98] Neil Chakraborti and Jon Garland, *Hate Crime: Impact, Causes & Responses* (2nd edn, SAGE 2015), p 16. See also Home Office, 'Hate Crime, England and Wales, 2021 to 2022' (6 October 2022).
[99] Law Commission (n 96), para 1.3.

The first set of specific criminal offences were introduced in the Crime and Disorder Act 1998. Sections 28–32 set out 11 offences that can be prosecuted as 'racially aggravated' if the perpetrator demonstrates racial animosity during the commission of the crime (for example, by shouting racist abuse while assaulting a person), or if the perpetrator was motivated by racial animosity. The 11 offences include various types of assault, criminal damage, and harassment and stalking, and they carry harsher sentences than if committed without evidence of racial aggravation. For example, conviction of actual bodily harm usually attracts a maximum sentence of five years' imprisonment, but if it is racially aggravated as per the Crime and Disorder Act, the maximum penalty is seven years.[100]

The Criminal Justice Act 2003 complemented the 1998 Act by requiring judges and magistrates to 'enhance the penalty' of a person convicted of any crime that is aggravated by racial hostility but which is not covered by ss 28–32 of the Crime and Disorder Act 1998.[101] In other words, the person might not be convicted of a racially aggravated offence per se, but any racial animosity demonstrated by the commission of the offence will be reflected in harsher penalties. Taken together, the various laws cover a range of behaviours including violence against the person, criminal damage against a person's home or place of worship, verbal abuse and harassment, and the dissemination of materials that are designed to incite violence or hatred against racialized persons.

Assessment of hate crime laws

Hate crime laws are, as Gail Mason has written, 'an important symbol of state support for those who are victimised'.[102] The law also marks a change from the colonial era, when instances of racial hatred went unpunished and were sometimes encouraged. However, there are at least four reasons to be critical of the contemporary legal framework. First, it is not clear that victims of race hate crimes are being treated consistently. GRT communities have expressed particular concerns with the way in which they are treated by legal authorities. In 2018, the EHRC found that more people expressed openly hostile feelings towards GRT people than any other group of people, and other surveys have revealed that the majority of GRT people experience hate speech or hate crime on a virtually daily basis.[103] The Evidence for Equality

---

[100] Crime and Disorder Act 1998, s 29.
[101] Criminal Justice Act 2003, s 145.
[102] Gail Mason, 'Legislating against Hate' in Nathan Hall et al (eds), *The Routledge International Handbook on Hate Crime* (Routledge 2015).
[103] Friends, Families, and Travellers, 'Race Hate and Prejudice Faced by Gypsies and Travellers in England' (March 2023), p 3.

National Survey in 2023 revealed that 61.9 per cent of Gypsies and Travellers reported experiencing a racial assault, which was the highest percentage of all ethnic groups surveyed.[104] Yet GRT people often feel reluctant to report instances of hate crime because they distrust the authorities and have faced racial discrimination from the police.[105] This means that the extent of hate crime against GRT people is probably much higher than the reported figures suggest, and it also means that the legal framework is not wholly effective in protecting GRT people from abuse in the first place. Two examples highlight the problem with the implementation of hate crime laws. In 2003, a 15-year-old Irish Traveller called Johnny Delaney was beaten to death by two teenagers who reportedly said, while kicking Delaney, that he deserved to be beaten because he was "only a Gypsy". The police recorded and investigated the incident as a race hate crime, with evidence from witnesses to the attack. However, the trial judge disagreed, and the perpetrators received sentences of four and a half years for manslaughter, rather than an enhanced sentence. After the ruling, the Detective Chief Inspector implicitly criticized the trial judge by expressly repeating his belief that the attack was racially motivated.[106] Another problematic case is that of Barry Smith, who was killed by three people after one of those people had lost her job for racially abusing Smith at her workplace. The police treated the killing as racially motivated, but the trial judge ruled that the racist comments at the workplace were a separate incident to the killing, even though the killing had been sparked by the incident at the workplace.[107] We see here how legal constructions of crime are not coterminous with how racial hatred manifests itself in practice.

A second problem with the legal framework is the evidential burden. To secure a conviction or enhanced sentence, prosecutors must provide evidence of the actual crime *and* of the racist animosity that animated the crime in question. There is a long and non-exhaustive list of potential evidence: testimony from the complainant and witnesses of verbal racist slurs made during the commission of the offence; evidence that the accused is a member of a racist organization, or has expressed racist hatred in the past; previous convictions for race hate offences; possession of symbols or signs associated with racism, such as swastikas; electronic messages that suggest the victim was targeted because of their racial background; conduct that is clearly directed at the victim's racial identity, such as the cutting off of dreadlocks; and contemporary events that might have triggered or agitated

---

[104] Nissa Finney et al (eds), *Racism and Ethnic Inequality in a Time of Crises: Findings from the Evidence for Equality National Survey* (Policy Press 2023), p 58.
[105] Friends, Families and Travellers (n 103), p 4.
[106] BBC News, 'Boys Guilty of Killing "Gypsy"' (28 November 2003).
[107] Katharine Quarmby, 'Calls for Barry Smith Murder to Be Recognised as Race Hate Crime' *Travellers' Times* (4 November 2014).

tensions between racial groups. Despite this long list of potential evidence, though, practitioners and researchers have reported problems with evidence-gathering at the initial stages of investigation.[108] In cases without witnesses, for example, it can be difficult to secure evidence of racial animosity taking place during the commission of an offence. Practitioners have also reported difficulty with securing evidence in cases where the crime was *motivated* by racial hostility but no overt racial slurs were made during the commission of the offence. The authors of 'Hate Crime and the Legal Process' highlight the disjoint between the workings of the police and the workings of the CPS and suggest that greater efforts could be made by the CPS to train police officers on what evidence would be helpful at trial, so that the police can focus on gathering that evidence at the initial stages of investigation.[109]

A third problem is that the legal framework reinforces the view that crimes committed out of racial animosity are extraordinary events that are contrary to the normal course of day-to-day life in society. For example, when sentencing Paul Taylor and Michael Barton for the racist murder of Anthony Walker in 2005, Justice Leveson stated that the crime was a 'racist attack of a type poisonous to any civilised society'.[110] This reflects and reinforces the narrow view of racism as something that is not compatible with the normal social order, thus masking the structural nature of racial injustices. That is, Leveson failed to appreciate that the acts of Taylor and Barton were symptomatic of structural racism *within* society rather than aberrations from 'civilized society'.

A fourth problem, which is perhaps the most significant, is the extent to which the use of the criminal law widens rather than narrows racial divisions. Mark Walters has argued that '[r]ather than reducing identity group hostilities, enhanced punishments may in fact serve to increase the individual, social and cultural harms of hatred'.[111] That is, the trial process and the experience of conviction tends to make the perpetrator more resentful of the racial group that they initially targeted. Victims of racial hatred crimes also report feeling that the process does not work for them. In 2014/15, for example, only 52 per cent of complainants said that they were satisfied with how the police dealt with their complaint, compared to 73 per cent for crime overall.[112]

---

[108] See Mark Walters et al, 'Hate Crime and the Legal Process: Options for Law Reform' (University of Sussex, October 2017), pp 75–80.
[109] Walters et al (n 108), p 80.
[110] Mark Oliver, 'Cousins Jailed for Racist Axe Murder' *The Guardian* (1 December 2005).
[111] Mark Walters, *Criminalising Hate: Law as Social Justice Liberalism* (Palgrave Macmillan 2022), p 210.
[112] Hannah Corcoran et al, 'Hate Crime, England and Wales, 2014/15' (Home Office 13 October 2015), p 1.

In this sense, racist hate crime laws might not actually advance the pursuit of racial justice and might in fact exacerbate racial tensions and divisions. Walters suggests that a restorative approach to dealing with instances of racial hatred should be pursued in the first instance, as these approaches 'facilitate the repairing of harm in a way that enables victims to move on, while offenders are reintegrated back into the community with a renewed sense of civic duty. Social condemnation is also expressed implicitly through the active participation in a process that asks participants to repair harms'.[113] Such an approach has been trialled in the London Borough of Southwark, in a project titled 'The Southwark Hate Crime Project'.[114] The results of the trial illustrate how a restorative approach which gives a voice to victims of racial hatred educated the perpetrator and also improved the emotional well-being of victims. In other words, the project supported the contention of critical race theorists who espouse the importance of centring the struggle for racial justice on the voices of those with lived experience. Interviews with participants in the project revealed that victims appreciated the opportunity to 'tell their "stories" about what had happened to them and how it had affected their lives and the lives of those around them. Important to these individuals was that they felt that someone was finally listening to them and empathising with their experiences of targeted abuse'.[115]

As with discrimination law, we can see how the shortcomings of the law on race hate crimes map on to the concerns of critical race theorists: a failure to address structural racism, narrow conceptions of who can be the victim of a race hate crime, a tendency to ignore the views of those with lived experiences of racial injustices, and the inappropriateness of adversarial proceedings.

Promoting racial justice

The Macpherson Inquiry which reported in 1999 suggested that one reason why the law on racial injustices up to that point was inadequate was because it was reactive, rather than proactive. That is, the law tended to only impose negative duties on individuals and organizations to refrain from committing racial injustices, rather than positive duties to promote racial equality and racial justice. The Labour government responded by enacting the Race Relations (Amendment) Act 2000 which strengthened the duty on public authorities to take race into account when making decisions, and this was in turn further strengthened by section 149 of the Equality Act 2010, which sets

---

[113] Walters (n 111), p 213.
[114] Walters (n 111).
[115] Walters (n 111), p 220.

out what is known as the Public Sector Equality Duty (PSED). The PSED imposes a duty on public authorities to have 'due regard' to the need to 'eliminate discrimination, harassment [and] victimization'; 'advance equality of opportunity'; and 'foster good relations' between people of different races when developing and implementing policies and practices.[116] The aim of this legal provision is, in part, to prevent racially problematic policies and practices from materializing in the first place. While there are some instances of the PSED having the desired effect, there are some shortcomings to the law as it currently stands.

One shortcoming lies in the absence of any duty to consider the impact of intersecting grounds of discrimination, harassment, and victimization. Thus, a public authority might have 'due regard' to whether a proposed policy directly or indirectly discriminates against Black people, but there is nothing that compels that authority to consider whether that policy will have a particular impact on Black women, for example. Public authorities in Scotland and Wales are required to have due regard to class as well as race, since a PSED for socio-economic inequalities was enacted in 2019 and 2021 respectively. The Runnymede Trust has urged England to follow suit, especially given the intersection of class and race inequalities: 'Given the racialised nature of socioeconomic inequalities in England, as a result of which BME people are more likely to live in poverty ... enforcing this duty is vital to eradicating inequalities in accessing public services.'[117]

A second problem with the PSED as it currently stands relates to the scope of the requirement to have 'due regard' to the need to eliminate racism and to foster good race relations. There are no set criteria that public authorities must use when checking proposed policies or practices, and this is particularly problematic because it means that there is no requirement for authorities to engage with people and communities who might be directly affected by the proposed actions. If the insights and expertise of those with lived experiences of racism are not being heard during the development of policies and practices that might adversely affect them, then the PSED is not as effective as it could be.

Authorities are encouraged to make use of Equality Impact Assessments (EIA), but even these are not cast-iron guarantees that problematic policies or practices will be revised or jettisoned. Authorities can still adopt policies even if the EIA reveals that the policy or practice might have discriminatory effects. The Home Office's EIA for the Police, Crime, Sentencing and Courts Bill reveals just how policy makers can pay lip-service to the PSED. In the

---

[116] The PSED applies to all nine protected characteristics in the Equality Act.

[117] The Runnymede Trust, 'England Civil Society Submission to the United Nations Committee on the Elimination of Racial Discrimination' (May 2021), p 7.

EIA, it is accepted that the proposed measures will adversely affect various ethnic groups such as Black communities and those of a GRT heritage to a greater extent than others. Despite these conclusions, the measures were pursued on the grounds that they can be 'objectively justified'. For example, on the provisions outlawing the use of certain roadside encampments, the EIA states:

> [T]he policy applies to everyone in the same way but may place those from GRT communities at a particular disadvantage. ... Although this policy may have an effect on these groups, the offence will apply to anyone who resides or intends to reside on land illegally in the conditions set out. Enforcement action will not be taken on the grounds of race or ethnicity, and instead will be based on whether any individual chooses to reside on land without permission and causes significant damage, disruption or distress, affecting the rights of others.[118]

This reasoning effectively justifies all instances of indirect discrimination, as it suggests that policies and laws which will have a discriminatory impact in practice will be justifiable if race is not explicitly a factor in the enforcement of that policy or law. Similarly, in the equality statement on the sentencing, release, probation, and youth justice measures in the Bill, it is acknowledged that 'BAME groups appear to be over-represented at most stages throughout the [criminal justice system]', and that the proposed Bill will add to this over-representation because the measures will likely result in 'some individuals with protected characteristics [being] over-represented'. But having acknowledged this, the Home Office concludes that 'our overall assessment is that such impacts would be justified as a proportionate means of achieving the legitimate aims of these reforms which are to ... restore confidence in our criminal justice system by ensuring that the public are better protected'.[119] This sort of reasoning though could be applied to virtually all criminal justice measures no matter how discriminatory those measures might be. It is, in effect, using the PSED to justify discrimination in the criminal justice system at large, which is the opposite of what the PSED is meant to be used for.

Yet another problem with the scope of the 'due regard' requirement is that EIAs and their equivalents are often siloed off from one another, and there is correspondingly no awareness of the cumulative impact of

---

[118] Home Office, 'Home Office Measures in the Police, Crime, Sentencing and Courts Bill: Equalities Impact Assessment' (updated 2 August 2023).

[119] Home Office, 'Overarching Equality Statement: Sentencing, Release, Probation and Youth Justice Measures' (updated 29 June 2023).

policies and practices, either within or across social systems. It might well be that a particular policy is likely to have discriminatory effects but can be 'objectively justified', but if numerous such policies are adopted, then we see the entrenchment of structural racism.

Legal challenges to authorities' engagement with the PSED have sometimes been unsuccessful because of the weaknesses with the 'due regard' requirement, with courts accepting that the authority merely needs to show that they have *considered* potentially discriminatory impacts of proposed policies. The case of *Diedrick*, decided in 2012, illustrates this. Until 2011, police forces had been required to record the self-defined ethnicity of people who were stopped and asked to account for themselves. When this requirement was removed, the claimant argued that the new policy would hinder efforts to ensure that stop and account powers were not exercised in a racially discriminatory manner and would damage relations between ethnic minorities and police officers. In the High Court, Justice Parker concluded that, under the PSED, the Secretary of State only had to have 'due regard' to the needs and concerns of racialized groups but did not necessarily have to adopt the course of action that would actually address those needs and concerns. In his words, the Secretary of State only needed to be 'fully alive' to concerns about racial discrimination but did not have to adopt a course of action that allayed those concerns.[120]

Notwithstanding these shortcomings, though, there have been some qualified successes in using the PSED. The case of *R(Bapio Action Ltd) v Royal College of General Practitioners*, decided in 2014, provides a more promising tale.[121] The claim was focused on the Clinical Skills Assessment (CSA), which prospective doctors are required to take when qualifying. In this sense, the case lay at the intersection of healthcare, education, and employment. There was considerable statistical evidence that certain racialized groups failed the assessment at a greater rate than non-racialized groups. In light of this, the British Association of Physicians of Indian Origin (BAPIO) argued that the Royal College of General Practitioners and the General Medical Council 'failed to fulfil the public sector equality duty ... and that the differences in outcome described are, in whole or in part, the result of that failure and establish against the Royal College alone that it has discriminated, directly or indirectly, against South Asian and BME doctors'.[122] Judge Mitting ruled against BAPIO on the grounds that, during the course of proceedings, the Royal College had identified ways to address the concerns raised, and

---

[120] *Diedrick v Chief Constable of Hampshire Constabulary and others* [2012] EWHC 2144 (Admin) [43].

[121] *R(Bapio Action Ltd) v Royal College of General Practitioners* [2014] EWHC 1416 (Admin).

[122] *Bapio* (n 121), [9].

that therefore the College should be given the opportunity to implement those measures.[123] Mitting also rejected the claims of direct and indirect discrimination. However, although the court found against BAPIO, the judge noted that the action had compelled the Royal College to take appropriate steps and 'that the bringing of this claim is likely in the end to produce something of benefit for the medical profession and so for the public generally'.[124] As such, in Mitting's view, '[t]his claim has served a useful purpose and the Claimant has achieved, if not a legal victory, then a moral success'.[125] As noted on BAPIO's website, '[s]ince 2014, when BAPIO led a legal challenge against the Royal College of General Practitioners there has been a seismic shift in transparency and reporting of the differential attainment data for all examinations and specialty progression reports by the UK GMC'.[126] Although BAPIO acknowledges that there is still much work to bridge the attainment gap, the case is illustrative of the benefits that even failed legal action can bring.

Other qualified successful uses of the PSED include a challenge to South Wales Police's (SWP) use of automated facial recognition technology (AFR). The SWP had undertaken an EIA when first deploying AFR, but the appellant argued that the approach taken to the EIA was inadequate because it had failed to account for the risk of indirect discrimination. The Court of Appeal agreed that although the SWP had considered the risk of direct discrimination, they 'have never sought to satisfy themselves, either directly or by way of independent verification, that the software program in this case does not have an unacceptable bias on grounds of race or sex'.[127] The Court emphasized that the PSED imposed a procedural duty on public authorities, and that it did not matter whether the use of AFR would in fact indirectly discriminate against people on the basis of race or sex. Moreover, the Court was at pains to emphasize that the PSED places a continuing duty on public authorities to review the potential discriminatory impact of policies and practices.

In November 2022, the Metropolitan Police announced a 'wholesale change' to its Gangs Matrix – a database of actual and suspected 'gang members' – after a PSED-based legal challenge initiated by UNJUST UK and Awate Suleiman. Racial justice campaigners had long argued that Black people were overrepresented on the database, pointing to the fact that many individuals on the database had no history of gang involvement.

---

[123] *Bapio* (n 121), [32].

[124] *Bapio* (n 122), [51].

[125] *Bapio* (n 122), [51].

[126] BAPIO, 'Bridging the Gap' (2020), p 1, Available from: https://www.bapio.co.uk/differential-attainment-in-healthcare-professionals

[127] *R(Bridges) v South Wales Police* [2020] EWCA Civ 1058 [199].

Aside from the discriminatory assumptions at play, the database had broader implications as the data were shared with third parties, thus putting people at risk of school exclusion, eviction from their homes, being stripped of welfare benefits, and in some cases deportation and having children taken into care.[128] Before the challenge could be ruled upon, the Met Police agreed that Black people are disproportionately represented on the database, agreed to remove the majority of individuals from the Matrix, and agreed to inform people who ask whether or not they are on the Matrix. Although this was described as a 'win' for racial justice campaigners,[129] it is notable that the Met did not agree to disband the Matrix altogether. There is a danger that this 'win' will serve to legitimize what remains of the Matrix, which is still racially discriminatory.

In February 2023, the PSED was again successfully used when challenging race discrimination in the prosecution of joint enterprise cases.[130] Liberty and JENGbA argued that the CPS was neglecting its duties under the PSED by not recording the ethnicities of persons prosecuted under the doctrine of joint enterprise. As with the Gangs Matrix challenge, the authority in question relented before the case reached court, and the CPS announced a pilot scheme to record data on the age, race, sex, and disability of those prosecuted under joint enterprise laws. Although this is a step in the right direction, we have already seen that the judiciary is reluctant to intervene with policies and practices on the basis of general statistics and will generally only act when a specific individual can show they have been specifically discriminated against.[131] As such, the use of the PSED to enforce data collection will only have limited effect.

Conclusion

Although it is not possible to cover every case that has involved a challenge to racial injustices, the examples in this chapter illustrate that the shortcomings of the contemporary legal system traverse different aspects of social life. In particular, courts have struggled to grapple with the problem of structural racism and have failed to appreciate how understandings of 'race' and 'racism' evolve. There has been a consistent failure to acknowledge the problem of

---

[128] BBC News, 'Gang Violence Matrix: Met Police to Overhaul Controversial Database' (12 November 2022).

[129] Liberty, 'Met to Overhaul "Racist" Gangs Matrix after Landmark Legal Challenge' (11 November 2022).

[130] Simon Hattenstone, 'Joint Enterprise Prosecutions to Be Monitored for Racial Bias' *The Guardian* (16 February 2023).

[131] General statistical evidence had little impact in the *JCWI* case (n 68), *Roberts* (n 77), or *Diedrick* (n 120).

intersectionality, or to listen to the views of those with lived experiences of racial injustices, and this has highlighted the drawbacks of legal action in the pursuit of racial justice.

Another set of cases to be considered are those where racism has played a central role in the injustice suffered, but there has been little to no mention of race in legal proceedings. An example of such cases can be found in inquests into deaths in state custody. It has long been established that Black men are more likely to face disproportionately severe levels of restraint, and thus die, at the hands of the police and other state officials. This is largely because of racially charged stereotypes of the 'dangerous, violent and volatile' Black man.[132] At the time of writing, Black people are seven times more likely to die than White people following the use of restraints either during, or following, police custody or contact.[133] But despite the number of inquests that have been held into the deaths of Black people in custody, the question of racism is not always addressed. The reasons are circular. Leslie Thomas KC and the charity INQUEST have reported that there 'is an entrenched discomfort among coroners about including race in inquests'[134] because racial discrimination is rarely ever explicit in such cases, and coroners prefer to keep the scope of the inquest narrow and focus on matters that are directly causative of death.[135] This in turn leads lawyers to keep race out of the conversation, as doing otherwise risks antagonizing the coroner and jury.[136] The more that lawyers leave the issue out of legal representations, though, the more that the legal system fails to address the role of racism in deaths in custody. In a review into race and deaths in custody, the charity INQUEST quoted a lawyer who expressed regret that they did not raise the role of race: "[T]here's been a number of cases where I should have run race and I didn't. And that's to my eternal shame."[137] It is incumbent on lawyers to challenge racial injustices when such injustices have occurred or are likely to occur, and it is to the concept of such 'antiracist lawyering' that we now turn.

---

[132] Rt Hon Dame Elish Angiolini DBE QC, 'Report of the Independent Review of Deaths and Serious Incidents in Police Custody' (January 2017) [5.18]. See also Joint Committee on Human Rights, 'Deaths in Custody' (third report, 14.12.2004, HL Paper 15-1), paras 227 and 256; Raekha Prasad, '"I Can't Breathe": Race, Death and British Policing' (INQUEST, 20 February 2023).

[133] Prasad (n 132), p 38.

[134] Thomas (n 29), p 426; Prasad (n 132), p 118.

[135] Prasad (n 132), p 118.

[136] Prasad (n 132), pp 119–20.

[137] Prasad (n 132), p 120.

5

Antiracist Lawyering

Introduction

I have so far painted a rather bleak picture for lawyers and campaigners concerned with racial justice. The legal system, we have seen, was used to create the conditions for structural racism to develop in the colonial era, and it now allows structural racism to thrive. It does this while portraying itself as pro-racial justice, thus making the task of identifying and addressing law's racism more difficult. It is perhaps little surprise, then, to find some activists describing the legal system as part of the problem rather than part of the solution.[1] But law is not an autonomous being with a mind of its own, and its content and application will reflect the mindsets of the people using the legal system. If legal actors are trained in 'antiracism', then they can help generate antiracist legal processes and outcomes. In this chapter, I set out four principles of 'antiracist lawyering': reflection, creativity, collaboration, and accountability. These principles will help lawyers address the six tenets of Critical Race Theory (CRT) that I have so far used to frame the limitations of the law. That is, these elements will help lawyers (i) promote understandings of structural racism; (ii) promote understandings of race as a social construct; (iii) grapple with intersectionality; (iv) avoid prioritizing the interests of the 'White British' population; (v) centre the voices of those with lived experiences of racial injustices; and (vi) recognize when legal processes might be inappropriate or counterproductive.

To explain what reflective, creative, collaborative, and accountable lawyering entails, we will first get to grips with the idea of 'antiracism'

---

[1] In a roundtable discussion on antiracist struggles, Shanice Octavia McBean outlined the shortcomings of the legal system and argued that "these legal processes are not working for us, what can we do differently? How can we wrench justice from the system and not play the system on its own terms?" See Sophia Siddiqui, 'Anti-racist Organising Today: A Roundtable Discussion' (2023) 65 *Race & Class* 119, 128.

more generally. With this definition in mind, we will see that 'antiracist lawyering' can be classed as a form of 'social justice lawyering', and the idea of social justice lawyering is therefore engaged with to develop an account of antiracist lawyering that encompasses reflection, creativity, collaboration, and accountability.

Defining antiracism

Ibram X. Kendi writes that an antiracist is a person who takes active steps to dismantle racist policies.[2] There are two aspects of this that are worth stressing: first, the emphasis on taking *active* steps to combat racism; and second, the focus on racist *policies* rather than racist ideas. We can consider these in turn.

Kendi draws a distinction between the person who claims that they are 'not racist' and the antiracist person who takes active steps to tackle racism. The former may well not act or speak in an overtly racist manner, but they tend to focus on their own interpersonal racial prejudices at the expense of recognizing and grappling with the problem of structural racism. As such, they might not realize how their seemingly race-neutral and innocuous actions and decisions might sustain structural racism. Examples of such innocuous actions were provided in the discussion of structural racism in Chapter 1, such as the parent who sends their child to a 'good' school but which tends to be in an affluent and predominantly White area.[3] We can see why, then, Kendi implores people to take the more active stance of antiracism, which involves doing more than merely refraining from saying or doing overtly racist things. An antiracist recognizes the need to look beyond the scope of their own interpersonal racism, and the need to take broader action to ensure that racism in society does not flourish unchallenged.

The second aspect of Kendi's definition that is worth emphasizing is the focus on challenging racist *policies*. This is because it is racist policies which breed racist ideas. 'The history of racist ideas', Kendi writes, 'is the history of powerful policy-makers erecting racist policies out of self-interest, then producing racist ideas to defend and rationalize the inequitable effects of their policies'.[4] As people consume these ideas, they develop antipathy towards people of different races. We have seen, for example, how the self-interested desire to accumulate wealth, territory, and power led to imperialism, and how pseudo-scientific accounts of racial differences were deployed to defend and rationalize the harms that imperialism inflicted on

---

[2] Ibram X. Kendi, *How to Be an Antiracist* (The Bodley Head 2019).
[3] See Chapter 1, n 22 and accompanying text.
[4] Kendi (n 2), p 230.

indigenous people. And we have seen how the consumption of these ideas laid the foundations for structural racism to thrive today. An antiracist must therefore identify policies that breed racist ideas and beliefs, call out such policies, and work positively and proactively to replace such policies with antiracist policies.[5]

To be 'antiracist', then, is to take active steps to eliminate the sorts of racist policies that create and sustain structural racism, even when one is not being overtly racist or consciously contributing to racist policies. According to Kendi, this requires 'persistent self-awareness, constant self-criticism, and regular self-examination'.[6] These traits are required because even those who claim to be antiracist have been conditioned to examine the world through a lens that has been constructed by structural racism. They must therefore work hard to ensure that they do not replicate these prejudices, however inadvertently. We can use the work of the American sociologist W.E.B. Du Bois to explain this.

Writing in the early 1900s, Du Bois was concerned about the various harms that Black people had been suffering in the decades after the abolition of slavery in the United States in 1865. In documenting these harms, he introduced the concepts of 'the veil' and 'double-consciousness'.[7] He recounts a time when he was excluded from a childhood activity because of his skin colour and explains how he was 'shut out from [White people's] world by a vast veil'.[8] The veil, Du Bois writes, hides Black people so they can never fully participate in social and political life. The veil, though, also influences how Black people view and understand themselves, as well as how they perceive the outside world. He writes that the veil 'only lets [a Black person] see himself through the revelation of the other world',[9] namely the world as construed by Whites. It is for this reason that Black Americans have a 'double-consciousness [in the] sense of always looking at one's self through the eyes of others'.[10]

The concept of 'double-consciousness' is multi-faceted. First, it reflects the idea that the pervasiveness of racism is so deep and wide that racialized people might have consumed narratives of racism which lead them to understand and judge themselves through standards and frameworks constructed by White people. Thus, a racialized person might alter their behaviour so that they align with the standards set out by the White

---

[5] Kendi (n 2), pp 231–2.
[6] Kendi (n 2), p 23.
[7] W.E.B. Du Bois, *The Souls of Black Folk: Authoritative Text, Contexts, Criticism* (first published 1903, W.W. Norton 1999), pp 10–11.
[8] Du Bois (n 7), p 10.
[9] Du Bois (n 7), p 11.
[10] Du Bois (n 7), p 11.

population, which in turn contributes to the racist idea that White norms are preferable. Second, with respect to the fact that Du Bois was focusing on the plight of Black Americans, the concept of 'double-consciousness' highlights how the dual identities of Black Americans pull in opposite directions. They are at once 'Black' and 'American'. A Black American, Du Bois writes, 'ever feels his two-ness – an American, a Negro; two souls, two thoughts, two unreconciled strivings; two warring ideals in one dark body, whose dogged strength alone keeps it from being torn asunder'.[11] This is a 'double-consciousness' because the Black American considers themselves to be, on the one hand, 'free' by virtue of the American social and political emphasis on freedom; and, on the other hand, 'not-free' by virtue of the historical and social binds that have subjugated Black people in America.

Kendi suggests that this concept is better described as a 'dueling consciousness'[12] since Black Americans have to balance a desire to be themselves with a pull towards assimilating with White ideals and expectations. This might be for subconscious reasons, or for more conscious reasons such as a desire to progress socially or professionally. Nikesh Shukla has expressed a similar idea in the context of the United Kingdom, explaining the difficulties that immigrants have when trying to uphold their cultural traditions and customs on the one hand, while on the other hand feeling the need to jettison such traditions and adopting the traditions of the 'White British' population in order to be accepted.[13]

We can take this analysis and apply it to the challenge faced by the lawyer in England and Wales today who wants to promote racial justice. They too have a double or duelling consciousness, in that they want to promote antiracist ideals on the one hand, but on the other hand they are conditioned to work and think within the parameters and language of a legal system that does not necessarily align with the requirements of antiracism. In other words, they too must balance 'two warring ideals' – the ideals of antiracism and the ideals of their professional duties and training. It is with this definition of antiracism and the challenge of the lawyer's 'duelling consciousness' in mind that we can understand why antiracist lawyering can be classed as a type of 'social justice lawyering', and why this requires reflective, creative, collaborative, and accountable lawyering.

---

[11] Du Bois (n 7), p 11. See also Bharat Malkani, 'The Souls of Black Folk, by W.E.B. Du Bois' in Faith Gordon and Daniel Newman (eds), *Leading Works in Law and Social Justice* (Routledge 2021).

[12] Kendi (n 2), p 29.

[13] Nikesh Shukla (ed), *The Good Immigrant* (Unbound 2017).

Social justice lawyering

If antiracism is about actively challenging and changing racist policies and structural racism, then antiracist lawyering is a form of lawyering that is geared towards the promotion of social justice. Many labels have been attached to lawyers who seek to effectuate broader social change through their work, including 'cause lawyering', 'progressive lawyering', 'activist lawyering', 'radical lawyering', and 'movement lawyering'.[14] Whichever term is used, there are controversies with this approach to lawyering. These can be separated into three categories: concerns with the ethics and professionalism of social justice lawyering, concerns with elitism and paternalism, and concerns with counterproductivity. Taking these concerns seriously helps shape a principled approach to antiracist lawyering.

Ethics and professionalism

A central concern with lawyering for social change is the perceived disjoint between activism and professionalism. An antiracist lawyer faces a tension between, on the one hand, the antiracist's commitment to activism and partisanship, and, on the other hand, the lawyer's professional and ethical commitments to neutrality and independence. The regulatory regimes for solicitors and barristers in England and Wales put this tension into sharp relief. The Solicitors' Regulation Authority makes it clear that solicitors must always act 'with independence' and 'in the best interests of each client'.[15] This suggests that the pursuit of broader social justice objectives such as racial justice should be avoided if such objectives threaten the solicitor's actual or perceived independence or the interests of the client. Barristers are required to follow similar guidelines. The Bar Standards Board sets out a Code of Conduct which demands, for example, that barristers 'promote fearlessly and by all proper and lawful means the client's best interests'. This must be done 'without regard to [the barrister's] own interests' and without regard to 'the consequences to any other person'.[16] The Code also prohibits barristers from withholding their services to a

---

[14] See, respectively: Austin Sarat and Stuart A. Scheingold (eds), *Cause Lawyering: Political Commitments and Professional Responsibilities* (Oxford University Press 1998); Jacqueline Kinghan, *Lawyers, Networks and Progressive Social Change: Lawyers Changing Lives* (Hart Publishing 2021); Adam Wagner, 'It's Not "Activist Lawyers" This Government Hates, But the Laws Themselves' *New Statesman* (28 August 2020); Michael Mansfield, *Memoirs of a Radical Lawyer* (Bloomsbury 2010); Ife Thompson, 'Black Lives Matter UK: For Lasting Change, We Need "Movement Lawyers"' (EachOther, 3 August 2020).

[15] 'SRA Principles' (Solicitors Regulation Authority, 30 May 2018).

[16] 'Code of Conduct', Rule C15 (Bar Standards Board 2015).

client merely because 'the nature of the case is objectionable to you or to any section of the public', or because 'the conduct, opinions or beliefs of the prospective client are unacceptable to you or to any section of the public'.[17] We can see why this Code might prevent a lawyer from being an antiracist, as the Code requires lawyers to potentially defend someone accused of violating laws against racism, thus potentially contributing to the perpetuation of racist policies and ideas.

There are good reasons for the requirement that lawyers set aside personal and moral opinions and objectives in their work and act with neutrality and independence. Their primary role is to ensure that all persons have access to justice, and thus the principles of neutrality, independence, and zealous advocacy on their client's behalf are essential to the working of the justice system. As Jacqueline Kinghan writes: '[The] very concept of the cause lawyer challenges the traditional ethical assumptions of what it means to be a detached lawyer. Their independence and ability to firmly uphold the best interests of their client is called into question such that their partisanship is said to subvert the accepted norms of professional ethics.'[18] Although Kinghan does not necessarily subscribe to these concerns, she has nonetheless summarized the controversy neatly: '[L]awyers might struggle to uphold the clients' best interests as a neutral advocate while at the same time being committed to their *own* goals.'[19] For these reasons, she observes that 'many lawyers ... see campaigns as being too overtly political and feel constrained by their professional status as lawyers such that they refrain from using it as a tool for change'.[20]

Elitism and paternalism

Writing in 1975, not long after the North Kensington Law Centre was established, Diana Leat cautioned that law centres might inadvertently further disempower people, as they become dependent on such centres whenever a social problem arises. Similarly, the more that people turn to lawyers in law centres for help, the greater the power inequalities between legal professionals and clients.[21] Clive Grace and Patrick Lefevre make a similar point, arguing that lawyers should facilitate community activism but not take the role of activist themselves.[22] This argument applies with particular

---

[17] 'Code of Conduct', Rule C28 (Bar Standards Board 2015).
[18] Kinghan (n 14), p 30.
[19] Kinghan (n 14), p 28.
[20] Kinghan (n 14), p 108.
[21] Diana Leat, 'The Rise and Rôle of the Poor Man's Lawyer' (1975) 2 *British Journal of Law and Society* 166.
[22] Clive Grace and Patrick Lefevre, 'Draining the Swamp' (1985) 7 *Law & Policy* 97.

force when lawyers use a case to advance a broader social goal such as racial justice. In these instances, the lawyer runs the risk of disempowering their client if they place their understanding of the pursuit of racial justice over and above the client's immediate interests. A lawyer might give the impression that 'they know best', which can in turn entrench social inequalities as the client comes to be in service to the legal profession – or at least in service to those lawyers who are prioritizing the pursuit for racial justice – rather than the other way round.

The concern that social justice lawyering is elitist or paternalistic shares links with what Azfar Shafi and Ilyas Nagdee have termed 'antiracism from above'.[23] Shafi and Nagdee document the rise of the Black Power movement in Britain from the late 1960s, drawing attention to the movement's radicalism and focus on community organizing. They term this 'antiracism from below'. They then trace how, after the riots that took place across England in 1981 in response to racially discriminatory policing, Thatcher's government set about neutralizing the radicalism of the Black Power movement. This was achieved by imposing 'antiracism from above' which involved creating spaces within existing power structures for antiracists to work in, thus giving the appearance of taking antiracism seriously while simultaneously constraining their radicalism. For example, the work of Black Power community groups was siphoned off into the work of civil society organizations funded by public money. This meant that the work of antiracism was now constrained by funding conditions and charity laws.[24] It also meant that the voices of those on the ground were ignored in favour of those who were working within existing positions of power. The turn towards legal help can engender a similarly problematic power dynamic, where antiracist work becomes the preserve of professionally qualified lawyers who are working within existing legal frameworks that do not accommodate the views and experiences of racialized people who have traditionally been marginalized. In other words, the radicalism of antiracism becomes neutered by the lawyer's adherence to legal norms and discourses.

Counterproductivity

A third concern with social justice lawyering, and antiracist lawyering in particular, is that it might be counterproductive. Leslie Thomas KC explains why a lawyer might refrain from raising race-related issues during inquests into deaths in custody, though his argument applies to legal proceedings

---

[23] Azfar Shafi and Ilyas Nagdee, *Race to the Bottom: Reclaiming Antiracism* (Pluto Press 2022).
[24] Shafi and Nagdee (n 23), pp 75–7.

more generally: '[W]e don't want to be accused of "playing the race card". There will often be less contentious arguments to run with so why risk damaging our client's case with such a disagreeable topic?'[25]

These concerns with social justice lawyering can guide and constrain the antiracist lawyer's work, so that they can make more effective use of the legal system to tackle racial injustices while still meeting their professional and ethical obligations. To reconcile their 'duelling consciousness', and to ensure that they do not disempower their clients or jeopardize their case, antiracist lawyers must be reflective, creative, collaborative, and accountable.

Principles for antiracist lawyering

A lawyer who seeks to promote racial justice might not initially understand the complex relationship between law and the struggle for racial justice, because orthodox legal education and training do not expose aspiring lawyers to the ways in which the law can create and sustain racial injustices. In 2021, the Howard League for Penal Reform and Black Protest Legal Support published a guide for antiracist lawyers working within the criminal justice system with the express aim of 'liberat[ing] [members of the legal profession] from the constraints imposed by traditional legal training'. As they explained, 'legal training in England and Wales ... does not equip lawyers to be antiracist'[26] because legal training does not emphasize law's partiality. Lawyers are generally trained to believe that law is impartial and are rarely trained to understand how the legal system creates and entrenches racial injustices. If they are not educated about law's partiality, then they will be bound to reproduce law's racism. As the authors of the guide state, 'lawyers might become complicit in that racism'[27] by adopting strategies and tactics that entrench racialized discourses. For example, a lawyer not schooled in the idea of structural racism might not recognize how a seemingly race-neutral practice or policy is steeped in a history of racial prejudice. In many respects, then, the principles of reflection, creativity, collaboration, and accountability can be read as an attempt to fill current gaps in legal education and training. Although we will consider these elements of antiracist lawyering in turn, it should be borne in mind that they work simultaneously and symbiotically.

---

[25] Leslie Thomas, *Do Right and Fear No One: A Life Dedicated to Fighting for Justice* (Simon & Schuster 2022), p 426.
[26] Howard League for Penal Reform, 'Making Black Lives Matter in the Criminal Justice System: A Guide for Antiracist Lawyers' (Howard League for Penal Reform 2021), p 5.
[27] Howard League for Penal Reform (n 26), p 5.

Reflective lawyering

It was noted earlier that antiracists must engage in 'persistent self-awareness, constant self-criticism, and regular self-examination'[28] to ensure that they do not fall into the trap of perpetuating racial injustices because of the way they have been conditioned to think and act. We can use the term 'reflection' to capture these three required traits and see why the antiracist lawyer must constantly reflect on their own biases, on their role as a lawyer, and on the system they are working in to ensure they do not perpetuate racial injustices or entrench the sorts of power inequalities that have been highlighted by critiques of social justice lawyering.

In a study of racial justice activists in America, published in 2019, Paul Gorski and Noura Erakat identified racism *within* racial justice movements as a central reason for 'burnout' among racial justice activists of colour, and the first task for the antiracist lawyer is to reflect on their own biases and prejudices. As they write:

> [R]acial justice activists ... of color identified among many sources of burnout the way they were treated by white racial justice activists within their movements – not white people in general, but white activists – as one primary cause. They shared how they grew emotionally and physically exhausted coping with the ways white activists carried their privilege and entitlement into racial justice movements – how it deteriorated their well-being, contributing to their burnout.[29]

Although the study was focused on racial justice groups in the United States, it is clear that those who claim to be working to advance racial justice in the UK might similarly bring their 'privilege and entitlement' and biases to bear on their work. The Association of Chief Executives of Voluntary Organisations and Voice4Change England recognized this when writing in June 2020 that '[t]he charity sector has a problem with racial and ethnic diversity. Black, Asian and Minoritised Ethnic (BAME) people are under-represented in the sector and those who are in charities can be subject to racism and antagonism not faced by white colleagues'.[30] On 12 October 2020, a report was published which revealed instances of racial discrimination

---

[28] Kendi (n 2), p 23.
[29] Paul C. Gorski and Noura Erakat, 'Racism, Whiteness, and Burnout in Antiracism Movements: How White Racial Justice Activists Elevate Burnout in Racial Justice Activists of Color in the United States' (2019) 19 *Ethnicities* 784, 786.
[30] Sanjiv Lingayah et al, 'Home Truths: Undoing Racism and Delivering Real Diversity in the Charity Sector' (Voice4Change England and the Association of Chief Executives of Voluntary Organisations 2020), p 9.

at Amnesty International, which is widely regarded as the world's pre-eminent human rights organization.[31] The problem of racism within the charity sector is acute enough to justify the existence of an organization called #CharitySoWhite, which aims to tackle racism within the sector.[32]

For these reasons, initiatives to encourage reflection within legal organizations should be welcomed. Following the series of racial justice protests in the summer of 2020, Liberty – the legal charity that has spearheaded many actions against racial injustice – set out the role that self-reflection would play in the development of their own antiracist practices. Martha Spurrier, the Director of Liberty, wrote on the organization's website that '[i]f we can't recognise the racism in our organisations and our sector, we are little better than the Government and the police who deny it in theirs. And if we don't confront our part in perpetuating systems of inequality, we have no hope of dismantling them'. She explained that antiracist work includes 'looking at ourselves [and carrying out] a deep and critical analysis of [our] culture and ways of working'.[33]

This is not to suggest that reflecting on one's own prejudices and ways of working will, by itself, lead to antiracist lawyering. We saw in the previous chapter, for example, that Liberty's challenge to the Gangs Matrix database did not conclude with an antiracist outcome, as the policy remains in place. Antiracists therefore also need to reflect on the processes of the legal system, and how these processes might stymy their adoption of antiracist strategies and tactics. This calls for creative and collaborative lawyering.

Creative lawyering

Reflecting on the limits of the legal system in tackling things such as structural racism and intersectionality requires a lawyer to think creatively about how to push those limits, so that they are able to make best use of the law without crossing the line into unethical or unprofessional lawyering.[34] The barrister and founder of Black Protest Legal Support, Ife Thompson, provides an example of creative antiracist lawyering.[35] She was representing a 17-year-old Black male who had been charged with possession of cannabis and obstructing a police officer. He had initially fled from the police because they were in plain clothes and did not show their identification when they

---

[31] Nazia Parveen, 'Amnesty International Has Culture of White Privilege, Report Finds' *The Guardian* (20 April 2021).
[32] See the organization's website: https://charitysowhite.org
[33] Martha Spurrier, 'We Stand in Solidarity with Black Lives Matter' (Liberty, 11 June 2020).
[34] Raymond H. Brescia, 'Creative Lawyering for Social Change' (2019) 35 *Georgia State University Law Review* 529.
[35] Ife Thompson, 'Discrimination and Policing: Case Study (Nov 22)' (Legal Action Group, November 2022).

confronted him. One of the officers caught up with him and subjected him to several knee and hand strikes in order to gain control over the boy's arms. Even though the 17-year-old now knew that they were police officers, he fled again. This led to his arrest and charge. When Thompson spoke to her client, she used her knowledge of racial trauma to understand why he had fled. He told her that 'he had seriously high levels of anxiety when he was around police, especially when subjected to a stop and search', and that 'he had only run away because he was scared of the police due to his past experiences as a person of colour'. At this point, Thompson advised her client to speak with a racial trauma expert to see if his past experiences and anxieties had played a role in his decision to run away. She made the case for a racial trauma expert to attend court: '[A]n expert of this sort would … show that my client did not have the required mens rea to wilfully obstruct the police as he was subject to violent policing during the encounter that would have triggered a trauma-based response leading him to avoid staying around the police.' The appointment of a racial trauma expert, and the argument that a Black person's reaction to the police might be based on race-based trauma, is not something that a traditionally trained lawyer would immediately think to do, but her approach worked. After reviewing the evidence, the CPS decided that it would not be in the interests of justice to pursue the prosecution. Leslie Thomas has also stated that, in his experience of representing the families of Black people who have died in custody, 'these cases could benefit from having a race expert on board to explain why the use of [prejudicial] language and such tropes amounts to unconscious bias' on the part of officers who have been implicated in the person's death.[36]

An antiracist approach to lawyering would involve undertaking similar measures to that taken by Thompson, who says that lawyers 'need to find new and creative ways to call out [racial] injustices and shape them into our arguments at court'.[37] It was noted in the previous chapter that the government and the Chair of the Grenfell Inquiry refused to include the question of structural or institutional racism within the remit of the Inquiry. However, this did not stop some of the lawyers from continuously raising the issue of structural racism during the proceedings, thus keeping it at the forefront of people's minds.[38] Likewise, lawyers involved in inquests into deaths in custody have expressed an awareness that the role of racial tropes should be raised in proceedings even if race and racism cannot be shown to be a direct cause of death.[39] In this sense, creative antiracist lawyering

---

[36] Thomas (n 25), p 427.
[37] Thompson (n 35).
[38] Thomas (n 25), p 412.
[39] Raekha Prasad, '"I Can't Breathe": Race, Death and British Policing' (INQUEST, 20 February 2023), p 120.

also involves raising the topic of racism even when racism is not necessarily within the remit of legal proceedings. And it involves identifying legal provisions that can be used to tackle racial injustices even if such provisions were not written with racism in mind. We saw in Chapter 2, for example, how Sharp identified the Habeas Corpus Act as a tool for challenging Somerset's captivity, even though the Act had not been written to address slavery. Recently, lawyers for racial justice activists who have taken part in protests have secured acquittals for their clients when charged with various public order offences by creatively construing the struggle for racial justice as a defence to such charges.[40]

Similarly, lawyers can also make use of the numerous provisions of international and foreign laws that address the problem of racism, even when these provisions are not directly applicable in England and Wales. Such norms can be used to persuade judges to interpret domestic laws in line with international standards on racial justice. The International Convention on the Elimination of All Forms of Racial Discrimination 1956 (ICERD) is the main instrument of international law that can provide advocates with a wealth of arguments in domestic legal proceedings, although for reasons that are beyond the scope of this work, we should not assume that the international legal system is an antiracist legal system.[41] Similarly, the European Union Race Directive of 2000, which used to be applicable to the UK before its withdrawal from the EU, can still be invoked to highlight what racism is, and how it can and should be tackled in the legal system.[42] Indeed, the courts of England and Wales have shown an awareness of international and foreign law on racism, and it is imperative for antiracist lawyers to make use of the opportunities presented by this.[43]

Collaborative lawyering

Creative lawyering of the type described in the previous section requires the input of those with expert knowledge of race and racism, and it is in this sense

---

[40] The Colston Four case was discussed in the Introduction to this book. See also the Brook House Three case: Griff Ferris et al, 'We Took Direct Action against the UK's Racist Policies, and a Jury Acquitted Us: Resistance Can Succeed' *The Guardian* (16 June 2023).

[41] For a collection of articles that grapple with the relationship between international law and racial justice, see the Symposium on Race, Racism, and International Law (2023) 117 *American Journal of International Law Unbound* 26.

[42] Race Equality Directive 2000/43/EC.

[43] Bob Hepple has outlined some of the cases in which the courts have been cognizant of international law, and he urges courts to interpret the Equality Act 2010 in the spirit of the values enshrined in comparable international laws. See Bob Hepple, *Equality: The Legal Framework* (2nd edn, Hart Publishing 2014), p 220.

that creative lawyering involves collaboration, or 'integrated advocacy'.[44] Collaborative lawyering entails working not just with other like-minded lawyers but also with communities and grassroots organizations, the media, educational settings, policy makers, and other non-legal authorities in order to embed antiracist discourses into legal services, and in order to provide a holistic service to the client.[45] In the previous chapter on legal challenges to racial injustices, we saw that legal outcomes are rarely in and of themselves sufficient to ameliorate the effects of such injustices. The schoolchild who has been racially discriminated against because of their hairstyle, for example, will need help with re-entering the education system, and antiracist lawyering therefore requires engaging with educational specialists. We also saw in Chapter 3 that exclusion from school increases the risk of coming into contact with the criminal justice system, and the child in question will therefore benefit from some advice on how to avoid this. Similarly, those suffering some sort of injustice in the employment and housing sectors will need assistance in the job and housing market as well as legal redress.

A holistic legal service would therefore encompass the provision of support for a range of non-legal issues and social needs. For example, the law firm Commons Law CIC employs a specialist who 'works in parallel with our lawyers to help clients who require support with a range of issues such as debt, employment, family or housing instability or mental illness'.[46] The traumatizing effects of racial injustices often need attending to at the same time as the legal wrong in question, and lawyers representing victims of racism, or defending racialized people caught up in the criminal justice system, can engage with therapists who specialize in working with racialized people.[47]

Collaborative lawyering is also essential to identifying and tackling the problem of intersectional injustices. A lawyer not trained in antiracism might overlook how other characteristics have shaped a person's opportunities, treatment, or outcomes in social interactions and processes. It makes sense, for example, to engage with feminist organizations such as Southall Black Sisters when gender is an issue in the case too.

Embedding a commitment to racial justice within working practices can help lawyers understand how to work collaboratively with other specialist organizations. This is because a commitment to racial justice entails a commitment to amplifying the voices of those affected by racism, which

---

[44] Andrea Giampetro-Meyer et al, 'How Antiracist Lawyers Can Produce Power and Policy Change' (2021) 24 *Journal of Gender, Race, and Justice* 237.
[45] Ife Thompson refers to this as 'movement lawyering'. See Thompson (n 14).
[46] See Commons Law CIC: https://www.commons.legal/crisis-navigation
[47] Specialist organizations include Black, African, and Asian Therapy Network, and Black Minds Matter.

in turn means engaging with community groups. The Black South West Network, for example, explicitly aims to broker relationships between those with an interest in advancing racial justice (which could include lawyers), and those communities who are affected by racial injustices, so that the former can benefit from the expertise of the latter.[48]

Accountable lawyering

In her account of helping a young client who was facing charges of obstructing the police, Thompson recounts that the suspect told her that he has learning difficulties, which is something that he had not revealed to either the undercover police officer who arrested him, or the first lawyer who had originally advised him to plead guilty.[49] Thompson does not claim a cause-and-effect here, but it is possible that the suspect only revealed this to her because she had earned his trust by taking his anxieties around racism and the police seriously. This illustrates why it is important for lawyers to train themselves in racial justice and to follow Sivanandan's advice to see events from the perspective of those with lived experience.[50] Doing so enables them to build a rapport with their client, which ensures that the client is being treated with due respect. This in turn will enable the lawyer to elicit all relevant facts and issues. Thus, in addition to reflection, creativity, and collaboration, lawyers must ensure that they perceive themselves as accountable to their client.

Accountable lawyering can also ensure that the lawyer does not disempower their client if they use their client's issue to advance the broader aim of racial justice. Spurrier was cognizant of this when setting out how her organization would pursue antiracist policies. She noted that the Senior Management Team at Liberty is White and made a commitment to 'redesigning our recruitment process, reviewing our policies and working on processes and structures to include greater diversity of experience and expertise and to create a genuinely inclusive organisational culture'.[51] This was an acknowledgement of the importance of 'lived theory', noting that those with lived experiences of racial injustice must be placed front and centre of campaigning and legal action.[52] Thomas makes a similar point when

---

[48] See Black South West Network: https://www.blacksouthwestnetwork.org/about/brokering-relationships

[49] Thompson (n 35).

[50] Avery F. Gordon, 'On "Lived Theory": An Interview with A. Sivanandan' (2014) 55 *Race & Class* 1 (discussed in Chapter 1).

[51] Spurrier (n 33).

[52] Giampetro-Meyer et al (n 44), p 241 ('Movement lawyering's distinguishing features are constituent accountability and integrated advocacy').

recounting his experiences of representing families at the inquest in 2004 into the New Cross Fire, which had occurred in 1981. Thirteen young Black people died, with another young Black man taking his own life two years later because of the trauma. At the time, the community had felt aggrieved that the police and politicians did not seem to care about the victims of the tragedy. It had been suspected that the fire was caused by a racially motivated attack, but the police investigation was ineffectual, and the deaths were not acknowledged by the state in the way that tragedies usually are. The initial coroner's inquest resulted in an open verdict and was described as a 'farce' by the Chair of the New Cross Parents' Committee, which had been formed to pursue justice for the deceased.[53] The families and communities did not relent in their cause, and a second inquest was opened nearly 25 years after the fire. Thomas writes that he 'accepted the case, thinking that it was likely to be a highly politicised inquest, a wide-ranging investigation that would look at the sins of the '80s, the endemic racism and the National Front, and the failings of the police'. However, he soon came to realize that many of his clients did not want politics to play a role in the inquest. In their view, the first inquest had been tainted by over-politicization, which, they felt, had prevented the truth from emerging about what happened that night in 1981. Thomas writes that this 'was a real eye-opener for me, because it made me realise that what mattered *wasn't* the lawyers' political spin on a case, which is sometimes very easy to do, but *what was best for the clients*'.[54]

Conclusion

The principles for antiracist lawyering outlined in this chapter are not intended to be comprehensive or definitive but are instead proposed as a starting point for aspiring or practising lawyers to think about when pursuing antiracist objectives in their work. Lawyers will always have to work within a framework that is limited but can use these principles when determining what legal strategies and tactics will ameliorate racial injustices, and when making sure that they do not entrench racial injustices through legal action.

---

[53] Quoted in Thomas (n 25), p 262.
[54] Thomas (n 25), p 266 (emphasis in original).

Conclusion

The Shamima Begum case: 21st-century racial injustices meet 17th-century legal norms

This book started with the story of the Colston Four and noted that the case brought the 17th-century trade in enslaved people before the legal system of the 21st century. As the rest of the book has highlighted, this was not quite the juxtaposition that it might have appeared to be, because the operation of the law in the 21st century very much allows the structural racism wrought by Britain's history of imperialism to survive, if not thrive, in England and Wales. This is not to say that law's role in facilitating racial injustices today mirrors or replicates law's role in the colonial era – the law today does not officially sanction enslavement or other types of racial injustices that were part of colonial rule. However, as we have seen, there are continuities between the past and present because the types of racial injustices which are challenged in the legal system today have their roots in the colonial era, and in the legal system of that era. In this sense, we have seen the reverse of the Colston Four case: contemporary racial injustices of the 21st century often confront legal norms and processes that have been shaped by historic discourses on race and law, which can sometimes be traced as far back as the 17th century.

A case which illustrates this point vividly is that of Shamima Begum, who was born in the United Kingdom in 1999, and was a British citizen under section 1(1) of the British Nationality Act 1981. In February 2015, when she was 15 years old, Begum left her home in Bethnal Green with two friends and travelled to Syria to join the Islamic State of Iraq and the Levant (ISIL), a militant group that is notorious for its brutal violence and acts of terror, particularly against Western liberal democracies such as the UK. Reactions to the girls' involvement with ISIL were mixed. Some sections of the British media were unforgiving, with Allison Pearson writing a year later in *The Daily Telegraph* that the 'jihadi girls will only have themselves to blame' for whatever happened to them next.[1] Others expressed concern

---

[1] Allison Pearson, 'The Jihadi Girls Will Only Have Themselves to Blame' *The Daily Telegraph* (26 February 2016), p 23.

for the girls' welfare, with Nicky Morgan, the Education Secretary, stating that she hoped they would be safely returned to the UK.[2]

Begum's friends died soon after they left England, but in 2019, aged 19 years old, she was discovered alive in a refugee camp in Northern Syria by a British journalist. Begum was resoundingly vilified in the British press when she said that although she wanted to return to the UK, she did not regret joining ISIL.[3] The political reaction matched the media's portrayal of her as an enemy of the UK, and the Home Secretary exercised his powers to revoke her British citizenship. The British Nationality Act 1981 permits the Home Secretary to strip a person born British of their citizenship if two conditions are met. First, it must be considered 'conducive to the public good' to do so.[4] Although it is arguably more 'conducive to the public good' for Begum to be detained in the UK where she can be monitored, rather than left in a refugee camp abroad, Sajid Javid, the Home Secretary, declared it was in the public interest to revoke her citizenship because of her associations with ISIL. Second, the 1981 Act only permits citizenship to be stripped if the affected person will not be left stateless.[5] Javid said that Begum would not be rendered stateless because her parents had been born in Bangladesh, and she would therefore qualify for Bangladeshi citizenship. It is this second limb of the test that illustrates how the present cannot be disconnected from Britain's past. Put simply, one can only satisfy the second limb if they have dual nationality, and this means that people racialized as something other than White British are more susceptible to having their citizenship revoked, because they are more likely to have dual nationality. That is, a person born to White British parents, and a person born to parents who were born abroad, can both have been born in the UK and lived almost identical lives in the UK, but the latter will be subject to citizen-stripping

---

[2] Alexandra Topping, 'Education Secretary Writes to School of Girls Believed to Have Fled to Syria' *The Guardian* (25 February 2015), Available from: https://www.theguardian.com/world/2015/feb/25/education-secretary-nicky-morgan-syria-bethnal-green-academy

[3] For a summary of headlines and media coverage, see Harriet Farnham, 'What the Media Circus Surrounding Shamima Begum Can Teach Us about Gender and Nation' (LSE Engenderings, 3 April 2019), Available from: https://blogs.lse.ac.uk/gender/2019/04/03/gender_and_nation. For an example, see Sophie Law, 'ISIS Bride Shamima Begum Might NEVER Be De-radicalised Because She Has Shown "No Remorse or Regret" for Running Away to Syria, UK Counter-Terror Expert Warns' *The Daily Mail* (16 February 2019), Available from: https://www.dailymail.co.uk/news/article-6712341/Shamima-Begum-challenge-radicalise-counter-extremism-expert.html?ico=topics_pagination_desktop

[4] British Nationality Act 1981, s 40(2).

[5] British Nationality Act 1981, s 40(4).

whereas the former will not.⁶ Although the latter might include White-skinned people from Australia, Canada, or New Zealand, for example, they are much more likely to be people racialized as something other than White given the history of British colonialism.⁷ In her review of the Windrush scandal, Williams suggested that the law on citizen-stripping 'arguably created a second tier of citizenship'.⁸ Just as colonial laws created a two-tiered legal system demarcated along racial lines, so too does the contemporary legal framework for immigration, nationality, and citizenship.

The inequities in the law on citizen-stripping are objectionable in principle but are even more troubling when we consider the practical effects of this sanction. Domestic courts, international legal authorities, and political philosophers have emphasized that the right to citizenship, or the right to nationality, is of fundamental importance because it is effectively 'the right to have rights'.⁹ This is because a person can only exercise their general legal rights in a political community if they are first classed as a citizen of that community. While in theory people like Begum have the option of exercising their rights in their other state of nationality, in practice this is not always straightforward. Bangladeshi authorities, for example, stated that she would not be welcomed to Bangladesh given her links with ISIL,¹⁰ leading Jonathan Sumption, a former justice of the UK Supreme Court, to describe her Bangladeshi citizenship as 'a legal fiction' because it has 'no practical reality'. As Sumption writes, this is not a situation that is unique to Begum, with many other former British citizens being left in similar circumstances.¹¹ In other words, being deprived of citizenship is akin to being deprived of legal personhood – a term that we considered in Chapter 2 when considering how

---

[6] United Nations Special Rapporteur on Counter-Terrorism and Human Rights, 'The Human Rights Consequences of Citizenship Stripping in the Context of Counter-Terrorism with a Particular Application to North-East Syria' (Office of the High Commissioner for Human Rights 2022), pp 14–15.

[7] The Home Office does not publish statistics on the demographics of people deprived of their citizenship, but the Institute of Race Relations has published research which asserts that 'the vast majority of those deprived are Muslim men with south Asian or middle Eastern/north African heritage'. See Frances Webber, 'Citizenship: From Right to Privilege' (Institute of Race Relations, September 2022).

[8] Wendy Williams, 'Windrush Lessons Learned Review' (19 March 2020), p 56.

[9] See *Pham v Secretary of State for the Home Department* [2018] EWCA Civ 2064 [30] and [49]; *Trop v Dulles* 356 US 86 (1958) (101–2); United Nations Special Rapporteur on Counter-Terrorism and Human Rights (n 6), p 4; Hannah Arendt, *The Origins of Totalitarianism* (first published 1951, Penguin Classics 2017), chapter 9.

[10] 'Shamima Begum Will Not Be Allowed Here, Bangladesh Says' *BBC News* (21 February 2019), Available from: https://www.bbc.co.uk/news/uk-47312207

[11] Jonathan Sumption, Letter to the Editor, *The Guardian* (26 February 2023), Available from: https://www.theguardian.com/uk-news/2023/feb/26/the-real-scandal-of-the-shamima-begum-citizenship-case

legal authorities in the 17th and 18th centuries responded to questions about the legal status of enslaved people. This is not to equate Begum with enslaved people of that era, but rather to make the point that Begum's case is the reverse of the Colston Four case. Whereas the latter case brought 21st-century legal proceedings to bear on a 17th-century phenomenon, Begum's case brought a 17th-century legal tool (denial of legal personhood to racialized people) to bear on a modern-day phenomenon (racialized discourses of terrorism).

Given the severity of being deprived of citizenship, Begum challenged Javid's decision and applied for leave to enter the UK so that she could provide effective instructions to her lawyers and take part in legal proceedings. Javid refused her request, and the ensuing legal proceedings therefore broadly revolved around two questions: whether the Home Secretary's decision to deprive her of citizenship was lawful, and whether Begum's right to a fair trial was infringed by the refusal to grant her leave. The case made its way through the Special Immigration Appeals Commission, the Divisional Court, the Court of Appeal, and finally the UK Supreme Court, where all questions were resolved in favour of the Home Secretary. The Court held that on the question of citizen-stripping, the judiciary should broadly defer to the judgement of the Home Secretary since the question involves matters of national security. On the question of her right to fair trial, the Court held that this right did not necessitate granting her leave to enter the UK if the Home Secretary considered her a threat to national security.[12]

The case as a whole speaks to several of the themes that have permeated this study of law's relationship with racial justice. First, it speaks to the ways in which law has been used to structuralize racism in society, and the way in which legal authorities have then set limits on law's capacity to tackle structural racism. The revocation of Begum's citizenship (based on legislation), and the limits placed by the judiciary on the use of law to challenge the Home Secretary's decision to remove her legal personhood (based on the principle of deference to the executive), must be understood within the historical context of the use of law to structuralize racism by denying racialized people, such as the enslaved, legal personhood and certain legal rights. Second, the case highlights the legal system's inability to grapple with intersectional harms. Begum has at times been cast as a victim, given that she was a child when she was manipulated into travelling to Syria, where she was subjugated by adult men. She has also been portrayed as 'heartless', 'arrogant', and an 'unapologetic monster' because she does not conform to societal stereotypes of

---

[12] *R (Begum) v Special Immigration Appeals Commission & Anor* [2021] UKSC 7. See in particular [134]–[136]. In 2023, the Special Immigration Appeals Commission rejected another challenge from Begum, ruling that the Home Secretary had acted lawfully notwithstanding evidence that Begum had been trafficked as a child. See *Begum v Secretary of State for Home Department* [2023] H.R.L.R. 6 (Sp Imm App Comm).

femininity, or stereotypes of the demure Muslim wife.[13] The Supreme Court, though, was either unable or unwilling to grapple with the complexities of intersectionality. In supporting the Home Secretary's determination that she posed a threat to national security, the Court acknowledged that there were differences between men and women members of ISIL, stating that women were primarily 'wives of fighters and mothers of their children'. However, the Court then decided that these differences were immaterial, ruling instead that '[a]ny individual, male or female, who returned to the United Kingdom having spent a prolonged period of time in ISIL-controlled territory was likely to have developed the capability to carry out an attack'.[14] There was no recognition of her status as a child when she was manipulated into travelling to Syria, or how her sex compounded her vulnerabilities. Third, the case was another example of law's reluctance to hear the voices of racialized people, since Begum was denied the chance to enter the UK so she could engage effectively with legal proceedings.

These issues – law's inability, or legal officials' unwillingness, to grapple with the structuralized nature of racism, intersectionality, and the lived experiences of racialized people – are just three of the six concepts that have informed the analysis of the limits of law in the struggle for racial justice. We have seen throughout that law has also been involved in the construction of the idea of 'race', while legal officials have simultaneously placed limits on the use of law to address evolving understandings of race and racism. For example, we saw in Chapter 4 that people of Gypsy, Roma, and Traveller (GRT) heritage have struggled to make use of hate crime laws because legal authorities are reluctant to conclude that violence towards GRT people is racially motivated. And in the case of *Taiwo*, we saw that the courts were unable to understand the role of immigration law in the construction of racial categories.[15]

We have also seen that the law has often only advanced the interests of racialized people when to do so does not inconvenience those classed as White British. The passage of the Race Relations Act in 1965, for example, was only possible because of the passage of the Commonwealth Immigrants Act in 1962, which meant that the requirement to treat racialized people without discrimination was only applicable in the context of encouraging racialized people to adapt their way of life so that they could integrate with White communities.[16] And we have seen that legal processes are sometimes inappropriate, if not antithetical, to the struggle for racial justice. Adversarial

---

[13] Farnham (n 3).
[14] *R (Begum) v Special Immigration Appeals Commission & Anor* [2021] UKSC 7, [17] and [19].
[15] See, respectively, Chapter 4, n 104 and n 63 and accompanying text.
[16] See 'The development of laws to tackle racial injustices: 1965–93', in Chapter 4.

processes, for example, can exacerbate racial tensions rather than ease them. This, we saw, is a particular problem in the context of the law on race hate crimes.

Although we have focused on the limits of law and legal action in the struggle for racial justice, we have also seen that racial justice campaigners and lawyers have been brave and creative in using the law to advance their cause. From Sharp's novel use of the Habeas Corpus Act in the 1770s, to the Mangrove Nine's unique legal strategy in 1971, and to the establishment of guides to antiracist lawyering and the development of holistic approaches to legal action in the 2020s, it is clear that although legal action will not in and of itself bring an end to all racial injustices, legal action can at least alleviate some of those injustices and is an important cog in the machinery of racial justice. To underscore the utility of law, and to end this book on a relatively hopeful note, we can briefly explore how law is being used by nationals of other countries to challenge the legacy of British colonial rule abroad.

The use of law to challenge the legacy of colonialism abroad

The post-World War years saw the breakup of the British Empire, but independence from British rule did not undo the effects of colonialism in these newly formed states overnight. The legacy of colonialism has manifested itself in myriad ways. First, social, legal, and political structures remain in place in many former colonies. Second, for reasons outlined subsequently, many states have retained the colonial emphasis on 'law and order'.[17] Third, contemporary deleterious living conditions in many former British colonies have their roots in imperialism and colonial rule. As a consequence, international, regional, and domestic legal systems have been deployed to undo this complex colonial legacy. Legal challenges to the use of the death penalty in former colonies, the use of legal action by Kenyans who suffered under British rule in the 1950s, and the legal case for reparations for slavery are just three examples that illustrate the growing use of law in the struggle for racial justice. We can consider these in turn.

Legal challenges to the death penalty

We saw in Chapter 2 that criminal justice systems played a key role in maintaining rule and imposing racial hierarchies in the colonies. The death penalty, which was introduced to many colonies by British authorities,

---

[17] Patrick Gathara, 'Colonize and Punish' *New Internationalist* (13 April 2022), Available from: https://newint.org/features/2022/02/07/colonize-and-punish

is a case in point.[18] In Barbados, for example, enslaved persons faced different procedures in capital cases from those who were not enslaved, illustrating clearly how punishments were used to create and sustain racial divisions.[19] When slavery was abolished across the Empire in 1833, the White population in places like Barbados called for even more robust and stricter criminal justice measures to keep what they perceived to be a dangerous and unruly population under control.[20] These calls only solidified in the aftermath of events like the Morant Bay rebellion in Jamaica in 1865. Therefore, as the use of the death penalty declined in Britain, it conversely expanded in places like Barbados as White planters sought to maintain order.[21]

When Barbados secured independence from British rule in 1966, it adopted a new constitution that contained provisions relating to the protection of individual rights. This could have been a moment to abolish the death penalty, but independence from formal British rule did not bring independence from the legal structures and societal mores that had prevailed under colonial rule. Newly independent states wanted to prove to themselves and the international community that they could self-govern without descending into chaos and anarchy, and the ruling classes were heavily influenced by the use of criminal justice measures to maintain order.[22] It followed that many colonial-era measures of control, such as the death penalty, were retained by newly independent states in legal systems that mimicked the systems of colonial rule.

Like many other states that severed themselves from British rule, Barbados agreed to keep the Judicial Committee of the Privy Council (JCPC) in London as the last appellate tribunal in its legal system. This meant that appeals in death penalty cases soon started to be heard by British-based judges in a London-based court. At first, the JCPC adopted a non-interventionist approach, refusing to intervene with the administration of capital punishment in the former colony. From the 1990s, though, the Council issued a series of rulings that drastically curtailed the use of capital punishment in places that were under its jurisdiction. Many of these were litigated in part by British-based lawyers who used standards of international human rights law in their arguments. Cases included challenges to the length of time people

---

[18] On British colonial rule and the death penalty generally, see Saul Lehrfreund, 'Undoing the British Colonial Legacy: The Judicial Reform of the Death Penalty' in Carol S. Steiker and Jordan M. Steiker (eds), *Comparative Capital Punishment* (Edward Elgar Publishing 2019).

[19] Lynsey Black et al, 'The Death Penalty in Barbados: Reforming a Colonial Legacy' [2023] 12 *International Journal for Crime, Justice and Social Democracy* 27, 28.

[20] Black et al (n 19), p 28.

[21] Black et al (n 19), p 29.

[22] Black et al (n 19), pp 29–30.

spent on death row, to the processes relating to the prerogative of mercy, and to the use of mandatory death sentences.[23] Although none of these explicitly addressed the question of race, it was becoming increasingly clear that the law could be used to challenge a punishment that was historically bound up with the racial injustices of colonial rule. But in many states, the existence of the death penalty itself was immune from legal challenge by virtue of 'savings clauses' in domestic constitutions, which protected certain laws and practices such as the death penalty from constitutional challenge.[24]

In 2005, Barbados removed itself from the jurisdiction of the Privy Council in favour of the Caribbean Court of Justice (CCJ) instead, as a means of severing its remaining ties to the former imperial state. And in 2018, the CCJ ruled the mandatory death penalty in Barbados to be unconstitutional, notwithstanding the savings clause in the constitution. In its ruling, the Court emphasized that laws should not be 'calcified to reflect the colonial times',[25] a statement which effectively opens the door to legal challenges to other vestiges of racialized colonial rule.

Justice for Kenyans

Legal action has also been used to compel the British government to pay compensation to over 5,000 Kenyans who had suffered torture and other forms of ill-treatment during the suppression of the Mau Mau uprising in the 1950s.[26] In 2013, the Foreign Secretary William Hague acknowledged the harms inflicted by colonial officials and offered an apology: "The British government recognises that Kenyans were subject to torture and other forms of ill-treatment at the hands of the colonial administration. The British government sincerely regrets that these abuses took place and that they marred Kenya's progress towards independence."[27] The government had initially refused to pay compensation, though, and only relented when the High Court ruled that the Kenyans had an arguable legal case and permitted their claims to proceed to trial. The case therefore illustrated the benefits of using legal action to compel political action, although it should be noted that as part of the out-of-court settlement, the government continued to deny legal liability for the wrongs inflicted under the colonial administration.

---

[23] For an outline of how and why the Privy Council's approach evolved, see Lehrfreund (n 18).
[24] Lehrfreund (n 18), p 283.
[25] *Nervais and Severin v The Queen* [2018] CCJ 19 (AJ) [65].
[26] See Chapter 2, n 80 and accompanying text.
[27] 'Mau Mau Torture Victims to Receive Compensation – Hague' *BBC News* (6 June 2013), Available from: https://www.bbc.co.uk/news/uk-22790037

The legal case for reparations for slavery

The payment of compensation to Kenyans has encouraged descendants of the enslaved to mount a legal case for reparations for slavery. Countries of the Caribbean Community (CARICOM) have suggested making a complaint under the CERD, which requires state parties such as the UK to take effective measures to ensure that laws and policies do not have the effect of perpetuating racial discrimination. CARICOM has argued that the official British policy of refusing to apologise for slavery or to make reparations for the trade in enslaved people has perpetuated racial injustices in CARICOM nations, thus violating the UK's obligations under CERD. They note, for example, that illiteracy and public health crises, which disadvantage and discriminate against CARICOM nationals, are the legacies of slavery. Lord Anthony Gifford has explained why he supports CARICOM's plans: '[W]hy do the peoples of the Caribbean suffer racial discrimination and racial disadvantage? It is because the UK and other European nations committed crimes against humanity against their ancestors and have never paid a penny of compensation.'[28] Patrick Robinson, a judge on the International Court of Justice, has stated that the refusal to apologise or to offer reparations is not legally sustainable. In his words, payment of reparations is "required by history and it is required by law". This is because, in part, "[r]eparations have been paid for other wrongs [such as those in Kenya] and obviously far more quickly, far more speedily".[29]

This brief account of these three developments illustrates the promises of antiracist lawyering that was outlined in Chapter 5. Each has involved reflection, creative use of the law, collaboration, and accountability to those affected by racial injustices.

Conclusion

Throughout this book, we have seen that law's historical and contemporary relationship with racial justice is complicated. At times, law has been explicitly used to create and entrench racial injustices, but at other times the

---

[28] Lord Anthony Gifford, 'Key Legal Aspects of the Claim for Reparation' (2019) 68 *Social and Economic Studies* 249, 252. Also see Esther Stanford-Xosei, 'Why We Still Need Holistic Reparations for Slavery' *The Independent* (30 October 2022), Available from: https://www.independent.co.uk/voices/reparations-slavery-africa-black-history-month-b2213721.html

[29] Aamna Mohdin, 'UK Cannot Ignore Calls for Slavery Reparations, Says Leading UN Judge' *The Guardian* (22 August 2023), Available from: https://www.theguardian.com/world/2023/aug/22/uk-cannot-ignore-calls-for-slavery-reparations-says-leading-un-judge-patrick-robinson

legal system has been successfully used to advance racial justice. At times, the racism of law has been explicit; at other times, it has been veiled. And the relationship spans both time and space: the nuances and complexities of this relationship traverse several centuries and different aspects of social life. The brief discussion in this chapter of the use of law by Barbadians, Kenyans, and the broader Caribbean community shows that the paradoxical relationship also transcends and traverses national boundaries and jurisdictions. And this account also shows how antiracist lawyering spans time, subjects, and boundaries. Although the legal system is not the panacea to the ills of racial injustices, and although the struggle for racial justice is a perpetual one, lawyers and activists can draw on the insights of Critical Race Theory and doctrines of antiracism to at least ameliorate some of the effects of racial injustices, and to contribute to broader efforts to promote racial justice.

References

4in10, Just for Kids Law, and Children's Rights Alliance for England, 'Race, Poverty and School Exclusions in London' (2020), Available from: https://londonchallengepovertyweek.org.uk/wp-content/uploads/2020/10/RacePovertyandSchoolExclusions_FV-1.pdf

Abuya, E.O., Krause, U., and Mayblin, L., 'The Neglected Colonial Legacy of the 1951 Refugee Convention' (2021) 59 *International Migration* 265.

Adébísí, F., 'The Only Accurate Part of "BAME" Is the "And" …' (African Skies blog, 8 July 2019), Available from: https://folukeafrica.com/the-only-acceptable-part-of-bame-is-the-and

Adébísí, F., *Decolonisation and Legal Knowledge: Reflections on Power and Possibility* (Bristol University Press 2023).

Akala, *Natives: Race and Class in the Ruins of Empire* (Two Roads 2018).

Alexander, C. and Shankley, W., 'Ethnic Inequalities in the State Education System in England' in B. Byrne, C. Alexander, O. Khan, J. Nazroo, and W. Shankley (eds), *Ethnicity, Race and Inequality in the UK: State of the Nation* (Policy Press 2020).

Amnesty International, 'Submission to the Windrush Lessons Learned Review' (October 2018), Available from: https://www.amnesty.org.uk/files/Resources/AIUK%20to%20Home%20Office%20Windrush%20Lessons%20Learned%20Review.pdf

Anderson, B., *Us and Them? The Dangerous Politics of Immigration Control* (Oxford University Press 2013).

Anderson, D.M., *Histories of the Hanged: Britain's Dirty War in Kenya and the End of Empire* (Weidenfeld & Nicolson 2005).

Angiolini, E., 'Report of the Independent Review of Deaths and Serious Incidents in Police Custody' (January 2017), Available from: https://www.gov.uk/government/publications/deaths-and-serious-incidents-in-police-custody

Anthony, H. and Crilly, C., 'Equality, Human Rights and Access to Civil Law Justice: A Literature Review' (Equality and Human Rights Commission 2015).

Arendt, H., *The Origins of Totalitarianism* (first published 1951, Penguin Classics 2017).

Art Against Knives, Kids of Color, No More Exclusions, Northern Police Monitoring Project, INQUEST, Joint Enterprise Not Guilty by Association, et al, 'Holding Our Own: A Guide to Non-policing Solutions to Serious Youth Violence' (2023), Available from: https://www.libertyhumanrights.org.uk/wp-content/uploads/2023/04/HoldingOurOwn_Digital-SinglePages.pdf

Atrey, S., *Intersectional Discrimination* (Oxford University Press 2019).

Atrey, S., 'Structural Racism and Race Discrimination' (2021) 74 *Current Legal Problems* 1.

Back, L. and Solomos, J. (eds), *Theories of Race and Racism: A Reader* (3rd edn, Routledge 2022).

Baksi, C. 'Landmarks in Law: When the Mangrove Nine Beat the British State' *The Guardian* (10 November 2020), Available from: https://www.theguardian.com/law/2020/nov/10/landmarks-in-law-when-the-mangrove-nine-beat-the-british-state

Baldwin, J., 'As Much Truth as One Can Bear', *The New York Times Book Review* (14 January 1962).

Ball, E.L., Seijas, T., and Snyder, T.L. (eds), *As If She Were Free: A Collective Biography of Women and Emancipation in the Americas* (Cambridge University Press 2020).

Banks, T.L., 'Elizabeth Key, Seventeenth-Century Virginia (US)' in E.L. Ball, T. Seijas, and T.L. Snyder (eds), *As If She Were Free: A Collective Biography of Women and Emancipation in the Americas* (Cambridge University Press 2020).

BAPIO, 'Bridging the Gap' (2020), Available from: https://www.bapio.co.uk/differential-attainment-in-healthcare-professionals

Bayly, C.A., 'The Second British Empire' in R. Winks and W.R. Louis (eds), *The Oxford History of the British Empire: Volume V; Historiography* (Oxford University Press 1999).

BBC News, 'Boys Guilty of Killing "Gypsy"' (28 November 2003), Available from: http://news.bbc.co.uk/1/hi/england/merseyside/3246518.stm

BBC News, 'Mau Mau Torture Victims to Receive Compensation – Hague' (6 June 2013), Available from: https://www.bbc.co.uk/news/uk-22790037

BBC News, 'Shamima Begum Will Not Be Allowed Here, Bangladesh Says' (21 February 2019), Available from: https://www.bbc.co.uk/news/uk-47312207

BBC News, 'Campaigners Criticise Government Race Report' (31 March 2021), Available from: https://www.bbc.co.uk/news/uk-56592331

BBC News, 'Gang Violence Matrix: Met Police to Overhaul Controversial Database' (12 November 2022), Available from: https://www.bbc.co.uk/news/uk-england-london-63568880

Bell, D., '*Brown v. Board of Education* and the Interest-Convergence Dilemma' (1980) 93 *Harvard Law Review* 518.

Berlant, L.G., *Cruel Optimism* (Duke University Press 2011).

Bhopal, K., '"What about Us?" Gypsies, Travellers and "White Racism" in Secondary Schools in England' (2011) 21 *International Studies in Sociology of Education* 315.

Birthrights, 'Systemic Racism, Not Broken Bodies: An Inquiry into Racial Injustice and Human Rights in UK Maternity Care' (2022), Available from: https://www.birthrights.org.uk/wp-content/uploads/2022/05/Birthrights-inquiry-systemic-racism_exec-summary_May-22-web.pdf

Bingham, T.H., *The Rule of Law* (Penguin Books 2011).

Black, L., Seal, L., Seemungal, F., Malkani, B., and Ball, R., 'The Death Penalty in Barbados: Reforming a Colonial Legacy' (2023) 12 *International Journal for Crime, Justice and Social Democracy* 27.

Bonilla-Silva, E., 'What Makes Systemic Racism *Systemic*?' (2021) 91 *Sociological Inquiry* 513.

Boodia-Canoo, N.S., 'Researching Colonialism and Colonial Legacies from a Legal Perspective' (2020) 54 *The Law Teacher* 517.

Booth, R., 'Landlord Admits It Made Assumptions about Family in Mouldy Rochdale Flat' *The Guardian* (22 November 2022), Available from: https://www.theguardian.com/society/2022/nov/22/landlord-assumptions-family-mouldy-rochdale-flat-boroughwide-housing

Booth, R., 'Social Landlord in England Said Mould Was "Acceptable" in Refugees' Homes' *The Guardian* (28 March 2023), Available from: https://www.theguardian.com/world/2023/mar/28/social-landlord-england-said-mould-acceptable-refugees-homes

Bowleg, L., '"Once You've Blended the Cake, You Can't Take the Parts Back to the Main Ingredients": Black Gay and Bisexual Men's Descriptions and Experiences of Intersectionality' (2013) 68 *Sex Roles* 754.

Brantlinger, P., 'Kipling's "The White Man's Burden" and Its Afterlives' (2007) 50 *English Literature in Transition, 1880–1920*, 172.

Brescia, R.H., 'Creative Lawyering for Social Change' (2019) 35 *Georgia State University Law Review* 529.

Bridges, L., 'The Lawrence Inquiry: Incompetence, Corruption, and Institutional Racism' (1999) 26 *Journal of Law and Society* 298.

Bridges, L., 'Race, Law and the State' (2001) 43 *Race & Class* 61.

Brown, M., 'Race, Science and the Construction of Native Criminality in Colonial India' (2001) 5 *Theoretical Criminology* 345.

Brown, M. and Booth, R., 'Death of Two-Year-Old from Mould in Flat a "Defining Moment", Says Coroner' *The Guardian* (15 November 2022), Available from: https://www.theguardian.com/uk-news/2022/nov/15/death-of-two-year-old-awaab-ishak-chronic-mould-in-flat-a-defining-moment-says-coroner

Bulman, M. and Kelly, N., 'Revealed: UK Has Failed to Resettle Afghans Facing Torture and Death Despite Promise' *The Observer* (4 December 2022), Available from: https://www.theguardian.com/world/2022/dec/03/revealed-uk-has-failed-to-resettle-afghans-facing-torture-and-death-despite-promise

Bunce, R. and Field, P., 'Mangrove Nine: The Court Challenge against Police Racism in Notting Hill' *The Guardian* (29 November 2010), Available from: https://www.theguardian.com/law/2010/nov/29/mangrove-nine-40th-anniversary

Burgum, S. and Powell, R., 'The Policing Bill Will Criminalise Gypsy and Traveller Families: There Is a Better Approach' (*The Conversation*, 25 January 2022), Available from: https://theconversation.com/the-policing-bill-will-criminalise-gypsy-and-traveller-families-there-is-a-better-approach-174487

Burns, G., Interview with Margaret Thatcher (*World in Action*, 27 January 1978), Available from: https://www.margaretthatcher.org/document/103485

Byrne, B., Alexander, C., Khan, O., Nazroo, J., and Shankley, W. (eds), *Ethnicity, Race and Inequality in the UK: State of the Nation* (Policy Press 2020).

Casey, L., 'An Independent Review into the Standards of Behaviour and Internal Culture of the Metropolitan Police Service' (March 2023), Available from: https://www.met.police.uk/SysSiteAssets/media/downloads/met/about-us/baroness-casey-review/update-march-2023/baroness-casey-review-march-2023a.pdf

Cathcart, B., *The Case of Stephen Lawrence* (Penguin 2000).

Chakraborti, N. and Garland, J., *Hate Crime: Impact, Causes & Responses* (2nd edn, SAGE 2015).

Chamberlain, M.E., *The Scramble for Africa* (3rd edn, Routledge 2013)

Charmantier, I., 'Linnaeus and Race' (Linnean Society of London nd), Available from: https://www.linnean.org/learning/who-was-linnaeus/linnaeus-and-race

Clarke, B. and Williams, P., '(Re)Producing Guilt in Suspect Communities: The Centrality of Racialisation in Joint Enterprise Prosecutions' (2020) 9 *International Journal for Crime, Justice and Social Democracy* 116.

Clayton, G. and Firth, G., *Immigration and Asylum Law* (9th edn, Oxford University Press 2021).

Commission on Race and Ethnic Disparities, 'The Report of the Commission on Race and Ethnic Disparities' (2021), Available from: https://www.gov.uk/government/publications/the-report-of-the-commission-on-race-and-ethnic-disparities

Corcoran, H., Lader, D., and Smith, K., 'Hate Crime, England and Wales, 2014/15' (Home Office, 13 October 2015), Available from: https://assets.publishing.service.gov.uk/government/uploads/system/uploads/attachment_data/file/467366/hosb0515.pdf

Cork, T., 'How Bristol Challenged Colston for 100 Years' *Bristol Post* (7 June 2021), Available from: https://www.bristolpost.co.uk/news/bristol-news/how-bristol-challenged-colston-100-5496144

Cotter, W.R., 'The *Somerset* Case and the Abolition of Slavery in England' (1994) 79 *History* 31.

Counsel Magazine, 'Obituary: Ian MacDonald' (20 November 2019).
Courts and Tribunals Judiciary, 'Judicial Diversity and Inclusion Strategy 2020–2025' (2020), Available from: https://www.judiciary.uk/wp-content/uploads/2020/11/Judicial-Diversity-and-Inclusion-Strategy-2020-2025-v2.pdf
Crenshaw, K., 'Demarginalizing the Intersection of Race and Sex: A Black Feminist Critique of Antidiscrimination Doctrine, Feminist Theory and Antiracist Politics' (1989) 1 *University of Chicago Legal Forum* 139.
Crenshaw, K., *On Intersectionality: Essential Writings* (New Press 2022).
Crenshaw, K., Gotanda, N., Peller, G., and Thomas, K. (eds), *Critical Race Theory: The Key Writings That Formed the Movement* (New Press 1995).
The Daily Telegraph, 'Home Secretary Announces Gurkhas Can Stay in Britain' (21 May 2009).
Dalrymple, W. and Anand, A., 'The East India Company' (16 August 2022), Available from: https://www.globalplayer.com/podcasts/42KuVh
Davies, K.G., *The Royal African Company* (Octagon Books 1975).
Davis, A.Y., *Freedom Is a Constant Struggle: Ferguson, Palestine, and the Foundations of a Movement* (Frank Barat ed, Haymarket Books 2016).
De Groot, L., 'New Baring Foundation Funding for Racial Justice' (Baring Foundation, 4 February 2021), Available from: https://baringfoundation.org.uk/blog-post/new-baring-foundation-funding-for-racial-justice
Delgado, R. and Stefancic, J. (eds), *The Derrick Bell Reader* (New York University Press 2005).
Delgado, R. and Stefancic, J., *Critical Race Theory: An Introduction* (3rd edn, New York University Press 2017).
Department for Business, Energy & Industrial Strategy, 'Government Response to Baroness McGregor-Smith' (nd).
Department for Education, 'Promoting Fundamental British Values as Part of SMSC in Schools' (November 2014), Available from: https://assets.publishing.service.gov.uk/government/uploads/system/uploads/attachment_data/file/380595/SMSC_Guidance_Maintained_Schools.pdf
Department for Education, 'GCSE Results (Attainment 8)' (18 March 2022), Available from: https://www.ethnicity-facts-figures.service.gov.uk/education-skills-and-training/11-to-16-years-old/gcse-results-attainment-8-for-children-aged-14-to-16-key-stage-4/latest
Department for Education, 'Permanent Exclusions and Suspensions in England' (updated 8 August 2023), Available from: https://explore-education-statistics.service.gov.uk/find-statistics/permanent-and-fixed-period-exclusions-in-england
Dorsett, S. and Hunter, I. (eds), *Law and Politics in British Colonial Thought* (Palgrave Macmillan US 2010).
Dorsett, S. and McLaren, J., *Legal Histories of the British Empire: Laws, Engagements and Legacies* (Routledge 2014).

Du Bois, W.E.B., *Black Reconstruction in America: 1860–1880* (first published 1935, Free Press 1998).

Du Bois, W.E.B., *The Souls of Black Folk: Authoritative Text, Contexts, Criticism* (first published 1903, W.W. Norton 1999).

Dummett, A., *A Portrait of English Racism* (Penguin 1973).

Eddo-Lodge, R., *Why I'm No Longer Talking to White People about Race* (expanded edn, Bloomsbury Publishing 2018).

'Editorial' (1975) 16 *Race & Class* 231.

El-Enany, N., *(B)Ordering Britain: Law, Race and Empire* (Manchester University Press 2020).

Elkins, C., *Legacy of Violence: A History of the British Empire* (The Bodley Head 2022).

Equality and Human Rights Commission, 'New Legal Fund to Tackle Race Discrimination' (23 November 2021), Available from: https://www.equalityhumanrights.com/media-centre/news/new-legal-fund-tackle-race-discrimination

Equality and Human Rights Commission, 'Contractor Who Suffered Monkey Chants and Racial Abuse at Probation Service Wins Payout' (24 August 2023), Available from: https://www.equalityhumanrights.com/contractor-who-suffered-monkey-chants-and-racial-abuse-probation-service-wins-payout

Farnham, H., 'What the Media Circus Surrounding Shamima Begum Can Teach Us about Gender and Nation' (LSE Engenderings, 3 April 2019), Available from: https://blogs.lse.ac.uk/gender/2019/04/03/gender_and_nation

Ferris, G., Micklethwaite, R., and Lynch, C., 'We Took Direct Action against the UK's Racist Policies, and a Jury Acquitted Us: Resistance Can Succeed' *The Guardian* (16 June 2023), Available from: https://www.theguardian.com/commentisfree/2023/jun/16/direct-action-uk-policies-deportations-to-jamaica

Finney, N., Nazroo, J., Bécares, L., Kapadia, D., and Shlomo, N. (eds), *Racism and Ethnic Inequality in a Time of Crises: Findings from the Evidence for Equality National Survey* (Policy Press 2023).

Fitzpatrick, P., 'Racism and the Innocence of Law' (1987) 14 *Journal of Law and Society* 119.

Fitzpatrick, P. (ed), *Nationalism, Racism, and the Rule of Law* (Dartmouth Publishing 1995).

Fitzpatrick, P. and Hunt, A., 'Critical Legal Studies: Introduction' (1987) 14 *Journal of Law and Society* 1.

Fredman, S. (ed), *Discrimination and Human Rights: The Case of Racism* (Oxford University Press 2001).

Fredman, S., *Discrimination Law* (3rd edn, Oxford University Press 2022).

Friends, Families, and Travellers, 'Race Hate and Prejudice Faced by Gypsies and Travellers in England' (March 2023, updated October 2023), Available from: https://www.gypsy-traveller.org/wp-content/uploads/2023/03/Race_hate_and_prejudice_faced_by_Gypsies_and_Travellers_in_England_Briefing.pdf

Fryer, P., *Staying Power: The History of Black People in Britain* (Pluto Press 2018).

Gamble, J. and McCallum, R., 'Local Child Safeguarding Practice Review: Child Q' (City of London & Hackney Safeguarding Children Partnership, March 2022).

Garner, S. and Selod, S., 'The Racialization of Muslims: Empirical Studies of Islamophobia' (2015) 41 *Critical Sociology* 9.

Gathara, P., 'Colonize and Punish' *New Internationalist* (13 April 2022), Available from: https://newint.org/features/2022/02/07/colonize-and-punish

Gentleman, A., *The Windrush Betrayal: Exposing the Hostile Environment* (Guardian Faber 2020).

Gentleman, A., 'Windrush Scandal Caused by "30 Years of Racist Immigration Laws" – Report' *The Guardian* (29 May 2022), Available from: https://www.theguardian.com/uk-news/2022/may/29/windrush-scandal-caused-by-30-years-of-racist-immigration-laws-report

Giampetro-Meyer, A., Brooke, S., and James, J., 'How Antiracist Lawyers Can Produce Power and Policy Change' (2021) 24 *Journal of Gender, Race, and Justice* 237.

Gifford, A., 'Key Legal Aspects of the Claim for Reparation' (2019) 68 *Social and Economic Studies* 249.

Gil-Riaño, S., 'Relocating Anti-racist Science: The 1950 UNESCO Statement on Race and Economic Development in the Global South' (2018) 51 *The British Journal for the History of Science* 281.

Gilroy, P., 'The Myth of Black Criminality' (1982) 19 *The Socialist Register* 47.

Glendon, M.A., *Rights Talk: The Impoverishment of Political Discourse* (Free Press 1995).

Gopal, P., *Insurgent Empire: Anticolonial Resistance and British Dissent* (Verso 2019).

Gordon, A.F., 'On "Lived Theory": An Interview with A. Sivanandan' (2014) 55 *Race & Class* 1.

Gordon, F. and Newman, D. (eds), *Leading Works in Law and Social Justice* (Routledge 2021).

Gorski, P.C. and Erakat, N., 'Racism, Whiteness, and Burnout in Antiracism Movements: How White Racial Justice Activists Elevate Burnout in Racial Justice Activists of Color in the United States' (2019) 19 *Ethnicities* 784.

Goulbourne, H., *Race Relations in Britain since 1945* (St Martin's Press 1998).

Grace, C. and LeFevre, P., 'Draining the Swamp' (1985) 7 *Law & Policy* 97.

Gulliver, K., 'Racial Discrimination in UK Housing Has a Long History and Deep Roots' (LSE British Politics and Policy Blog, 12 October 2017), Available from: https://blogs.lse.ac.uk/politicsandpolicy/racial-discrimination-in-housing

Hall, N., Corb, A., Giannasi, P., and Grieve, J.G.D. (eds), *The Routledge International Handbook on Hate Crime* (Routledge 2015).

Hall, S. (ed), *Policing the Crisis: Mugging, the State, and Law and Order* (Macmillan 1978).

Hall, S., *Stuart Hall: Selected Writings on Race and Difference* (P. Gilroy and R.G. Wilson eds, Duke University Press 2021).

Hall, S., 'Race, the Floating Signifier: What More Is There to Say about "Race"?' in P. Gilroy and R.G. Wilson (eds), *Stuart Hall: Selected Writings on Race and Difference* (Duke University Press 2021).

Hall, S., McIntosh, K., Neitzert, E., Pottinger, L., Sandhu, K., Stephenson, M.-A., et al, 'Intersecting Inequalities: The Impact of Austerity on Black and Minority Ethnic Women in the UK' (Women's Budget Group and Runnymede Trust 2017).

Hansen, R., 'The Kenyan Asians, British Politics, and the Commonwealth Immigrants Act, 1968' (1999) 42 *The Historical Journal* 809.

Hansen, R., 'The Politics of Citizenship in 1940s Britain: The British Nationality Act' (1999) 10 *Twentieth Century British History* 67.

Harkness, D., 'Ireland' in R. Winks and W.R. Louis (eds), *The Oxford History of the British Empire: Volume V; Historiography* (Oxford University Press 1999).

Hattenstone, S, 'Joint Enterprise Prosecutions to Be Monitored for Racial Bias' *The Guardian* (16 February 2023), Available from: https://www.theguardian.com/law/2023/feb/16/joint-enterprise-prosecutions-to-be-monitored-for-racial-bias

Hawes, D. and Perez, B., *The Gypsy and the State: The Ethnic Cleansing of British Society* (2nd edn, Policy Press 1996).

Hayes, G., Doherty, B., and Cammiss, S., 'We Attended the Trial of the Colston Four: Here's Why Their Acquittal Should Be Celebrated' (*The Conversation*, 7 January 2022), Available from: https://theconversation.com/we-attended-the-trial-of-the-colston-four-heres-why-their-acquittal-should-be-celebrated-174481

Heath, A.F. and Di Stasio, V., 'Racial Discrimination in Britain, 1969–2017: A Meta-analysis of Field Experiments on Racial Discrimination in the British Labour Market' (2019) 70 *The British Journal of Sociology* 1774.

Hepple, B., *Equality: The Legal Framework* (2nd edn, Hart Publishing 2014).

Herman, D., *An Unfortunate Coincidence: Jews, Jewishness and English Law* (Oxford University Press 2011).

Hickson, K., 'Enoch Powell's "Rivers of Blood" Speech: Fifty Years On' (2018) 89 *The Political Quarterly* 352.

Higher Education Statistics Authority, 'Undergraduate Degree Results' (22 November 2022), Available from: https://www.ethnicity-facts-figures.service.gov.uk/education-skills-and-training/higher-education/undergraduate-degree-results/latest#by-ethnicity-over-time

Hirsch, A., *Brit(ish): On Race, Identity and Belonging* (Vintage Publishing 2018).

Home Office, 'Hate Crime, England and Wales, 2021 to 2022' (6 October 2022), Available from: https://www.gov.uk/government/statistics/hate-crime-england-and-wales-2021-to-2022/hate-crime-england-and-wales-2021-to-2022

Home Office, 'Overarching Equality Statement: Sentencing, Release, Probation and Youth Justice Measures' (updated 29 June 2023), Available from: https://www.gov.uk/government/publications/police-crime-sentencing-and-courts-bill-2021-overarching-documents/overarching-equality-statement-sentencing-release-probation-and-youth-justice-measures

Home Office, 'Home Office Measures in the Police, Crime, Sentencing and Courts Bill: Equalities Impact Assessment' (updated 2 August 2023), Available from: https://www.gov.uk/government/publications/police-crime-sentencing-and-courts-bill-2021-equality-statements/home-office-measures-in-the-police-crime-sentencing-and-courts-bill-equalities-impact-assessment

Howard League for Penal Reform, 'Making Black Lives Matter in the Criminal Justice System: A Guide for Antiracist Lawyers' (Howard League for Penal Reform 2021), Available from: https://howardleague.org/publications/making-black-lives-matter-in-the-criminal-justice-system

Hussain, N., *The Jurisprudence of Emergency: Colonialism and the Rule of Law* (University of Michigan Press 2003).

Iganski, P., 'Hate Crimes Hurt More' (2001) 45 *American Behavioral Scientist* 626

Institute of Race Relations, 'Criminal Justice System Statistics' (14 September 2023), Available from: https://irr.org.uk/research/statistics/criminal-justice

Isaac, D., 'Reflections on the EHRC' (2020) 6 *European Human Rights Law Review Reflection* 578.

Jefferson, T., 'Policing the Riots: From Bristol and Brixton to Tottenham, via Toxteth, Handsworth, etc' (2012) 87 *Criminal Justice Matters* 8.

Jerome, L., Elwick, A., and Kazima, R, 'The Impact of the Prevent Duty on Schools: A Review of the Evidence' (2019) 45 *British Educational Research Journal* 821.

Joint Committee on Human Rights, 'Black People, Racism and Human Rights' (2019–21, HL 165, HC 559).

Joint Committee on Human Rights, 'Deaths in Custody' (third report, 14.12.2004, HL Paper 15-1).

Kearsley, J 'Awaab Ishak: Report to prevent future deaths' (16 November 2022), Available from https://www.judiciary.uk/wp-content/uploads/2022/11/Awaab-Ishak-Prevention-of-future-deaths-report-2022-0365_Published.pdf

Kendi, I.X., *How to Be an Antiracist* (The Bodley Head 2019).

Kinghan, J., *Lawyers, Networks and Progressive Social Change: Lawyers Changing Lives* (Hart Publishing 2021).

Kirkby, A., 'Briefing on New Police Powers for Encampments in Policing, Crime, Sentencing and Courts Bill: Part 4' (Friends, Families and Travellers, 24 March 2021).

Kirkup, J. and Winnett, R., 'Theresa May Interview: "We're Going to Give Illegal Migrants a Really Hostile Reception"' *The Daily Telegraph* (25 May 2012), Available from: https://www.telegraph.co.uk/news/0/theresa-may-interview-going-give-illegal-migrants-really-hostile

Kolsky, E., *Colonial Justice in British India* (Cambridge University Press 2010).

Lammy, D., 'The Lammy Review: An Independent Review into the Treatment of, and Outcomes for, Black, Asian and Minority Ethnic Individuals in the Criminal Justice System' (2017), Available from: https://assets.publishing.service.gov.uk/media/5a82009040f0b62305b91f49/lammy-review-final-report.pdf

Lamont, T., 'How the Trial of the Colston Four Was Won: The Inside Story' *New Statesman* (2 April 2022), Available from: https://www.newstatesman.com/long-reads/2022/04/the-inside-story-of-the-trial-of-the-colston-four

Law Centres Network, 'Law Centres Cap Off an Intensive Year with a Focus on Racial Justice' (Law Centres Network, 22 December 2022), Available from: https://www.lawcentres.org.uk/policy/news/news/law-centres-cap-off-an-intensive-year-with-a-focus-on-racial-justice

Law Commission, 'Hate Crime Laws: Final Report' (Law Com No 402, 2021).

Law Society, 'Access Denied? LASPO Four Years On: A Law Society Review' (June 2017).

Law, S., 'ISIS Bride Shamima Begum Might NEVER Be De-radicalised Because She Has Shown "No Remorse or Regret" for Running Away to Syria, UK Counter-Terror Expert Warns' *Daily Mail* (16 February 2019), Available from: https://www.dailymail.co.uk/news/article-6712341/Shamima-Begum-challenge-radicalise-counter-extremism-expert.html?ico=topics_pagination_desktop

Lawrence, D., 'An Avoidable Crisis' (2021), Available from: https://www.lawrencereview.co.uk

Leah, N., 'Confronting the Yorke–Talbot Slavery Opinion and Its Legacy within English Law' (Gatehouse Chambers, July 2021), Available from: https://gatehouselaw.co.uk/confronting-the-yorke-talbot-slavery-opinion-and-its-legacy-within-english-law

Leat, D., 'The Rise and Rôle of the Poor Man's Lawyer' (1975) 2 *British Journal of Law and Society* 166.

Lehrfreund, S., 'Undoing the British Colonial Legacy: The Judicial Reform of the Death Penalty' in C.S. Steiker and J.M. Steiker (eds), *Comparative Capital Punishment* (Edward Elgar Publishing 2019).

Lester, A. and Bindman, G., *Race and Law* (Penguin Books 1972).

Levin, C., *The Reign and Life of Queen Elizabeth I* (Springer International Publishing 2022).

Levin, C., 'Elizabeth's England and Others' in Carole Levin, *The Reign and Life of Queen Elizabeth I* (Springer International Publishing 2022).

Liberty, 'Met to Overhaul "Racist" Gangs Matrix after Landmark Legal Challenge' (11 November 2022), Available from: https://www.libertyhumanrights.org.uk/issue/met-to-overhaul-racist-gangs-matrix-after-landmark-legal-challenge

Lingayah, S., Wrixon, K., and Hulbert, M., 'Home Truths: Undoing Racism and Delivering Real Diversity in the Charity Sector' (Voice4Change England and the Association of Chief Executives of Voluntary Organisations 2020).

Lobban, M., *Imperial Incarceration: Detention without Trial in the Making of British Colonial Africa* (Cambridge University Press 2021).

Lorde, A., 'The Master's Tools Will Never Dismantle the Master's House' in A. Lorde (ed), *Sister Outsider: Essays and Speeches* (first published 1984, Crossing Press 2007).

Lukes, S., de Noronha, N., and Finney, N., 'Slippery Discrimination: A Review of the Drivers of Migrant and Minority Housing Disadvantage' (2019) 45 *Journal of Ethnic and Migration Studies* 3188.

Mahmud, T., 'Colonialism and Modern Constructions of Race: A Preliminary Inquiry' (1999) 53 *University of Miami Law Review* 1219.

Malik, K., *Strange Fruit: Why Both Sides Are Wrong in the Race Debate* (Oneworld 2008).

Malkani, B., 'The Souls of Black Folk, by W.E.B. Du Bois' in F. Gordon and D. Newman (eds), *Leading Works in Law and Social Justice* (Routledge 2021).

Malkani, B., 'The Pursuit of Racial Justice through Legal Action: An Overview of How UK Civil Society Has Used the Law 1990–2020' (Baring Foundation 2021), Available from: https://baringfoundation.org.uk/resource/the-pursuit-of-racial-justice-through-legal-action

Mansfield, M., *Memoirs of a Radical Lawyer* (Bloomsbury 2010).

Marshall, P.J., 'The First British Empire' in R. Winks and W.R. Louis (eds), *The Oxford History of the British Empire: Volume V; Historiography* (Oxford University Press 1999).

Mason, G., 'Legislating against Hate' in N. Hall, A. Corb, P. Giannasi, and J.G.D. Grieve (eds), *The Routledge International Handbook on Hate Crime* (Routledge 2015).

Matiluko, O., 'Decolonising the Master's House: How Black Feminist Epistemologies Can Be and Are Used in Decolonial Strategy' (2020) 54 *The Law Teacher* 547.

McCallum, D., 'Safer Bristol Partnership: Multi-agency Learning Review following trhe Murder of Bijan Ebrahimi' (Safer Bristol Executive Board, 17 January 2014, updated 25 October 2017), Available from: https://www.bristol.gov.uk/files/documents/1225-multi-agency-learning-review-following-the-murder-of-bijan-ebrahimi/file

McGregor-Smith, R., 'Race in the Workplace: The McGregor-Smith Review' (Department for Business, Energy and Industrial Strategy 2017), Available from: https://www.gov.uk/government/publications/race-in-the-workplace-the-mcgregor-smith-review

McLaren, J., 'The Uses of the Rule of Law in British Colonial Societies in the Nineteenth Century' in S. Dorsett and I. Hunter (eds), *Law and Politics in British Colonial Thought* (Palgrave Macmillan US 2010).

Macpherson, W., 'The Stephen Lawrence Inquiry' (Cmd 4262-I, 1999).

Meer, N., *The Cruel Optimism of Racial Justice* (Policy Press 2022).

Mills, C.W., *Black Rights/White Wrongs: The Critique of Racial Liberalism* (Oxford University Press 2017).

Mills, C.W., 'I – Racial Justice' (2018) 92 *Aristotelian Society Supplementary Volume* 69.

Mitchell, P., *Imperial Nostalgia: How the British Conquered Themselves* (Manchester University Press 2021).

Mohdin, A., '"The Law Is Breaking Children": Black People in UK Tell UN of Daily Injustices' *The Guardian* (27 January 2023), Available from: https://www.theguardian.com/world/2023/jan/27/black-people-in-uk-tell-un-of-daily-injustices

Mohdin, A., 'UK Cannot Ignore Calls for Slavery Reparations, Says Leading UN Judge' *The Guardian* (22 August 2023), Available from: https://www.theguardian.com/world/2023/aug/22/uk-cannot-ignore-calls-for-slavery-reparations-says-leading-un-judge-patrick-robinson

Mohdin, A. and Aguilar García, C., 'Defendants of Colour More Likely to Be Charged than White People, Finds CPS Study' *The Guardian* (7 February 2023), Available from: https://www.theguardian.com/world/2023/feb/07/defendants-of-colour-more-likely-to-be-charged-than-white-people-finds-cps-study

Mohdin, A., Walker, P., and Parveen, N., 'No 10's Race Report Widely Condemned as "Divisive"' *The Guardian* (31 March 2021), Available from: https://www.theguardian.com/world/2021/mar/31/deeply-cynical-no-10-report-criticises-use-of-institutional-racism

Mohdin, A. and Walker, P., 'Bodies Credited in UK Race Review Distance Themselves from Findings' *The Guardian* (12 April 2021), Available from: https://www.theguardian.com/world/2021/apr/12/bodies-credited-in-uk-race-review-distance-themselves-from-findings

Monteith, K., Quinn, E., Dennis, A.L., Joseph-Salisbury, R., Kane, E., Addo, F. et al, 'Racial Bias and the Bench: A Response to the Judicial Diversity and Inclusion Strategy (2020–2025)' (University of Manchester 2022).

Moore, J.M., 'The "New Punitiveness" in the Context of British Imperial History' (2015) 101 *Criminal Justice Matters* 10.

Morgan, J. and Querton, C., 'Access to Protection for Women Seeking Asylum in the UK' in J. Freedman and G. Colby (eds), *Feminist Representations: Sexual Violence Against Women, Asylum, Voice and Testimony* (Proceedings of the British Academy series, Oxford University Press, forthcoming).

Morrison, S., 'Colston 4 Found Not Guilty of Criminal Damage to Slave Trader's Statue' *The Bristol Cable* (5 January 2022), Available from: https://thebristolcable.org/2022/01/colston-4-found-not-guilty-of-criminal-damage-to-slave-traders-statue/

Möschel, M., *Law, Lawyers and Race: Critical Race Theory from the United States to Europe* (Routledge 2016).

Nijjar, J., 'Echoes of Empire: Excavating the Colonial Roots of Britain's "War on Gangs"' (2018) 45 *Social Justice* 147.

Nijjar, J., 'Sociological Imagination, "Lived Theory" and Black Liberation: The Legacy of A. Sivanandan' (2018) *The Sociological Review Magazine*, Available from: https://thesociologicalreview.org/collections/sivanandan/sociological-imagination-lived-theory-and-black-liberation-the-legacy-of-a-sivanandan

Office of the High Commissioner for Human Rights, 'Lived Experiences Key to Achieve Racial Justice and Equality' (United Nations, 25 October 2022), Available from: https://www.ohchr.org/en/stories/2022/10/lived-experiences-key-achieve-racial-justice-and-equality

Office of the High Commissioner for Human Rights, 'UK Illegal Migration Bill: UN Refugee Agency and UN Human Rights Office Warn of Profound Impact on Human Rights and International Refugee Protection System' (United Nations, 18 July 2023), Available from: https://www.ohchr.org/en/press-releases/2023/07/uk-illegal-migration-bill-un-refugee-agency-and-un-human-rights-office-warn#:~:text=The%20Bill%20extinguishes%20access%20to,matter%20how%20compelling%20their%20circumstances

Oldham, J., 'New Light on Mansfield and Slavery' (1988) 27 *Journal of British Studies* 45.

Oliver, M., 'Cousins Jailed for Racist Axe Murder' *The Guardian* (1 December 2005), Available from: https://www.theguardian.com/uk/2005/dec/01/ukcrime.race

Olusoga, D., *Black and British: A Forgotten History* (revised edn, Picador 2021).

Parveen, N., 'Amnesty International Has Culture of White Privilege, Report Finds' *The Guardian* (20 April 2021), Available from: https://www.theguardian.com/world/2021/apr/20/amnesty-international-has-culture-of-white-privilege-report-finds

Pearson, A., 'The Jihadi Girls Will Only Have Themselves to Blame' *The Daily Telegraph* (26 February 2016).

Perera, J., 'How Black Working-Class Youth Are Criminalised and Excluded in the English School System' (Institute of Race Relations 2020).

Potter, H., *Law, Liberty and the Constitution: A Brief History of the Common Law* (Boydell Press 2015).

Powell, E., 'Rivers of Blood' speech (Conservative Association meeting, 20 April 1968), Available from: https://www.telegraph.co.uk/comment/3643823/Enoch-Powells-Rivers-of-Blood-speech.html

Prakash, G., *Another Reason: Science and the Imagination of Modern India* (Princeton University Press 1999).

Prasad, R., '"I Can't Breathe": Race, Death and British Policing' (INQUEST, 20 February 2023).

Quarmby, K., 'Calls for Barry Smith Murder to Be Recognised as Race Hate Crime' *Travellers' Times* (4 November 2014), Available from: https://www.travellerstimes.org.uk/news/2014/11/calls-barry-smith-murder-be-recognised-race-hate-crime

Rattansi, A., *Racism: A Very Short Introduction* (Oxford University Press 2007).

Refugee Council, 'An Analysis of Channel Crossings & Asylum Outcomes: November 2021' (November 2021), Available from: https://www.refugeecouncil.org.uk/wp-content/uploads/2021/12/Channel-crossings-and-asylum-outcomes-November-2021.pdf

Riley, C.L., *Imperial Island: A History of Empire in Modern Britain* (The Bodley Head 2023).

Robertson, J., *The Enlightenment: A Very Short Introduction* (Oxford University Press 2015).

Roberts-Wray, S.K., 'The Adaptation of Imported Law in Africa' (1960) 4 *Journal of African Law* 66.

Robins, J. and Newman, D., *Justice in a Time of Austerity: Stories from a System in Crisis* (Bristol University Press 2021).

Runnymede Trust, 'England Civil Society Submission to the United Nations Committee on the Elimination of Racial Discrimination' (May 2021), Available from: https://www.runnymedetrust.org/publications/civil-society-report-to-united-nations-cerd

Ryder, K.C.M. and Wilson, A., '"The Black Must Go Free": How a Legal Ruling on "Windrush Day" in 1772 Is as Relevant as Ever on Windrush Day 2021' (Matrix Chambers, 22 June 2021), Available from: https://www.matrixlaw.co.uk/resource/webinar-the-black-must-go-free-how-a-legal-ruling-on-windrush-day-in-1772-is-as-relevant-as-ever-on-windrush-day-2021

Saini, A., *Superior: The Return of Race Science* (4th Estate 2019).

Sanghera, S., *Empireland: How Imperialism Has Shaped Modern Britain* (Penguin Books 2021).

Sarat, A. and Scheingold, S.A. (eds), *Cause Lawyering: Political Commitments and Professional Responsibilities* (Oxford University Press 1998).

Scarman, L.J., 'The Brixton Disorders 10–12 April 1981' (Cmd 8427, 1981)

Scott, D., 'Abolitionism Must Come from Below: A Critique of British Anti-slavery Abolition' (2020) OpenLearn, Available from: https://www.open.edu/openlearn/society-politics-law/sociology/abolitionism-must-come-below-critique-british-anti-slavery-abolition

Shafi, A. and Nagdee, I., *Race to the Bottom: Reclaiming Antiracism* (Pluto Press 2022).

Shankley, W. and Finney, N., 'Ethnic Minorities and Housing in Britain' in B. Byrne, C. Alexander, O. Khan, J. Nazroo, and W. Shankley (eds), *Ethnicity, Race and Inequality in the UK: State of the Nation* (Policy Press 2020).

Sharp, G., *A Representation of the Injustice and Dangerous Tendency of Tolerating Slavery; Or of Admitting the Least Claim of Private Property in the Persons of Men, in England* (Benjamin White, 1769).

Shilliam, R., *Race and the Undeserving Poor: From Abolition to Brexit* (Agenda Publishing 2018).

Shukla, N. (ed), *The Good Immigrant* (Unbound 2016).

Siddique, H., 'Judiciary in England and Wales "Institutionally Racist", Says Report' *The Guardian* (18 October 2022), Available from: https://www.theguardian.com/law/2022/oct/18/judiciary-in-england-and-wales-institutionally-racist-says-report

Siddiqui, S., 'Anti-racist Organising Today: A Roundtable Discussion' (2023) 65 *Race & Class* 119.

Sivanandan, A., 'Race, Class, and the State: The Black Experience in Britain' (1976) 17 *Race & Class* 347.

Sivanandan, A., 'RAT and the Degradation of Black Struggle' (1985) 26 *Race & Class* 1.

Sivanandan, A., *Communities of Resistance: Writings on Black Struggles for Socialism* (first published 1990, Verso 2019).

Sivanandan, A., 'The Great Cop Out: Public Accountability, Not Public Relations' (1998–99) 47 *Campaign Against Racism and Fascism* 2, Available from: https://irr.org.uk/app/uploads/2017/05/no.47.pdf

Solanke, I., *Discrimination as Stigma: A Theory of Anti-discrimination Law* (Hart Publishing 2016).

Solomon, E., 'The Illegal Migration Bill Has Passed, and Here's What Will Happen: Children Lost, Abused and Exploited' *The Guardian* (18 July 2023), Available from: https://www.theguardian.com/commentisfree/2023/jul/18/illegal-migration-bill-children-abused-exploited-law

Sorrenson, M.P.K., *Origins of European Settlement in Kenya* (Oxford University Press 1968).

Special Rapporteur on Counter-Terrorism and Human Rights, 'The Human Rights Consequences of Citizenship Stripping in the Context of Counter-Terrorism with a Particular Application to North-East Syria' (Office of the High Commissioner for Human Rights 2022).

Spurrier, M., 'We Stand in Solidarity with Black Lives Matter' (Liberty, 11 June 2020), Available from: https://www.libertyhumanrights.org.uk/issue/we-stand-in-solidarity-with-black-lives-matter

Stanford-Xosei, E., 'Why We Still Need Holistic Reparations for Slavery' *The Independent* (30 October 2022), Available from: https://www.independent.co.uk/voices/reparations-slavery-africa-black-history-month-b2213721.html

Steeds, M. and Ball, R., *From Wulfstan to Colston: Severing the Sinews of Slavery in Bristol* (Bristol Radical History Group 2020).

Steiker, C.S. and Steiker, J.M. (eds), *Comparative Capital Punishment* (Edward Elgar Publishing 2019).

Sumption, J., 'Letter to the Editor' *The Guardian* (26 February 2023), Available from: https://www.theguardian.com/uk-news/2023/feb/26/the-real-scandal-of-the-shamima-begum-citizenship-case

Suthakaran, A., 'How Can We South Asians Dismantle Racism in Our UK Communities?' (EachOther, 27 August 2020), Available from: https://eachother.org.uk/how-can-we-south-asians-dismantle-racism-in-our-uk-communities

Symposium on Race, Racism, and International Law (2023) 117 *American Journal of International Law Unbound* 26.

Tabili, L., 'The Construction of Racial Difference in Twentieth-Century Britain: The Special Restrictions (Coloured Alien Seamen) Order, 1925' (1994) 33 *Journal of British Studies* 54.

Tharoor, S., *Inglorious Empire: What the British Did to India* (Penguin Books 2017)

Thomas, L., *Do Right and Fear No One: A Life Dedicated to Fighting for Justice* (Simon & Schuster 2022).

Thompson, I., 'Black Lives Matter UK: For Lasting Change, We Need "Movement Lawyers"' (EachOther, 3 August 2020), Available from: https://eachother.org.uk/black-lives-matter-uk-for-lasting-change-we-need-movement-lawyers/

Thompson, I., 'Discrimination and Policing: Case Study (Nov 22)' (Legal Action Group, November 2022), Available from: https://www.lag.org.uk/article/213357/discrimination-and-policing-case-study-nov-22-

Topping, A., 'Education Secretary Writes to School of Girls Believed to Have Fled to Syria' *The Guardian* (25 February 2015), Available from: https://www.theguardian.com/world/2015/feb/25/education-secretary-nicky-morgan-syria-bethnal-green-academy

Topping, S., 'The Nasty Stench of Racism Pervades the Tragedy of Little Awaab Ishak' *Manchester Evening News* (20 November 2022), Available from: https://www.manchestereveningnews.co.uk/news/greater-manchester-news/nasty-stench-racism-pervades-tragedy-25523795

Townsend, M., 'Grenfell Families Want Inquiry to Look at Role of "Race and Class" in Tragedy' *The Guardian* (26 July 2020), Available from: https://www.theguardian.com/uk-news/2020/jul/26/grenfell-families-want-inquiry-to-look-at-role-of-race-and-class-in-tragedy

Travis, A., 'Immigration Bill: Theresa May Defends Plans to Create "Hostile Environment"' *The Guardian* (10 October 2013), Available from: https://www.theguardian.com/politics/2013/oct/10/immigration-bill-theresa-may-hostile-environment

Tuitt, P., *Race, Law, Resistance* (GlassHouse Press 2004).

Tuitt, P., 'A Concise Note on Peter Fitzpatrick's "Racism and the Innocence of Law"' (2021) 17 *International Journal of the Law in Context* 36.

United Nations Committee on the Elimination of Racial Discrimination (CERD), 'Concluding Observations on the Combined Twenty-First to Twenty-Third Periodic Reports of the United Kingdom of Great Britain and Northern Ireland' (3 October 2016, CERD/C/GBR/CO/21-23).

United Nations Special Rapporteur on the and Promotion and Protection of Human Rights and Fundamental Freedoms while Countering Terrorism, 'The Human Rights Consequences of Citizenship Stripping in the Context of Counter-Terrorism with a Particular Application to North-East Syria' (Office of the High Commissioner for Human Rights 2022).

Vanhala, L., 'Framework for Better Use of the Law by the Voluntary Sector' (Baring Foundation 2016).

Vanhala, L., 'Successful Use of Strategic Litigation by the Voluntary Sector on Issues Related to Discrimination and Disadvantage: Key Cases from the UK' (Baring Foundation 2017).

Veiga, A., Pina-Sánchez, J., and Lewis, S., 'Racial and Ethnic Disparities in Sentencing: What Do We Know, and Where Should We Go?' (2023) 62 *The Howard Journal of Crime and Justice* 167.

Verma, R., '"It Was Standard to See Signs Saying 'No Blacks, No Dogs, No Irish"' (EachOther, 29 November 2018), Available from: https://eachother.org.uk/racism-1960s-britain

Vincent, C., 'Belonging in England Today: Schools, Race, Class and Policy' (2022) 58 *Journal of Sociology* 324.

Wagner A., 'It's Not "Activist Lawyers" This Government Hates, But the Laws Themselves' *New Statesman* (28 August 2020), Available from: https://www.newstatesman.com/politics/2020/08/its-not-activist-lawyers-this-government-hates-but-the-laws-themselves

Walters, M., *Criminalising Hate: Law as Social Justice Liberalism* (Palgrave Macmillan 2022).

Walters, M., Wiedlitzka, S., Owusu-Bempah, A., with Goodall, K., 'Hate Crime and the Legal Process: Options for Law Reform' (University of Sussex, October 2017).

Walvin, J., *The Zong: A Massacre, the Law and the End of Slavery* (Yale University Press 2019).

We Are Bristol History Commission, 'The Colston Statue: What Next?' (2021), Available from: https://www.bristol.gov.uk/files/documents/1825-history-commission-full-report-final/file

Webb, D.A., 'The *Somerset* Effect: Parsing Lord Mansfield's Words on Slavery in Nineteenth Century America' (2014) 32 *Law and History Review* 455.

Webber, F., 'Citizenship: From Right to Privilege' Institute of Race Relations (September 2022).

Weber, J.-J., *Language Racism* (Palgrave Macmillan 2015).

Wiecek, W.M., 'Somerset: Lord Mansfield and the Legitimacy of Slavery in the Anglo-American World' (1974) 42 *University of Chicago Law Review* 86.

Wiener, M.J., *An Empire on Trial: Race, Murder, and Justice under British Rule, 1870–1935* (Cambridge University Press 2009).

Williams, E.E., *Capitalism and Slavery* (first published 1964, Penguin Books 2022)

Williams, P., 'Criminalising the Other: Challenging the Race–Gang Nexus' (2014) 56 *Race & Class* 18.

Williams, P. and Clarke, B. 'Dangerous Associations: Joint Enterprise, Gangs and Racism' (Centre for Crime and Justice Studies 2016), Available from: https://www.crimeandjustice.org.uk/publications/dangerous-assoc iations-joint-enterprise-gangs-and-racism

Williams, W. 'Windrush Lessons Learned Review' (2020), Available from: https://www.gov.uk/government/publications/windrush-lessons-learned-review

Wilson, A., *In Black and White: A Young Barrister's Story of Race and Class in a Broken Justice System* (Endeavour 2021).

Winks, R. and Louis, W.R. (eds), *The Oxford History of the British Empire: Volume V; Historiography* (Oxford University Press 1999).

Winter, C. and Mills, C., 'The Psy-Security-Curriculum Ensemble: British Values Curriculum Policy in English Schools' (2020) 35 *Journal of Education Policy* 46.

Working Group of Experts on People of African Descent, 'UN Experts Condemn UK Commission on Race and Ethnic Disparities Report' (Office of the High Commissioner for Human Rights, 19 April 2021), Available from: https://www.ohchr.org/en/press-releases/2021/04/un-experts-condemn-uk-com mission-race-and-ethnic-disparities-report?LangID=E&NewsID=27004>

Working Group of Experts on People of African Descent, 'UK: Discrimination against People of African Descent Is Structural, Institutional and Systemic, Say UN Experts' (Office of the High Commissioner for Human Rights, 27 January 2023), Available from: https://www.ohchr.org/en/press-releases/2023/01/ uk-discrimination-against-people-african-descent-structural-institutional

Zander, M., 'How Law Centres Started Out' (Law Centres Network 2020), Available from: https://www.lawcentres.org.uk/about-law-centres/how-law-centres-started-out

Index

References to endnotes show both the page number and the note number (231n3).

A

activism 7, 10, 22, 36, 42, 44, 118–9, 125, 126–7, 129
Adébísí, Folúkẹ́ 25
Africa
  British Empire and 16, 28, 50, 52
  imperialism 51–2
  independence 60–1
  Indians in 46–7, 61
  post WW II 58
  slavery 1, 40–1, 59
  see also Kenya; Rwanda; Uganda
Alexander, Claire 70
Aliens Act (1905) 55
Aliens Order (1920) 56
Amnesty International 129–30
Anderson, Bridget 55
antiracism 7, 25, 90, 121–3, 124, 125–35
Arendt, Hannah 54
Asians 6, 18, 24, 25, 61, 71, 79–80, 117–8
Association of Chief Executives of Voluntary Organisations 129
Asylum and Immigration Act (1996) 67
Asylum and Immigration Appeals Act (1993) 67, 90
asylum seekers 67, 90, 91
Atkins, Lord 47, 95, 96
Atrey, Shreya 11, 80–1, 106, 107, 108

B

Bahl, Dr Kamlesh 107
Bahl v The Law Society (2004) 107
Baldwin, James 8
BAME (Black and Asian Minority Ethnic) 6, 24, 25, 71, 74, 75, 116, 129
BAPIO (British Association of Physicians of Indian Origin) 117–18
Bar Standards Board 125
Barbados 142–3
Baring Foundation 94
Barton, Michael 113

Begum, Shamima 8, 136–40
Bell, Derrick 12, 38
Berlant, Lauren 8
Berlin Conference (1884–5) 51–2
Bindman, Geoffrey 11, 44, 45, 46, 69, 86, 87
Black Equity Organisation 25
Black Lives Matter 11–12, 81
Black Power movement 127
Black Protest Legal Support 128, 130
Black South West Network 134
Black people
  Africans 24
  Asian prejudices against 25
  BAME and BME 6, 24
  Caribbeans 24, 70, 77
  communities 53
  considered 'inferior' 15, 16, 52
  criminal justice and 72, 74–5, 77, 116
  early 20th century 55–6
  education 70, 72, 105–6
  EIA and 116
  employment 76–7, 100
  Gangs Matrix database and 49, 75, 118–19
  healthcare 79–80
  housing 78
  immigration 57–8, 60
  police force and 103–5, 120
  racialization and 9, 13, 16
  racism against 39–40, 74, 78, 82–3, 103–5, 123–4
  slavery 1, 16, 31–3, 34–9, 40–4, 59
  US 20, 123–4
  women 6, 17–19, 33, 80
BME (Black and Minority Ethnic) 6, 24, 25, 71, 76, 77, 115, 117
Bobb-Semple, Colin 40
Bonilla-Silva, Eduardo 14, 15
Boodia-Canoo, Nandini 51
Bowleg, Lisa 19
Bridges, Lee 13–14, 91
Bristol 1, 2, 81

164

INDEX

British Empire
  Africa and *see* Africa: British Empire and
  attempt to preserve 58–9
  capitalism 28
  disintegration 7, 54, 141
  law 4, 6–7, 23, 27, 28, 30, 48
  racial injustices 4, 7, 45
  racism 14, 16, 40, 58, 66
  slavery 3, 16, 20, 21, 39, 44
  subjects 55–6, 60
British Nationality Act (1948) 58–9
British Nationality Act (1981) 62–3, 136, 137
Brockway, Archibald Fenner 59–60
Brown v Board of Education (USA) 10–11, 20
Butts v Penny (1677) 33–4, 35, 36

C

Callaghan, James 61, 86
capitalism 8, 28, 34
Caravan Sites and Control of Development Act (1960) 60
Caribbean 1, 16, 28, 31, 35, 40, 49–50, 57–8, 142–5
CARICOM (Caribbean Community) 144
Carnarvon, Henry Herbert, Lord 29
Cartwright (1569) 31, 37
Casey, Baroness Louise 73
CCJ (Caribbean Court of Justice) 143
CERD (Committee on the Elimination of Racial Discrimination) *see* ICERD
Chamberlain v Harvey (1696) 34
#CharitySoWhite 130
Civil Rights Acts (USA) 10
Clarke, Kenneth 67
Clarkson, Thomas 21
class 6, 17–19, 80, 94, 97, 101, 115
colonialism
  capitalism and 28
  intersectionality and 18
  law and ix–x, 4n11, 5–7, 29–30, 31–45, 46–53, 92, 97, 136, 138, 141–2
  legacy of ix–x, 4n11, 53, 54, 55, 71–2, 74, 92, 141, 136, 141–2
  racial oppression and ix–x, 7
  racism and racial injustice 7, 34, 45–51, 59, 61, 75, 92, 96–7, 121, 136, 143
  slavery and 7, 31–45
Colston, Edward 1, 1n1, 2
Colston Four x, 2–3, 2n4–5, 8, 136, 139
Commons Law CIC 133
Commonwealth 58, 60–1, 62–4, 66–7
Commonwealth Immigrants Act (1962) 60–1, 86, 87, 140
Commonwealth Immigrants Act (1968) 60, 61, 86, 87
Communications Act (2003) 110
Constantine, Learie 84
COVID-19 47, 79–80
CPS (Crown Prosecution Service) 74, 113, 119, 131

CRC (Community Relations Commission) 85–6, 88
CRE (Commission for Racial Equality) 88–9, 91, 94
CRED (Commission on Race and Ethnic Disparities) 81, 82, 83
Crenshaw, Kimberlé 12, 17
Crichlow, Frank 88
Crime and Disorder Act (1998) 90, 111
Criminal Damage Act (1971) 2
criminal justice 4, 7, 69–70, 72–4, 77–8, 82–3, 92–4, 105, 116, 133, 141–2
Criminal Justice Act (2003) 90, 111
Criminal Justice and Public Order Act (1994) 90, 104
Criminal Tribes Act (1871) 48–9, 56, 75
CRT (Critical Race Theory)
  concepts 5–6, 7–8, 12, 15, 21, 22, 24, 26, 85, 121
  law and 11, 21, 93
  origins 10, 11
  UK and 11, 12
'cruel optimism' 8
CSA (Clinical Skills Assessment) 117

D

Daniel, Gloria 2
Davis, Angela 17
Davis, Lord Justice 103
Davy, William 37–8
de Cordova, Marsha 82
death penalty 141–3
Delaney, Johnny 112
Denning, Lord 89
Di Stasio, Valentina 76–7
Diedrick (2012) 117
disabilities 19, 91, 109, 110, 119
Disability Rights Commission 91
discrimination
  criminal law and 22, 73, 116
  direct 98–9, 118
  disabilities 19, 91
  education and 70–1, 105–6
  employment and 76–7, 100–101, 107
  gender 91
  healthcare and 79
  housing and 78, 101–3
  immigration laws and 55–6, 59, 61, 69
  indirect 99–101, 116, 118
  intersectionality and 68, 106–8
  laws on x, 3–4, 5, 7, 45–6, 84–93, 103–4, 115
  police force 4
  racial
    activism and 22
    CRED and 81
    criminal justice and 73, 104, 117, 119, 120, 127
    education and 70–1, 106
    employment and 76–7, 108
    healthcare and 79

165

housing and 78–9, 101–3
immigration laws and 55–6, 63, 69
institutional racism and 13, 81, 82–3
laws against 45–7, 59, 84–91, 97–8, 100–101
legal aid and 93–5
reparations for 144
sexual orientation 19
displacement 7
diversity 6, 25
Dolben's Act (1788) 43–4
Drake, Sir Francis 32
Du Bois, W.E.B. 16–17, 123–4
Dummett, Ann 86–7

E

East India Company 40, 45, 46, 48
Ebrahimi, Bijan 73–4
Eddo-Lodge, Reni 14
Ede, James Chuter 57
EDI (equality, diversity, inclusion) 25, 26
education 7, 9, 70–2, 92, 105–6, 117, 133
Egyptians Acts (1530, 1554) 27
EHRC (Equality and Human Rights Commission) 91, 94, 108, 111
EIA (Equality Impact Assessments) 115–17, 118
El-Enany, Nadine 55, 63, 66–7, 69
Eliot, Sir Charles 50
Elkins, Caroline 28
Empire Windrush see *Windrush*
employment 7, 9, 55, 70, 75–7, 85, 86, 95, 100–101, 107, 117, 133
Enterprise and Regulatory Reform Act (2013) 108
Equal Opportunities Commission 91
equality
imperialism and 28, 59
law and 3, 10, 28, 34, 43, 86, 87, 90–1, 93–4, 97, 99–100
liberalism and 43
problematic term 6, 25
racial 11, 20, 21, 58, 60, 70, 86, 88, 90–1, 93–4, 114
slavery and 34
social 8
Equality Act (2006) 90, 91, 97
Equality Act (2010) 3, 23, 90, 91, 97, 99, 100, 108, 109, 114
Equiano, Olaudah 42
equity 25, 26
Erakat, Noura 129
European Convention on Human Rights 97, 101, 104
European Union Race Directive 132
Eyre, Edward John 49

F

Finney, Nissa 78
Fitzpatrick, Peter 11, 96
Foot, Sir Dingle 87

Football (Offences) Act (1991) 110
Fryer, Peter 21, 40, 44

G

Gaitskell, Hugh 60
Gangs Matrix database 49, 75, 118–19, 130
gender 6, 17–19, 91, 101
Gentleman, Amelia 59, 65–6
Gibson, Lord Justice Peter 107
Gifford, Lord Anthony 144
Gilroy, Paul 74
Glynn, John 37
Gopal, Priyamvada 50
Gordon, Avery 21
Gordon, George William 49–50
Gorski, Paul 129
Government of India Act (1858) 40, 45–6, 48
Grace, Clive 126
Gregson, William 41
Grenfell Tower 42, 47, 79, 95–6, 131
GRT (Gypsy, Roma and Traveller)
criminal justice and 74
criminalization of 4, 49, 73, 90, 91
education and 70
EIA and 115–16
hate crimes against 111–12, 140
injustices against 16, 24, 98
laws allowing local authorities to close caravan sites 60, 90, 91
laws banning immigration of 27
'not conventionally White' 16, 17, 24
Gurkhas 56, 56n6
Gypsies see GRT

H

Habeas Corpus Act (1679) 36–7, 84, 132, 141
Hague, William 143
Hale, Lady 98, 100, 105
Hall, Stuart 12, 17, 74
Hansen, Randall 61n24
harassment 73, 88, 90, 108–9, 111, 115
Hargrave, Francis 38
Hasian, Marouf Jr 50
Hastings, Warren 40
Hattersley, Roy 63
Hawkins, Sir John 32
Hayter, Teresa 66
healthcare 7, 9, 79–80, 117
Heath, Anthony 76–7
Henley, Robert 36
Hepple, Bob 89
Herman, Didi 99
Hickinbottom, Lord Justice 102, 103
History of Jamaica (Edward Long) 40
Hobhouse, Wera 82
Hoffmann, Lord 109
Holroyd, Justice 39

INDEX

Holt, Chief Justice Sir John 34–5, 36
housing 7, 9, 13, 78–9, 85, 86, 90, 95–6, 101–3, 133
Howard League for Penal Reform 128
Human Rights Act (1998) 3, 90, 97
Hussain, Nasser 51

I

ICERD (International Convention on the Elimination of All Forms of Racial Discrimination) 132, 144
Illegal Migration Act (2023) 68–9
Immigration Act (1971) 62, 65
Immigration Act (1988) 64
Immigration Act (2014) 64, 65, 91, 101
Immigration Act (2016) 64, 91
Immigration and Asylum Act (1999) 64
immigration laws 7, 27, 49, 53–7, 60–9, 86–7, 91–2, 103, 138, 140
Immigration Restriction Act (1897) 55
imperialism
  'boomerang effect' 54, 72
  intersectionality and 19
  justification of 6, 18, 23, 27–30, 58, 122
  law and 6, 23, 27–30, 49, 58
  legacy 54, 66, 68, 141
  racism and 18, 49, 122, 136
  'Scramble for Africa' 51–2
inclusion 6, 25
India 20, 30, 40, 45–6, 48–9, 66, 84
Indians 25, 45–6, 47, 48, 61, 70–1
inequalities and injustices 10, 11, 13, 17, 21, 22, 24, 25, 85
INQUEST 120
Institute of Race Relations 14
interest-convergence x, 6, 20, 38, 59, 87
intersectionality
  class and x, 6, 17, 19, 49, 80
  imperialism and *see* imperialism: intersectionality and
  law and 19–20, 85, 97, 100, 106–8, 119–21, 130, 133, 139–40
  preferred term 26
  women and x, 6, 17–19, 33, 49, 68, 80, 100, 107, 115, 133
Isaac, David 94
Ishak, Awaab 78–9
ISIL (Islamic State of Iraq and the Levant) 136–7, 138, 140

J

Jamaica 37–8, 40–2, 49–50, 142
James, Grace 44
Javid, Sajid 137, 139
JCPC (Judicial Committee of the Privy Council) 142
JCWI (Joint Council for the Welfare of Immigrants) 64, 101, 102–3

JENGbA (Joint Enterprise Not Guilty by Association) 22, 119
Jews 16, 17, 24, 32, 55, 57, 89, 98–9
Johnson, Boris 81
Jones, Claudia 18

K

Kaderbhai (1931) 46–7, 95, 96, 103
Kay, Justice 104
Kendi, Ibram X. 15, 122–3, 124
Kenya 46–7, 50, 59, 60–1, 141, 143
Key, Elizabeth 32
Kikuyu 50
King, Dr Martin Luther Jr ix, xi
Kinghan, Jacqueline 126
Kipling, Rudyard 29

L

language 6, 24
law
  colonialism and *see* colonialism: law and
  CRT and *see* CRT: law and
  imperialism and *see* imperialism: law and
  intersectionality and *see* intersectionality: law and
  race hate crimes and 110–14
  racial justice and
    advancement of x, 3–4, 8, 20, 23, 46, 109–10, 134
    construction of 42
    expectations 3
    lawyers and xi, 7, 121–4, 125, 127, 128, 129, 132–4, 141
    legal aid 93–4
    limits 4, 23, 54, 81, 84–5, 140–1
    recent developments x, 2–3, 7, 81, 84–5, 87–9, 90–1, 132, 141
    relationship 4, 5, 6, 8, 9, 10–12, 17, 29, 54, 58, 60, 62, 139
  racialization and 48
  racism and 7, 11, 40, 45, 92, 96–7, 121, 139, 145
  structural racism and 5, 7, 14, 27, 84–5, 92, 96–7, 102, 104–5, 114, 119, 139–40
  'rule of' 23, 28–30, 42, 51, 58, 71
  slavery and
    1500s 31–2
    1600s 32–4
    1700s 34–44, 84
    1800s 44–5
    legacy 51, 123, 142
Law Centres 87–8, 94, 126
Law Society 93
Lawrence, Baroness Doreen 79
Lawrence, Stephen 13, 73, 84, 89, 110
lawyers
  'antiracist lawyering'
    accountability 121, 122, 128, 134–5
    collaboration 121, 122, 128, 132–4

concept 7, 120, 125
creativity 121, 122, 128, 130–2
reflection 121, 122, 128, 129–30
inquests into deaths of Black people in police custody 120, 131
racial justice and 124, 127, 141
social justice lawyering
antiracist lawyering as a form of 122, 124
counterproductivity and 125, 127–8
elitism and paternalism and 125, 126–7
ethics and professionalism of 125–6
Leat, Diana 126
Lee, John 42, 47
Lefevre, Patrick 126
legal aid 93–4
Legal Aid and Advice Act (1949) 93
Legal Aid, Sentencing, and Punishment of Offenders Act (2012) 93
Lester, Anthony 11, 44, 45, 46, 69, 86, 87
Leveson, Justice 113
liberalism 8, 21, 23, 28, 43, 58
Liberty 119, 130, 134
Linnaeus, Carl 52
lived theory x, 21, 134
Long, Edward 40
Lorde, Audrey 18, 19
Loving v Virginia (USA) 10–11

M

MacDonald Ian 88
Macpherson, Sir William 13, 73
Macpherson Inquiry 13, 73, 114
Major, John 67
Mandla v Dowell Lee (1983) 89
Mangrove Nine 88, 141
Mansfield, Lord 37–9, 40, 41, 42, 43, 58
Mason, Gail 111
Matiluko, Oluwaseun 19
Mau Mau 50, 59, 143
May, Theresa 64, 101
McBean, Shanice Octavia 121n1
McGregor-Smith, Baroness Ruby 76, 77
McLaren, John 29
Meer, Nasar 8
Mills, China 72
Mitting, Judge 117–18
Modern Slavery Act (2015) 100
Moore-Bick, Sir Martin 96
Morant Bay rebellion 142
Morgan, Jennifer 68
Morgan, Nicky 137
Muslims 16, 71, 77, 139–40

N

Nagdee, Ilyas 127
Namakula, Catherine 82
Natal (South Africa) 55
National Health Service 59
Nationality and Borders Act (2022) 68, 91

New Cross Fire 135
Nijjar, Jasbinder 75
North America 1, 16, 28, 31, 32, 40
Notting Hill 88
Nuñez, Hector 31–2

O

Odain, Lloyd 108–9
Olusoga, David 2, 31, 39, 52
OWAAD (Organisation of Women of African and Asian Descent) 18

P

Pakistan 58, 66, 67
Pakistanis 70–1, 77, 78
Parker, Justice 117
Pearne v Lisle (1749) 36
Pearson, Allison 136
Perera, Jessica 72
Phillips, Lord 98–9
Plassey, Battle of 45
Police, Crime, Sentencing and Courts Act (2022) 73, 91
police force 4, 13, 73, 75, 88, 89, 97, 104–5, 113, 117, 118–19, 120, 130–1
Powell, Enoch 61
Prakash, Gyan 48
Prevent Strategy 70, 71, 72
PSED (Public Sector Equality Duty) 23, 90, 115, 116–18, 119 *see also* Equality Act (2010)
Public Order Act (1936) 56–7
Public Order Act (1986) 110

Q

Querton, Christel 68

R

R (Bapio Action Ltd) v Royal College of General Practitioners (2014) 117
R (Roberts) v Commissioner of Police of the Metropolis and another (2015) 103–5
race
class and 94
definition 5, 6, 15–16, 17, 24
hierarchy 15, 16, 17, 24, 61
immigration law and 69
imperialism and 30
manufacturing of 55
relations 86, 115
social construct x, 5, 15, 17, 85, 99, 100, 121, 140
Race & Class 19
race hate crimes 109–14, 140, 141
Race Relations Act (1965) 54, 60, 84, 85, 86, 87, 97, 110, 140
Race Relations (Amendment) Act (1968) 85, 97
Race Relations (Amendment) Act (1976) 88, 89, 97, 100

INDEX

Race Relations (Amendment) Act (2000) 90–1, 97, 114
Race Relations Board 85, 86, 88
Racial and Religious Hatred Act (2006) 90
'Racial Bias and the Bench' (2022) 92
Racial Discrimination Bill 59–60
racial justice
  definition 5, 9
  education and 72
  interest-convergence and 38
  law and *see* law: racial justice and
  promotion of 114–15
  struggle for 8, 10, 17, 81, 85, 109, 128, 132, 140–1
  White people and 121, 129–30, 134
racism
  Black people and *see* Black people: racism against
  Britain 27
  criminal justice and 72–5
  definitions 15–16, 99
  education and 70–2
  employment and 75–7
  fight against 115
  housing and 78–9, 95–6
  imperialism and 29–31
  institutional 12, 13–14, 15, 80, 81, 82–3
  interpersonal 12–13, 14, 15, 15n25, 80
  law and *see* law: racism and
  police force and 73–5
  policies 122–3
  'scientific' 15, 24, 29, 40, 52, 59
  slavery and 16, 40, 139
  structural
    antiracist lawyering and 121, 125, 130–1
    colonialism and x, 46, 72, 75, 96–7, 136
    CRED and 81–2
    CRT and x, 12
    definition 5, 12, 15, 122
    education and 70
    entrenchment of 117
    healthcare and 47, 80
    housing and 42, 47, 96, 131
    identification of 81, 113
    immigration laws and 64, 67, 69
    law and *see* law: racism and: structural racism and
    today 82, 83, 123, 136
  systemic 12, 13, 14, 15, 80, 82, 95–6
  White people and 14, 16, 34, 123–4
Refugee Convention 67
Refugee Council 67
religion 16, 89, 91, 98–9, 109
Rhodes, Cecil 51–2
Roberts, Mrs 103–5
Roberts-Wray, Sir Kenneth 29
Robinson, Patrick 144
Roma *see* GRT
Roma Rights (2004) 98, 105

Royal African Company 1, 32, 36
Royal College of General Practitioners 117–18
Runnymede Trust 76, 78, 115
Rwanda 69

S

Saini, Angela 16n29
SBS (Southall Black Sisters) 18–19, 133
Scarman, Lord 73
Scott, David 20, 21
Sewell Report 81–2
sexual orientation 19, 91, 109, 110
Shafi, Azfar 127
Shankley, William 70, 78
Sharp, Granville 21, 36–7, 39, 40, 42, 84, 132, 141
Shukla, Nikesh 53, 124
Sierra Leone 56
Sikhs 89
Sivanandan, Ambalavaner 12, 14, 19, 21, 87, 134
slavery
  abolition 3, 20, 21, 44–5, 142
  Black people *see* Black people: slavery
  British Empire 1–2, 20
  campaigns against 3, 20, 21, 37, 38–9, 84
  Colston Four and 1–2, 8
  death penalty and 142
  justification of 7, 16, 33, 40, 59
  law and *see* law: slavery and
  modern 100
  racism and *see* racism: slavery and
  reparations 141, 144
  USA 123
Slavery Abolition Act (1833) 44, 46
Smith, Barry 112
Smith v Brown and Cooper (1701) 34
Smith v Gould (1706) 35
Solanke, Iyiola 106
Solicitors' Regulation Authority 125
Somerset, James 37, 38–9, 132
Somerset v Stewart (1772) 3, 36–7, 39, 39n48, 40, 44, 58
Sorrenson, M.P.K. 46
Special Restrictions (Coloured Alien Seamen) Order (1925) 56
Spurrier, Martha 130, 134
Stewart, Charles 37, 38
StopWatch 22
Stowell, Lord 44
Suleiman, Awate 118
Sumption, Jonathan 138
Systema naturae (Carl Linnaeus) 52

T

Taiwo v Olaigbe (2012) 100, 140
Talbot, Charles 35–6
Taylor, Paul 113
Tharoor, Shashi 29, 30
Thatcher, Margaret 62–3, 64, 66, 127
Thomas, Leslie, KC 30, 92, 120, 127–8, 134–5

Thompson, Ife 130–1, 134
Tilak, Bal Gangadhar 30
transgender 109
Travellers *see* GRT
Tuitt, Patricia 11, 96
two-tiered legal system 15, 27, 30, 31, 54, 138

U

Uganda 60
United Nations 21, 82, 87
United States 10–11, 14, 18, 39, 87, 123, 129
UNJUST UK 118
Upadhyaya, Mahesh 86

V

Vanhala, Lisa 22
victimization 74, 90, 108, 109, 115
Victoria, Queen 28
Vincent, Catherine 72
Voice4Change England 129
Voting Rights Act (USA) 10

W

Walker, Anthony 113
Walters, Mark 113, 114
West India Lobby 35
West Indies *see* Caribbean
White people
  activism and x, 21, 37
  criminal justice and 13, 74, 120
  education and 14, 70, 122
  employment and 14, 76–7
  housing and 13
  immigration laws and 55–6, 62–3, 137–8
  interest-convergence and 20, 85, 87, 140
  opportunities 9, 10
  other than White British 7, 9, 13, 14, 16, 17, 24, 26
  racial justice and *see* racial justice: White people and
  racism and *see* racism: White people and
  superiority 15, 29, 40, 52, 61
  supremacy 14, 55, 58–9
  two-tier legal system and 7, 27, 30
  'wages of whiteness' 17, 18
  Whiteness as norm 24, 25–6, 71
  working-class 16
Wiecek, William 35
Wilberforce, William 21
Williams, Patrick 75
Williams, Wendy 65–6, 138
Wilson, Alexandra 92
Winder, Robert 60
Windrush 57–8
Windrush Generation 4, 59, 65
Windrush Scandal 56, 63–6, 68, 138
Winnington, Sir Francis 36
Winter, Christine 72
Woolley, Lord Simon 81–2

Y

Yorke, Sir Philip 35–6

Z

Zander, Michael 87
Zong 40–2, 47, 51

www.ingramcontent.com/pod-product-compliance
Lightning Source LLC
Chambersburg PA
CBHW051549020426
42333CB00016B/2170